M000284260

Praise for

supersonic

An entertaining first-hand account of
pure rock 'n' roll madness
Daily Telegraph

This incredible book offers additional insights
into their turbulent upbringing, the making of
the band . . . the exclusive photos and brilliant
one-liners make for a sensational read
Sun

Supersonic is not quite an autobiography
. . . rather, it is a thorough and thoroughly
entertaining oral history
i news

supersonic

THE COMPLETE, AUTHORISED
AND UNCUT INTERVIEWS

CURATED BY SIMON HALFON

HEADLINE

Copyright © Nemperor Ltd, Burnage Films Ltd,
Big Brother Recordings Ltd, 2021.

The right of Simon Halfon to be identified as the Author of
the Work has been asserted by him in accordance with the
Copyright, Designs and Patents Act 1988.

First published in 2021 by
HEADLINE PUBLISHING GROUP

First published in paperback in 2023 by
HEADLINE PUBLISHING GROUP

1

Apart from any use permitted under UK copyright law, this publication may
only be reproduced, stored, or transmitted, in any form, or by any means,
with prior permission in writing of the publishers or, in the case of
reprographic production, in accordance with the terms of licences
issued by the Copyright Licensing Agency.

Every effort has been made to fulfil requirements with regard to
reproducing copyright material. The author and publisher will be glad
to rectify any omissions at the earliest opportunity.

See page 356 for picture credits.

Cover photograph © Jill Furmanovsky

Lyrics reproduced by kind permission of the publisher:
Dead Leg Music / Sony / ATV Music Publishing Ltd.

Cataloguing in Publication Data is available from the British Library

ISBN 978 1 4722 8547 8

Design by Perfect Bound Ltd
Colour reproduction by AltaImage

Printed and bound in Great Britain by Clays Ltd, Elcograf S.p.A.

Headline's policy is to use papers that are natural, renewable and recyclable
products and made from wood grown in well-managed forests and other
controlled sources. The logging and manufacturing processes are expected
to conform to the environmental regulations of the country of origin.

MIX
Paper | Supporting
responsible forestry
FSC
www.fsc.org
FSC® C104740

HEADLINE PUBLISHING GROUP
An Hachette UK Company
Carmelite House
50 Victoria Embankment
London EC4Y 0DZ

www.headline.co.uk
www.hachette.co.uk

Contents

Introduction

'How busy are you?' That was Noel's first question as he sat in our kitchen while I poured him a cup of strong tea, some time in the early months of 2014.

By that time, it had been over twenty years since he and I first met in Los Angeles, where I was living at the time. Oasis were shooting a video for a US version of their single 'Supersonic'. Back then, I was designing record sleeves, including for Paul Weller, and happened to mention to him on the phone beforehand that I was popping down to the set, as the director Nick Egan – another ex-pat – was a friend. Paul told me that I should introduce myself, not forgetting to tell Noel that he and I were mates. It was really that connection that served as a gold seal, firstly at the shoot and then that same evening at the Hollywood Roosevelt Hotel where I'd been invited to join the band for a light ale or two. This was where my friendship with Noel and Liam began and over the next couple of years I'd see them on a fairly regular basis when they'd breeze through town either for a gig or another video shoot.

To fill in the gaps very briefly between that first meeting and that cuppa with Noel twenty years on: by the middle of 1996 I was back living in London – a stone's throw from both Noel and Liam's houses in north-west London and we'd see a fair bit of each other.

Towards the end of the nineties I began designing LP covers for Oasis, and at the same time had the privilege of taking photos of the band at close quarters – whether it be at the studio, in Paris, Milan, and even on a return trip with them to the West Coast. The boys were always extremely welcoming and their own studio, Wheeler End, out in Buckinghamshire was a regular meeting spot. It felt like being a member of a gentlemen's club of sorts, where the time was split – for the most part – between chatting, laughing and listening to great music.

So there we were, 2014, in my kitchen. Noel tells me that August 2016 will be the twentieth anniversary of Oasis playing their two landmark gigs at Knebworth and asks if I might be interested in producing a short documentary to celebrate that. Would I? Needless to say, I immediately replied with a very enthusiastic 'Yes.' I was unbelievably flattered to be asked, to be honest.

It wasn't until later that evening that I really had a chance to think about the potential and the scale of this idea. It seemed to me that this was not a short TV 'walk down memory lane' documentary. It really felt like those first three years of the Oasis story, from being signed by Alan McGee to their landmark shows at Knebworth, were nothing short of a phenomenon. I had recently seen Asif Kapadia's excellent documentary *Senna* and I felt that this Knebworth celebration could be elevated to a theatrical feature-length documentary in very much the same way, and, like *Senna*, utilise archive footage alongside contemporary audio interviews to tell the story.

With this in mind I got in touch with James Gay Rees, who produced *Senna*, to see if they'd be interested in collaborating on this feature idea. James was in from the get-go. Asif came on board as an executive producer but wasn't available to direct the film as he was in the middle of making *Amy* and was committed to another project right after. We needed a director.

Prior to all this, I had already had some dealings with Mat Whitecross on another film project that, like most film projects, sadly didn't come to anything. I remembered being really impressed by his passion, understanding and commitment. Mat is a super-smart filmmaker. I also knew that because he had worked with, and been friends with, Coldplay since their student days, he'd have a real understanding of the dynamics of a rock band. We approached Mat and thankfully he, like me, couldn't say yes quick enough. He and his producing partner Fiona Neilson were now firmly on board.

All we needed now was for Liam to sign off on the idea. So Mat, James and myself headed up to a restaurant in Highgate to meet with him and his partner Debbie to talk them through the idea. He was keen but had two questions, 'Who is the hero and who is the villain?'

That was a key question and one that made it our resolve to be certain this film would be an absolutely fair and frank telling of the band's story. It's a tale that goes beyond the phenomenon to tell the story of a group that captured the zeitgeist, but with a tale of two brothers at its heart.

Throughout 2015, with Mat Whitecross at the helm, we were able to interview all the key players at great length and this enabled us to make *Supersonic* the film we had hoped it would be. We were very fortunate to have access to so many of those who were close to the band, including family members. All very kindly and candidly recounted their stories in great depth, over many, many hours.

Mat did an outstanding job weaving the stories together, creating a film that resonated on such an amazing level with the band, the fans and critics alike, even picking up some awards along the way. It wasn't just Liam who claimed that the film was 'biblical'. Fans of the film reached far and wide from the late George

Michael to Chris Martin to Paul Thomas Anderson to Ewan McGregor. Lena Dunham even hosted a screening in Los Angeles with Brad Pitt introducing the film. Yes, Brad Pitt. What was really surprising, though, was that the film really struck a chord with a whole new generation of kids that weren't even born when Oasis played Knebworth.

As the twenty-fifth anniversary of Knebworth approached, I thought it the perfect opportunity to revisit the transcripts of all the interviews recorded for the film. We had over sixteen hours in the can with Noel and twelve with Liam. It had not been physically possible to include it all in a two-hour documentary film, so the idea for a book, unabridged, made perfect sense. The good sense in this idea has been confirmed over the last few months, during which I have had the opportunity to revisit and dig deep into the full transcripts with all the key players.

As a result this book genuinely feels like the last word – a complete and true bookend to a documentary that I'm very proud of, and a real testament to a band that genuinely mattered, and still does to this day.

Simon Halfon
June 2021

Liam Oasis was definitely like a fucking Ferrari: great to look at, great to drive. It would spin out of control every now and again when you go too fast. I'd have that any day over the old Volvo – being in a band like that didn't interest me one bit. We just wanted to fucking take it to the max, every day, have a great time, every fucking day, and then if it ended tomorrow, it ended tomorrow.

Noel I would go back and fucking do that journey again in a heartbeat.

Liam I just wanted it all fucking there and then. The beginning, the middle bit and the end, right now. I just wanted it. Whatever the ending was I wanted it now, and whatever the middle bit was I wanted it now, and whatever the beginning was . . . I just wanted it all to happen in one big fuck-off explosion of madness.

Noel Everybody used to say, 'We are the best band in the world'. I am not sure anybody truly believed it. I actually fucking believed it. And I still believe it to this day. There was a period where we were fucking untouchable. It was only short – eighteen months, maybe two years – but we were up there with the greats.

Growing up

Noel I was born in Longsight in 1967 on 29th May. *Sgt Pepper* came out on 1st June and I do believe on hospital radio they were playing *Sgt Pepper* as I was born into the world and if that's not fucking true, that's the story I've been sticking to for the past forty-eight years.

Peggie Gallagher Paul arrived ten months after I was married, then Noel arrived a year after that again and everything was fine, it was going alright, or so I thought it was.

Paul Gallagher We had bowl heads, knitted jumpers, little shorts. She used to knit our clothes. Imagine, you've got no choice, you couldn't say, 'I don't want that, Mam,' 'cause she's just spent four years knitting you a jumper. We were dressed identical, maybe it was cheaper to do two instead of one.

Peggie Liam arrived five and a half years after. I don't know, I think there was always that bit of jealousy with Liam and Noel, because there was only Paul and Noel for so long. I idolised Paul and Noel because I had only the two of them. Noel was absolutely beautiful when he was a baby. Then, of course, Liam comes along, takes the limelight. You could tell the disagreement was there with them.

Noel We lived off a busy main road; Longsight Market was across the road from our house. It was a busy Mancunian suburb maybe two miles from the city centre. I don't romanticise my childhood, but it was alright. We had an outside toilet. It's grim up north and all that.

Peggie It was great, that was the best time with the kids. Everybody knew everybody, I knew hundreds of Irish people. If you went out shopping with the kids on Stockport Road, you'd always run into friends that you knew when you were young and their families. Going to church, going to school, everybody knew everybody. It was a great community for the Irish people then. I was down Longsight in a two-bedroom house – two up and two down – and that was demolished. We got rehoused to a place called Burnage, which was further south. Compared to Longsight, this was like fucking the Cotswolds. You had a front garden and a back garden instead of an alleyway and a front door that opened onto the street. But if you'd seen my rooms upstairs – you couldn't swing a bloody cat in them.

Paul You've got a three-bedroom council house, there's not a lot of space. You're going to get friction. That's what people don't understand, you know, since Liam was ten till seventeen, he shared a bedroom with Noel.

Noel Our Paul's always had his own room, *bastard*. It's something I've never quite forgiven him for. I got to share with Liam, which wasn't really a problem until we were teenagers and then he was just a pain in the arse . . . and has remained that way ever since.

Liam Paul had his own room, I shared one with Noel. Yeah, it was alright.

Noel I didn't hang around with Liam until I joined the band. Although I shared a room with him, five years is a generation apart. All his mates, when I was fifteen, they are all ten, you know, so that's massive. I'm leaving school at fifteen, he's ten years old. You're fucking smoking weed at fifteen, he's just out of short pants, so there is no relationship.

Liam I think we got on, I think. He was a bit of a stoner, a bit of a loner, one of them people that you'd throw stones at. He had a guitar so he was copping for it, you know what I mean? One of them, walking round with his guitar with his weird mates. Our Paul was a mod so he had a bit more about him, he wasn't so weird like Noel was.

Peggie Always very quiet, Noel. He would go upstairs and bury himself. Always strumming a guitar. Many's a time I went up and I knocked at the door and said, 'Bloody guitar, you get on my bloody nerves.' 'You leave my guitar alone,' he said. I used to do an awful lot of knitting and he'd be always drumming with the needles when he was young. It was in him. I used to go, 'He'll put that bloody knitting needle in his eye yet.'

Paul Noel was quiet, moody, skinny, withdrawn, he kept himself to himself. Then you've got Liam who is a livewire. Imagine Zebedee from the Magic Roundabout versus, I don't know, Mickey Mouse? You got a lot of noise.

Liam Noel's definitely a bit cagey, I'd call it shifty.

Noel I don't know why me and Liam would be so different, we both had the same childhood, do you know what I mean? I am more of a loner. I genuinely like my own company. I'm not a shy, can't-really-speak-to-anyone person . . . I'm very outgoing and fucking love my circle of friends and all that, but I don't need them . . . A few years in nick, in solitary confinement, that wouldn't bother me in the slightest.

Liam Anyone who could do a stretch, I would watch out for them. Anyone who says, 'Yeah, I could do fucking time,' that's scary. I couldn't do that. He definitely keeps himself to himself. He's a funny cunt without a doubt. He's great and all that, but he's a bit of a dick as well.

Noel Liam is a fucking major pain in the arse . . . there isn't actually a word that could adequately sum up his fucking buffoonery.

He was a devil, Liam, full of it.

Liam Our kid's more a thinker, I wasn't a thinker, I didn't have no time to think. It was just, 'Let's get straight into this fucking day.' I'd never sit there and scratch my chin and go, 'How am I going to play this Tuesday afternoon?' There was none of that. It was like, 'Let's fucking have Tuesday, full on, let's freak Tuesday out so it doesn't come back again. Let Tuesday tell Wednesday, "Fucking hell, you're in for it tomorrow, mate."'

Peggie He was a devil, Liam, full of it. Many's a time, I swear to God, if I caught him I would have broke the brush across his back, because he used to torment me in the kitchen.

Liam I used to have too much Weetabix, a lot of energy. Three in the morning, three when I get in from school and three before I go to bed. I was just fucking bouncing off the walls, man.

Peggie Liam was a mammy's boy, always with me. He'd always come looking for you to see where you were. They were all close, but I suppose Liam was always closer to me, because he was the youngest. Everybody loved him round here because he had a lot of time for older people. You'd be coming back from the shops there and he'd say, 'Let me carry that bag for you.' He used to go up and down Burnage Lane waving to everyone. The big wave. Everybody loved him round here.

Noel Liam, I would suggest, needs an audience. He is an ideal frontman.

Paul Total attention seeker, robbing your clothes, robbing your records, robbing your this, robbing your that, robbing your money.

Liam I was pretty confident all the way through life, you know what I mean – fuck knows, I guess just looking in the mirror and seeing what your reflection is, you kind of, if you look like a knob you're going to act like a knob, I guess, you know what I mean. I kind of dig the way I look so went for it. I'm definitely a bit of a show-off and that, always loved the attention and that and still do, but not to the point where it's like fucking Bonnie Langford or one of them little fucking brats with jazz hands.

Peggie I used to go to the school plays and he'd always look to see if he could spot you in the audience. Liam always wanted to be top of everything, from a small little boy. If he didn't get the main part, he didn't want to be in it. Noel was a different kettle of fish altogether.

Noel I didn't hate school, I wasn't like an anarchist – fuck school and fuck all the teachers and all that. When I joined there was a mix-up with another kid called Gallagher from another school. There was three top classes and two classes for headcases in our year. Due to a mix-up, I got put in the top class for a term. I was thinking, there is something not right here; I don't understand what that teacher is saying; I don't know what she is fucking going on about. Who are these fucking eggheads? Then I walked into another classroom one day and was like, 'Aha! Okay, right.' Took my rightful seat at the back of the class.

> We would just do fuck all, all day, apart from listen to music, get into mischief.

Liam School was alright, I enjoyed it, I mean I didn't learn anything, but I enjoyed the fucking about part of it. I guess that set me up for being in a band and being on tour. I liked being in a gang, I liked hanging out with me mates, you know what I mean. It was a good crack. I wasn't one of them, sitting on me own, thinking about stuff, I was definitely always up to some kind of shit.

Noel I don't look back on it with any fondness or any hate, do you know what I mean? It was just somewhere you had to go until you grew up, and then they fucking let you go and that was it. I didn't play truant, or 'wag it' as it used to be called, because I hated school, I did it because it was fucking boring. One of my mates lived right by the school and his mam and dad worked all day so you could stay at his house. We would just do fuck all, all day, apart from listen to music, get into mischief. Me mam got a job as a dinner lady and then that made things a bit trickier because you would always have to be around school at dinner time, but not in the morning or the afternoon.

Peggie Noel would go to school as brazen as you like. I was a dinner lady then and he'd come in and stand in the queue with these big Doc Martens on him. He'd get whatever he wanted, because it was free dinners, and then he'd always come back to me at the end with a biscuit that he didn't want and give it to me, as much as to say, 'This will get me out of trouble.' Then the teacher would say, 'Where is Noel?'

'I've just seen him, here; he was in front of me.'

'No, Mrs Gallagher, he's not been in school for three weeks.'

'I've just been talking to him; he's come up here with his tray and everything.' He was skipping over the wall, he was trouble.

Liam I got me hair shaved, ears pierced, told a couple of teachers to fuck off – like you do. Didn't do me homework, it got ate by an alien one day, all that nonsense. The usual. Didn't bother turning up because we were sitting at home playing pool, getting stoned, wagging it or whatever they call it these days. But yeah, but when I was there, it was a laugh.

Peggie I remember the teacher saying once to me, 'I don't know how you put up with him, Mrs Gallagher. I only have him a couple of hours a day, I have to go home and take a tablet. You've got to put up with him all the time.' I still meet that lady sometimes. She said, 'He was full of energy.' He was a devil, Liam.

Liam I enjoyed going to school, like I say, didn't learn much, but I liked it because I just fucked about. I remember just having a laugh. I weren't that clever at school, didn't pass any exams, wasn't interested, always looking out the window, just fucking flicking people on the ear and robbing shit and stuff. Just being the class clown and shit. Obviously at home there was a bit of tension and a bit of shit going down, so it was a bit of relief getting into school and hanging out with your mates and just fucking about. We were always running around fighting with schools and shit like that, it was a good crack. I wouldn't say I went round looking for trouble, but if someone started then I certainly wouldn't do a runner, you know what I mean. I wasn't like tough guy or that, there were a lot harder people than me. I had a few mates that knew how to knock people out.

Paul You have the cocks of the school; Liam was the cock of the school and then, one day, some rival school turned up and boshed him on the head with an 'ammer.

Liam With a hammer, yeah, that was in St Mark's. We were stood there having a cig in one of the fucking little areas round the back. The girls used to come over to our school to use our facilities, because ours were better, and I think we were talking to our mate's sister, she was about twelve so we were about fifteen. I remember all these lads coming down, I don't know what school they were from. They've come down, hoods up, and one of them's fucking punched her. So we got stuck in. I've hit this kid and this kid pulled out this little fucking hammer and went whack on me head. Then I've ended up in hospital, blood everywhere. Got out of fucking double maths, though, so that was alright. That was it. From that day on, it was like as if something had fucking clicked. I started hearing music,

Somebody hammered the music into him . . .

it started making sense. Up until then I wasn't into music. I know it sounds stupid, I probably said it before, but whoever he is, thank you.

Noel Somebody hammered the music into him . . . he's got a lot to answer for, hasn't he? I've got a perfect alibi for that – so it's nowt to do with me.

Proper jobs

Noel I left school in 1983. There wasn't a great deal to do in Manchester in 1983 if you were fifteen. What would we do? Nothing, is the answer to that. Sign on. Work for six, seven months until you got laid off. Or I would go and work with my old fella. When I didn't have shitty labouring jobs I would be hanging out with my mates in the local park, either picking magic mushrooms or fucking trying to get drugs – there is fuck all to do.

Peggie Noel didn't want to do any job, to be quite honest with you, Noel just wanted to laze around. It was all too much bother for Noel to do any job.

Liam I think I got kicked out of school when I was about fifteen. They found me a job working up the road, in a garden centre, and I done that for a bit, which was alright. It was a nice peaceful job, you'd sit there on this wood and it was pretty chilled and that. I can't remember what I was getting, I think I was getting 50 quid a week or something. I'd go to work, come down to my old school on my little BMX, and wave me 50 quid across the railings going, 'Knobheads!' to me mates who were still at school. So it was good. Then the bloke says, 'You've got to clean these toilets out.'

'I ain't fucking cleaning the toilets out, not a chance.'

So then he sacked me.

Peggie Liam didn't like work at all. He walked out, he wasn't cleaning no toilet for nobody. That was that.

Liam Never had a proper job, it was just like bits of shit. There was a guy from Levenshulme. He'd have a contract for us painting the fucking satellites at Jodrell Bank out in Cheshire. Or cleaning the shit up around these ICI factories. So we'd do that, they were alright. We'd just get stoned and fucking go and sit in the toilets for about an hour. Skin up and he'd be, 'Where's Gallagher?' We'd be in the toilet, crashed out with a brush between our legs, fucking snoring.

Noel I got a job for a sub-contractor to British Gas, putting in gas mains all over Manchester. I used to work out in the trenches, literally digging fucking holes for a living. Then for some reason I was put in the stockyard. Maybe I'd done my back in or something, which fucking plagues me to this very fucking day. No one would ever come to this fucking place and you could sit in there all fucking day listening to the radio. Or I would bring a ghetto blaster in and listen, just bring tapes in and stuff, you know, playing along to them.

There was a load of – let me get technical about this – big fucking iron caps they would put on the end of gas mains. Some of them needed shifting and one of them fell and broke my right foot.

Liam I done another job doing neon signs. I had to do the Granada TV sign in fucking November. You'd have to get harnessed over it – someone would fucking hold your legs and drop you down – and you'd be fucking changing light bulbs with no gloves on, freezing, for a tenner a day. I can't even change a light bulb. I'd just hang about there going, 'I can't work it,' so I got fucked off from that one.

Noel My old fella was a sub-contractor who would put concrete floors in flats. He was a proper grafter, a labourer, and instilled in us a work ethic. And he was a City supporter, which is a relief because we could have been fucking dirty reds and, let's face it, nobody would have wanted that.

Liam We'd do a bit of work on the buildings and that and he was still a dick, never pay you on time. You do big hours on this building site, grafting like fuck – proper graft, with grown big fucking Irishmen – and then you go down to get the wages off him the next weekend and he'd never be in.

Noel Family life was a bit like *The Royle Family* but with added violence and tension. Not all the time. It was the seventies and then leading into the eighties and Thatcher, unemployment and all that. My mam was working two jobs to try and make ends meet. They were bleak times. There wasn't a great deal to do apart from get into trouble. Smoke weed, sniff glue, listen to music, go to football. That was it. I don't look back on them with any romance whatsoever, but then again when I look back on them they don't fill me with any dread either, it was just growing up. I was arrested a few times, for shoplifting, robbery, all of which fucking haunt me to this day. I've still got a police record. If you're caught three times you pretty much know that you're not destined for a life of crime. If I'd have got away with it a bit more I might have been like a proper gangster, but I was shit at it.

Peggie I will tell you a funny thing about Noel, once he got up to some mischief and went to court. There was a hole in the bottom of his shoe, it was a big hole in the bottom and he had a piece of cardboard in it. I said, 'I tell you what, Noel, if you get half off your father, I'll give you the other half.' He said, 'Okay.' So I said to himself, 'Noel wants a pair of shoes.'

'Well, our Lord didn't have shoes, what does he want shoes for?'

And then I thought to myself, 'You are not right in the head.'

Liam If it wasn't for music, who fucking knows, I could either be dead or I could be in nick, simple. I don't think I'd have got my head together to do a normal job.

The tunes

Noel I guess music is a form of escapism for me. I've always enjoyed it and loved playing it and I guess as I've got older it means everything to me now. Everything I've got that is good in my life has come through my love of music. Of all things, I think the thing I value the most is being able to just shut the fucking living-room door, pick up the guitar and just sit and strum it for an hour, an hour and a half, and not even know what I am playing. It makes me feel great and it takes me somewhere else, whether I am playing it, writing it, doing it, talking about it. I do often wonder what do other people do? Some people actually play golf to unwind and fucking go to the gym, you know, or play video games, imagine that.

> Everything I've got that is good in my life has come through my love of music.

Liam I wasn't into it until later on, I was just into being out all night and playing football. Anyone with a guitar or in a band I thought was a bit suspect, you know what I mean. I would throw stones at them and shit like that. Hurl abuse at them when they were walking down the road. All these people go, 'Oh yeah, man, I was into like George Formby at age three.' Really? Well, I was into just shitting in me nappy, you know what I mean? I didn't get The Beatles at five, I got them at nineteen.

Noel I can tell you the first record that was bought for me. My old fella bought me, 'The Show Must Go On' by Leo Sayer because I'd seen him dressed as a clown on *Top of the Pops*. I don't know why I was fascinated with the clown, but anyway he bought me that on seven inch. Dad is a shit dad and a shit husband but I must kind of credit him for the musical side of us. He was a DJ and he had a record collection and all that, so there was always music in the house. Everyone in the Irish community knew who my old man was in Manchester, everyone. He was a DJ in the Irish social clubs and that's where I first heard Elvis, Motown and all that kind of thing.

Peggie He was a DJ for years and he was always into Irish music, country and western.

Paul We had to roadie for him, me and Noel. We got good at playing pool from doing that. He'd have an amp, two decks, speakers, records and he would be playing in some holy name club in Manchester, you'd get out, 'You two, carry that gear.' Fucking roadies at seven . . . 'There you go, there's a pound for some Coke, go and play pool.'

Liam Me old fella was playing the Chieftains, the Dubliners, Daniel O'Donnell and all that nonsense. He'd be playing that, Mam wasn't really playing music. I guess Noel was into The Smiths, he was into a bit of the Pistols. Paul was more a Jam fan, he was more of a mod. So there was always music round the house, but it just wasn't my time. Then when the Roses popped up, I sort of got into music.

Noel *Never Mind the Bollocks* as an album is probably the first record that I wished to own, because all the older lads on the estate where I lived had it and it had swearing in it. It said fuck and shit and it was like, 'Oh my God, swearing on a record.' I remember that being the first really important record.

Liam Our kid had the Roses albums and The Smiths and stuff, a band called The Bodines and all that Manchester stuff. Then our Bod had The Jam, The Style Council, UB40, he was more of a soul boy, more of a mod kind of thing.

Paul I thought Weller was amazing, even though he was from a different part of the country. My dad was against anything British, he wouldn't allow me to have a green parka. 'You can't be walking round with a target on your back.' He didn't understand, so I had to get a brown snorkel jacket and try and sneak patches on the arms, I must've looked a right dickhead.

Noel Once I discovered weed and guitars and The Jam and The Smiths and all that, what would you want to go out for? Everything I ever wanted in life was coming out of the speakers and I was playing along to it and it was going somewhere I felt, it was great.

Liam Obviously I was sharing a room with Noel so I would hear it all. I never really was a big Smiths head, our kid got heavily into them. I like Johnny Marr, I like the tunes and that, but Morrissey always just rubbed me up the wrong way. As I've got older I've kind of liked him, he's a funny cunt, but as a kid I couldn't really fucking stomach him, you know what I mean? So like I said, when the Roses popped up, that was where it was at for me. They were talking about their influences – Simon and

Garfunkel, Hendrix, The Yardbirds and stuff – so I started listening through them, kind of. Then I made my own way around the musical world and made my own thing. It's like an advent calendar, once you open that door you open another door, and it's just like this big long chain. Before you know it I was in Beatle world, and still am, and it's fucking amazing.

Liam Me old fella had a guitar, yeah. He didn't play it, used to just whack us with it. I think it was more of a fucking weapon than an instrument, you know what I mean?

Noel The guitar that I learnt on, the guitar that lit the fire, was behind our living-room door, stood against the wall. How it got there is anyone's guess. My dad could never play the guitar, my mam certainly couldn't, and my two brothers can't play it so I don't know why it was there.

Liam Our kid had a guitar and he'd be playing his guitar in his bedroom. Me and my mates, we'd be like, 'Fucking weird brother upstairs playing that guitar, shall we go out and smash some cunt's head in?'
    'Yeah, let's do that then.'
    Then we would come back and he would still be fucking playing the guitar. So my mates would be thinking he's a bit weird. But he wasn't super weird; he wasn't like the geezer out The Cure or anything.

Paul He'd just sit in his room, music on, he'd have a little amp, headphones, didn't see him for years.

Noel I didn't pick it up to become anything, I used to get grounded – well, they call it grounded now – I used to have to stay in a lot because I was a bit of a wild man at school, in the sense that I never fucking went. I was getting in trouble so I got to stay in a lot. I remember kind of strumming along, not strumming the full six strings but the odd string, to Joy Division basslines; I'd while away the hours of being stuck in your room. But I didn't really take the guitar seriously until

> # I didn't really take the guitar seriously until Liam asked me to join Oasis.

Liam asked me to join Oasis. I always had one, I was a bit into it, but not really that fucking arsed . . . It was something I did for pleasure, it was never going to be the career. I was just so lucky that that guitar was there and I was made to fucking stay in on curfew. Thank God for that.

Liam I played violin at one point, very badly, like everyone, I don't know anyone that plays violin well. Noel got guitar lessons, I think he was playing guitar in school and me mam decided to get me a fucking violin for some bizarre reason, which got booted to school, there and back. It wasn't cool, I looked pretty gangsterish with it, but it was shit when you whipped it out.

Peggie I put myself in debt for a violin, it was £30 at the time, and as soon as I paid it off he said, 'I'm not carrying that violin up to school, people will think I'm a sissy.'

Noel The first gig I ever went to was The Damned at the Apollo in 1980 in Manchester. The second gig I ever went to was Stiff Little Fingers, then I went to see Public Image and U2 – all at the Apollo. The reason for that was Shaun Dolan did the door at the Apollo, and he was married to one of my mam's family friends from the area where they were all born in Ireland. I was underage so we would go down there and he would wait till all the crowd had gone in, then he would let me and whoever I was with in to stand at the back. I think I was twelve or thirteen and it was in fucking Ardwick, which is in town, miles away from where we lived. I am going to these punk gigs, and they are pretty hairy things, you know. We'd go and stand at the back getting blown away.

Liam I think the first gig I went to see was The Stone Roses in the International One in Longsight. I was on the dole at the time so I borrowed like £15 off me mam. The ticket cost a tenner, bought it off some tout. I know a lot of people, you know, don't condone touts, but if it wasn't for that tout that day I wouldn't have seen The Stone Roses and I wouldn't have joined Oasis. So viva la tout. They weren't dressed in leather kecks or like The Cure or The Smiths and that. I always found them bands a little bit fucking odd because they weren't dressed like me. Then when I saw the Roses and the Mondays, I thought, 'You know what? I'll stop throwing stones and gobbing at them,' because they look a little bit like us. That made more sense to me. Seeing The Stone Roses, I just thought, 'You know what, you don't have to have a perm, you don't have to have leather kecks on, you don't have to be this fucking Jim Morrison poet dude to be in a band.' They weren't farting about on stage, they were just stood there playing the music – he didn't have flowers hanging out of his arse, you know what I mean? They just didn't seem pretentious to me, it seemed like it was just normal. There's four guys up there on that stage

I had two spliffs, bought two shitty beers, went down to the front, checked it out and thought, 'I'm having a bit of that.'

that looked like our kid's mates, that looked like my mates. Obviously they are older and have just sat and learned their instruments and are doing it right, you know what I mean. I thought I could do that, it doesn't look hard, it was that kind of thing. That ain't a diss on the Roses or anything, they just looked effortless and I think that's what it should be. A lot of people make too much out of this rock-and-roll thing. If it's cool, it looks effortless. There's no need for make-up and painting your fingernails and all that nonsense. At that gig, I had two spliffs, bought two shitty beers, went down to the front, checked it out and thought, 'I'm having a bit of that.' Went home, Mam said, 'What was the gig like?'

I said, 'Mega, I'm going to be in a band.'

Peggie Actually, I never thought Liam was interested in music, until he used to sit out there in the kitchen and say, 'I'm going to be famous one day, Mam.'

I said, 'Are you? Get off your bloody arse and get out and get a job.'

'Oh no, Mam,' he says, 'I'm telling you,' he says, 'I'm going to be really famous one day and you're going to be really proud of me.'

I said, 'Am I? Well, I hope it's before I start pushing up daisies, because we need the money now. What are you going to do, Liam?'

'I'm a singer.'

I said, 'I never heard you singing.'

'I'm going to be in a band,' he says, 'I'm telling you.'

That's the first I knew about it. 'Never mind talking a load of bull there, get out and get a job for yourself.'

The Inspirals

Noel The gig where I met Graham Lambert was an Anti-Clause 28 gig. The Mondays, the Roses and James played this gig. You put that gig on now it would be 175,000 people at it; then it was in the International Two, which was previously called the Carousel, the place where my mam and dad met, funnily enough. It was a huge, old, Irish dance hall and I remember being stood up in the balcony, watching The Stone Roses. I saw this guy just leaning on the balcony. There was a little red light where he was stood and I noticed he had a tape recorder. I went up to him and said, 'Are you taping this gig?' and he said, 'Yeah.'

So I said, 'If I give you my address, can you send me a copy of the tape?'

I was fucking obsessed with this band.

He said, 'Yeah.'

Lovely guy, we got chatting about music and he said, 'Who else are you into?' and I said I'd been to see Inspiral Carpets a few times. He said, 'I'm in Inspiral Carpets, and I was kind of like, 'Really? Fucking hell!' Pretty soon after that their lead singer left and Graham said, 'Do you want to come and audition for the singer's job because you know all the songs?' I went up and it soon became clear that my singing chops hadn't arrived just yet. Fair play to them, though, they didn't like fuck us off, they said, 'Well, fuck it, you can look after the gear then.' Brilliant.

Clint Boon* My first memories of Noel would be midway through 1988; he was a fan of the band and he

---

* Keyboard player and occasional vocalist of Inspiral Carpets.

used to come and see the Inspirals a lot. I remember a period, probably for a month or two, he had a broken leg so he was coming to gigs on crutches. It made an impact on us. He could sing, we all know that, but he just wasn't the kind of vocalist we wanted. We needed somebody with a bigger set of lungs really.

Noel So I became their roadie, worked in the office and all that, worked for them for years, it was fucking great.

Liam He was just buzzing, you know what I mean, he was around the music, around the Inspirals. At that time all this Manchester thing was going down, it was a good time, I guess, making a few quid, seeing the world. It was great.

Paul Noel just came back with all weird-looking clothes on. 'Where have you been?'
 'I've been on tour.'
 'Okay, who with?'
 'Inspiral Carpets.'
 If your brother goes away working on the other side of the world, you aren't going to go, 'Well done, brother, fantastic!' You're going to say, 'And? . . . You're missing the City games, mate, give a shit.'

Noel I thought, this is it, this'll do for me, this is fucking great, set up these guitars, play them before the band get up, fucking excellent. Get three hundred quid a week, fucking brilliant. What can be better? Drugs, women, booze, travelling the world, it doesn't get any better than that. In fact in many ways it is better than being in a fucking band.

Peggie I was excited because I was glad he'd got what he wanted to do, but God, I was worried about him – I'm an awful worrier, me, you know. You thought of drugs and I was always well clued-up to that. If they ever tried to pull the wool, I said, 'I know all about it, you don't have to tell me.'

Drugs, women, booze, travelling the world, it doesn't get any better than that.

Liam I used to do a bit with him, when they'd go down to London and they'd need a helping hand or something, someone to lug it about. I'd kind of jump in every now and again. I went to Konk Studios once, which is The Kinks' place. That was good.

Clint Boon Liam had often come along to gigs. He'd be in the dressing room with his mates and it always struck me how quiet he was, always so quiet and polite and appreciative. He'd never ask for anything, he'd never gone in the dressing room and helped himself to beer, which is what a lot of kids did, he would wait until he was asked if he wanted something, just dead polite.

Noel I met Mark Coyle the first day of their first major British tour, I was working for them on my own for quite a while and then the whole thing blew up. They were going on this tour and of course they had to have a huge fucking tour bus and a crew and all that. I met Mark Coyle sat at the back of the tour bus smoking weed and me and him got on like a fucking house on fire.

Mark Coyle That's how I met Noel, just walking into a room and he was on that side, pulling this fucking face, because the organisation that he was in, had just grown. This is his thing, he's the roadie for that band. Didn't speak to him for probably a couple of days, and as soon as we started talking, well, we were fucking best mates straight away. There is one thing I remember about Noel, he never had a fucking dirty hand. I'd load the truck, take charge of all the boxes going on, a fucking hard job. But he was very committed to the cause, he loved that band. He was a big fan of the Inspiral Carpets.

They were all terrified of him, he was just the boss all the way, from the minute I met him.

Clint Boon You'd never see him sweating, he is famous for not sweating. He was good at getting the local crew to do all the hard work and he'd stand there saying, 'Put that there, plug that in there.' During the gig you'd often look over and he'd be sat having a beer or he'd be looking bored, giving that knobhead sign to you.

Noel Me and Mark used to share a room, we had some great, funny fucking times, doing mushrooms and all sorts of mad shit . . . fucking proper laugh. We were the archetypal roadies, fucking hell, man, we went everywhere, all over the world, loads of fucking times. We loved it.

Clint Boon Touring the world, getting decent money, getting free booze every night, not having to worry about record sales and all that kind of stuff. He was just a passenger on this amazing vehicle that took him round the world a few times.

Noel The Inspirals were a fucking good laugh, really were. Clint Boon and Graham Lambert, they used to make me belly laugh all the time, we always had a good laugh with them.

Clint Boon He was confident, cocky, but in a good way, like a lot of Mancunians are. Not arrogant, just confident, very cool and infectious. He was always dead funny. On the night that he auditioned to be the singer he was singing one of the songs I'd written and in the middle of it he stopped and said, 'Who the fuck's written this? This is shite.' Never been one to bite his lip really, was he? We grew to love him, we came to see him as a brother.

Noel Me and Mark – lazy fuckers. I thought we were great. I mean, clearly we weren't because we did get fired, separately got fired, by the band for being unprofessional and somewhat unapproachable by various tour managers.

Clint Boon My favourite memories of Noel are when I'd go to see him in his flat at India House in Manchester. It's just like a little one-, maybe two-bedroom flat that he had there, and he'd sit on his bed and he'd play us these songs. You never felt like, this is genius, you know what I mean? I think we took the piss a bit at the time. It's probably the only time in Noel's career that somebody's

> I thought we were great. I mean, clearly we weren't because we did get fired ...

took the piss out of his songwriting, and he got the last laugh, didn't he?

Noel I wasn't sitting at the side of the stage tuning guitars thinking, 'One day this is going to be me,' you know what I mean? Not in the slightest. I thought that was it. I never thought, 'That could be me,' or 'I deserve to be there.' That never entered into my sphere of thinking at all, at all. I wasn't as egotistical as that. The ego thing came, coincidentally, accompanied by the massive bag of fucking cocaine, you know. There's a funny thing, isn't it?

The Rain

Liam My life then was going to sign on, getting me dole, cashing me cheque, going into Sifters, getting a record if the cover looked great, getting all me classics built up and that, buying some weed, going into Greggs, going back home and fucking blasting it out. I had to play it loud. I wanted it so fucking bad, man, and I was just obsessed with being in a band, just ob-fucking-sessed, man. Right up for it, thought I could do it and, in fact, knew I could do it, just needed to get people to write the songs, I guess, or to get a band and that. Definitely, I knew I could do it – without a doubt. That's all I wanted to do.

Peggie Liam was sure he was going to be famous. Then, of course, Bonehead started coming round and Tony McCarroll and Guigsy, that's when Liam formed the band.

> I wanted it so fucking bad, man, and I was just obsessed with being in a band ...

Paul Bonehead used to play keyboards and I used to see him round Westpoint when he had hair and this little Bontempi or whatever under his arm. I didn't see him for years and then he popped up with Liam.

Bonehead I probably got the name Bonehead when I was eight. In 1973, most people in my primary school did have long hair, which was the style of the time, and I didn't. It was just like straight down the barber's every Friday, you know, typical Irish Catholic parents and they're having none of it, no long hair in our house. They gave me my fifty pence and I had to go down, 'What is it? Usual short back and sides?' No long hair on our street. So, that was me nickname from the age of eight, you know, some kid, 'Ah, look at the bonehead!' and that was it. When I got to secondary school even the teachers referred to me as Bonehead, even when they were angry. *Bonehead*. It wasn't 'Arthurs'. That's when you knew you were in trouble, when you got the surname. It was Bonehead and has been ever since. When we got really well known we used to do interviews in France and they'd want to know why I was called Bonehead. I always used to tell them that if you went right back in my family history my real name is *Bonaparte Headimus*; and Bonehead was for short. People fell for it. The people that I grew up with weren't massive music fans. It was either football or music that you got into, and the circle of friends I associated with, it was football. It was United or City and nothing in between, that was it. They were big football fans and as we got older and we got to the age where we could go to pubs, it was football and drinking. But luckily my older brother was really into music. I shared a bedroom with him as we were growing up and he had a record player, an amp and two speakers, a really good, cool stereo system. He had a massive vinyl collection which was brilliant. He played guitar, he'd bought himself an amp and he was twanging that around the house, I used to have a go of it when he wasn't around. Friday night was pub night so I got to know Chris and Guigs just through people in the pub, who knew people who knew people. Everybody was into the Roses and the other bands coming out of Manchester.

'We're going to form a band, you know, do you want to be in it?'

Guigs was like, 'What shall I do?' Play bass, one note, dead easy. Chris can sing, get a microphone. Plugged it in in his garage and did it, badly, but it was great because all of a sudden Friday nights were Friday night in the garage making a racket through one amp and it was really good, it was cool. Guigs had never seen a bass guitar in his life. Chris had never sang in his life, we did a couple of gigs – we did one in the pub, which didn't even put gigs on, we just said to the landlord, 'We want to do a gig,' and he was, 'What do you mean, gig?' We used a drum machine, the same beat for every song, and somebody just said, 'Look, I know a guy from Levenshulme, Tony McCarroll.' I didn't know Tony, but he played drums, so we had a drummer then. It was a racket, it was crap, but it was brilliant as well.

Liam I knew Bonehead and I knew Guigs and they were in a band called The Rain that were playing pubs and stuff. I was impressed because they were in a band and I wanted to be in a band. They'd heard I was cool and was looking at being in a band, that I'd had my epiphany and all that bollocks. So then some lad come over to me and said, 'They've sacked Chris' – who was their singer – and then they've asked, 'Do you want to go down and meet them?'

I said, 'Yeah, go on, I'll give it a go.' Put me money where me mouth is kind of thing, so I did it and then they liked it.

Bonehead I knew who Liam was, and someone mentioned that Liam wanted to be in a band, he wanted to sing and that he actually could sing, you know.

Liam I think I went to Bonehead's house and just fucking sang, with him on guitar. I don't know what we fucking sang. So long ago. But he was like, 'Cool', and his missus Kate was going, 'Better than the last one anyway.' I mean it wouldn't have been fucking hard to beat him, he was shit.

Bonehead His look . . . I mean, he looked like Liam's always looked, you know? He had a great topcoat on and great haircut, a great walk, great voice.

Noel He had the haircut for sure and the walk and all that.

Liam I was fucking cool. I looked like a rock star even when I was digging holes in Manchester. I was cool then. People would clock my head even when I was wearing fucking overalls and had a fucking shovel in my hand. Full of shit with a pneumatic drill, I still looked cool. A lot of people look like that in Manchester and dress like that anyway, so I wouldn't say it was my look, it was a shared look with everyone.

> I looked like a rock star even when I was digging holes in Manchester.

Bonehead His voice was just like, whoa . . . Wasn't the Liam we all know; a bit softer and a lot more melodic.

Liam So they liked it and then they went, 'Right, look, do you want to be in this band?'

I says, 'Yeah, but we'll have to change that fucking name though 'cause it's terrible,' and we changed it to

Oasis and that was it. So, for the record, I was never in a band called The Rain.

Bonehead The Rain. I think he thought it was a crap name so Liam, being Liam, says, 'No, that's shit, we need to change the name.' I think he got it off an Inspiral Carpets tour poster, Swindon Oasis, the venue, I think it was. I was just like, 'Whatever, yeah, that'll do.' A name's a name; once people get familiar with your name, it's just the name of the band, isn't it?

Noel Halfway down Market Street in Manchester there was the Underground Market. There was this stall called Oasis – which sold Adidas trainers – where the Manchester look came from. We used to shop there and all that. What a great name, and what a fucking great story that would have been for the band. Unfortunately the fucking singer decides to tell somebody that I had an Inspiral Carpets tour poster up on my wall and on it was a place they played in Swindon called the Oasis Centre.

Liam It certainly wasn't about Swindon Oasis. There was a stall, I think it was in Affleck's Palace, that sold cool clothes. There was a song by the Mondays called Oasis, there was a kebab shop called Oasis, there was a taxi rank called Oasis . . . you're looking around and that name keeps coming up, all the time in my head. Oasis, just sounded good. I know a lot of people think it's shit, and it probably is a shit name, but everything's shit, innit? Until you make it good. The fucking Jam, that's a shit name, The Jam. But it isn't because they are good and they write good music. The Who's a shit name as well; The Beatles is a fucking shit name.

We wrote a couple of shit tunes, a tune called 'Take Me', which we even knew were shit at the time and still is to this day, but it was something. I wasn't interested in writing songs to be fair. We did it because Noel wasn't in the band at that time. It was like as soon as someone comes who knows what they are doing with melody and guitars, then they can have that gig, man. I was not arsed about that, I just wanted to be a fucking frontman. Bonehead wrote the music, I wouldn't even know how to look at a guitar. He'd just write it, send it over or whatever. I can't remember how it worked. I'd listen to it back and get a melody and write some shitty words down, still doing the same thing today, you know what I mean?

Bonehead Me and Liam together, we were never going to write an album for certain. I'm not a songwriter.

Liam We were nowhere near what it had to be. We could still be fucking there now doing it if we were doing it. Never, ever had the desire to want to write songs. I was not interested in that at all. We knew we were shit, never said we were good. I don't think the confidence came until we had the songs. We were just doing it, that's the main thing. We were just, you know, opening the door.

And then there were five

Liam I thought the main thing was getting Noel in the band. He was a songwriter, he'd been doing it for quite a bit, he was a lad. He was touring with the Carpets so he'd seen a bit. No one wants to be setting people's gear up all their life, that's like work, innit? That's graft, especially if you've got a talent. I thought, when he comes back and he sees that we're doing it instead of talking about it, he'll want to join our band and he'll do the business. Whether we are good or not. We weren't fucking great, but we were better than nothing. Get him in the band: he'll be the songwriter and I can just fart about. Then when he did get in the band and his songs were great I just thought all we need to do now is get a deal and then we'll tell them what we are about.

> Get him in the band: he'll be the songwriter and I can just fart about.

Noel I was doing a gig in Munich and I used to phone home to speak to me mam on a Sunday. I'd be at the phone box at the venue, somebody soundchecking a bass drum – boom, boom, 'one, two, sibilance, sibilance, one, two' – and I'm going, 'How you doing? I'm in Munich.'

'Where's Munich?'

'It's in Germany.'

'Where's Germany?' Fucking hell . . .

Chatting away about family stuff and then, 'How is Liam?'

'Oh, he's out rehearsing.'

'What for? Fucking hell, he's not joined the Shakespeare fucking group, has he?'

'No, he's in a band.'

'What?! Doing what?'

'He's the singer.'

'He can't fucking sing.'

'Oh, I don't know now. Well, he said he's the singer.' And that was it.

Got home and our Paul is going, 'Oh yeah, he's in this band. They are pretty fucking good, you know.'

Liam I think we were rehearsing in Longsight at the time, in some Irish centre. At that point it was good as it was going to be. Let's do a gig. It's like a footballer, you've got to go and get some time on the pitch under your belt.

Noel They were playing at the local band night. I went down to see them and I remember being pretty impressed. They had their own songs and Liam didn't look that out of place and I thought, 'Fucking hell, that's pretty good.'

Liam It was shit. I don't think there was anyone there, but at least we did it . . . It can't have been that fucking bad if he wanted to join.

Noel I'm not in Oasis at this point, I'm not in a band, I have no intention of being in a band, I'm just trying not to get sacked from this job because I fucking blagged my way into it and I'm an absolute chancer. It didn't dawn on me at all that I was going to join that band. They came up and said, 'What do you think?'

I said, 'It's fucking great.'

'We were thinking, would you fancy being our manager?'

'What? What the fucking hell are you talking about? No.'

'Because you know loads of people and all that.'

'No, I'm not sure about that, I think you can get a better manager than me.'

Liam We were asking him to manage us at first. I was thinking he might have a connection through the Inspiral Carpets and he was like, 'Fucking manage you, I'll write the songs for you.' He wanted to do it; we didn't put a gun to his head . . . The truth is he got on his hands and knees and said, 'Listen, I'll do anything, anything, just please let me be in your band.'

I said, 'Get up off your hands and knees, son, you're alright, you can do it.'

That's the main event. I think I've got a picture of it somewhere.

Noel A couple of weeks later Liam said, 'Come and fucking jam with us.' So I went and sat in with them playing their tunes and it was great. I think the second time I went I had a riff of something, I don't know what it was. Liam was going, 'Play them that fucking song that you played us.' It just went from there really. Once everybody joins in and you hear this thing that you've 'written' being played back to you in this room it's like, 'Wow! Fucking hell!' To hear your own stuff and saying, 'If you play that, why don't you play that there and I'll play that there.' It was really a mega moment. And then it went nowhere for two years.

Paul It was perfect for Noel because he'd seen Liam, he'd seen potential. Someone young, good looking; I believe I have got the songs, or I will have, put them together: magic. But there is no genius involved, it just happened.

Liam He'd gone from being the loner, the stoner, the little weirdo . . . He'd sort of come out of himself and I guess that's through drugs and pills and that. He started getting a bit more swagger. I just knew he'd be the one, he'd be great. Once he got sacked, he went, 'Fuck it, I'm going to have it with Oasis.' I'd like to thank the Inspiral Carpets for sacking him, well done.

Noel The actual reason why I got sacked is amazing. We were travelling all on the same bus, the band and the crew, and it's back in the day before open borders and all that. The band would sit at the front of the bus and all the fucking potheads would sit at the back. Somebody would come up and say, 'We are coming to the Spanish border.' The singer was asleep in his bunk. We had to clean the fucking bus up, there were drugs everywhere. The sniffer dogs got on and all that and there's a fucking scene. As the bus is pulling off, the lead singer wakes up, I'm stood up by his bunk – he says, 'Fucking hell, have they gone?' and I said, 'Yeah, they've gone,' and he said, 'What about the fucking drugs on the bus?' and I said, 'Fucking hell, there was shitloads of it everywhere,' and he said, 'Where did you hide them?' and I put my hands under his pillow and said, 'Under your pillow.' I got the sack about two weeks after that. One of my finest moments.

Clint Boon I think towards the end of '92 his heart wasn't in it. He'd already started with Oasis, he was writing with them, he was rehearsing with them when he had the chance. He was phoning home every night, talking to Liam about his ideas . . . I think it dawned on us that his heart was no longer with the Inspirals so we literally let him go. We give him £2,000 as a golden handshake, which was a lot of money back then.

Noel There is the myth that I kicked open the rehearsal room door to the theme tune from *The Good, the Bad and the Ugly* and said, 'Everybody stop what they're doing, I am here to make us all millionaires.' There wasn't that at all, I kind of fell into the whole thing by accident really. I never had a clear vision of anything until Liam asked me to join and then I turned into a megalomaniac. I always thought that we were greater than the sum of our parts, do you know what I mean?

> I never had a clear vision of anything until Liam asked me to join and then I turned into a megalomaniac.

Noel Somebody who'd worked for one of the three biggest bands in Manchester, Inspiral Carpets, really should have had a head start, but we didn't. But what we did have was the tunes and when the music was shit for that first eighteen months, two years, we never gave up.

Liam We weren't the best musicians and I

obviously weren't the best singer and that, but we just, I don't know, we just got our heads down and got on with it. I don't think there was any fucking plan, it was let's get some gigs under our belt and just learn our craft. We were very, very fucking serious about it.

Paul If there was a master plan there would be no Tony McCarroll in the band, and there probably would have been no Guigsy, and there probably would have been no Bonehead because he's balding. If you are going to do it that way, you are going to pick people with hair, aren't you?

Noel Imagine a band coming along now with a geezer like Bonehead, what is the first thing anybody would say to you? He's got to fucking go. I remember Alan McGee saying to us once, 'Can we no get him a fucking hat?' No, he is what he is; he's not even going to wear shades. In fact we should shave that bald patch, fucking paint a Union Jack on it.

> Bonehead was kind of the glue that held it all together.

Liam He was like the geezer, you know, the doctor off *Back to the Future*, the mad fucking doctor. He was always in mad bands and that, just always had some instrument on him. Fixing it or breaking it or trying to play it. He was kind of like that.

Noel He would lose his fucking mind on red wine. He'd also lose the use of his neck muscles when he was drunk.

I swear to God, when he'd get pissed, it was like his head was a medicine ball.

Liam I like Bonehead's style of playing, there's no frills. Even though now he thinks he is fucking Jimi Hendrix. Chill, man, that fucking straight rhythm, it's a dying art, man. That was our sound pretty much. Just a wall of sound and Noel over the top and Guigs just doing the root notes.

Noel Bonehead was kind of the glue that held it all together. I would say he was the most forward thinking, initially, because he had been in bands before Oasis. If anything, I would say Bonehead was probably, in the early days, the spirit of Oasis. He didn't give a fuck and why would you?

Bonehead What does he mean by the spirit of Oasis? I don't know. Maybe he said that because whenever Noel and Liam had a bit of a fight and it got more than heated, to the point that someone is going to have to come between them, I would always, always wait and watch and jump in between them. You can guarantee it would be me who would try and lighten it up the next morning, who'd come falling out of the lift doing a *Morecambe and Wise* stunt, half-drunk still, to lighten the atmosphere to get them all laughing so we could get on the bus. Maybe I was in that sense, yes.

Noel When it would be going off between me and Liam, he was the only one person that would try and get in between us and we would just completely ignore him. There would be a lull in the argument while he said his bit and then we would just go, 'Whatever,' and carry on fucking rowing about – I don't know, fur collars on jackets and shit.

Liam Bonehead. Mental fucker. Cannot describe how mental he is. Another brother, love him, still in touch with him. He's a top musician and all, he can play anything. But he's a mental cunt and I loved his mad side, so me and him would get up to mad shit together, you know what I mean?

Noel Guigs brought a calmness to it all, he never got flustered. Just a real, quiet fucking dude. Guigs didn't care about playing on records. Loved cricket and *Doctor Who* and weed and Man City. I'd say fifth after that was being in Oasis. I'd say that came a lowly fifth. I think he's got two prized possessions in his life, none of them are like fucking Ivor Novellos and shit, I think one of them is a Dalek that he bought off the BBC, another one is a fucking Ian Botham signed cricket bat or something. Just a recluse. We were in the band with him till 1998, so that was what, seven years. I reckon if I wrote down everything he said to me it would fill about a paragraph and a half. Bass players are a weird bunch though, aren't they? They are always the quiet ones.

Liam Guigsy, chilled-out motherfucker, man. Stoner. He is like fucking Bob Marley. Lovely lad, adore him, but just a complete and utter fucking stoner. He was into cricket, which I found dead weird. Fucking cricket, what the fuck's that about? He loved the music, man, loved it, he was deep into it, but maybe a bit too fucking deep. Sometimes you've got to come out of it and go, 'It's only music.'

Bonehead He is 'Lee Perry Guigs', he should have been a Rasta. How he ended up in a rock-and-roll band and not a reggae band I don't know.

Liam Tony McCarroll was good, had some good times with Tony, man. Tony was more into the Irish scene. We would go to the Irish pubs, he would hang about with all these Irish musicians. But he was cool, man.

Tony McCarroll I was knackered, you know, I was absolutely knackered, I never forget that, that moulded me, I had a different outlook on life. None of them lot, initially, had kids, none of them had that responsibility, tough on the shoulders of an eighteen-year-old. I don't think they appreciated it, they couldn't see why I wasn't as loud and brash as them, which I could never be. I wasn't with Paula for so long, the mother of Gemma, me child, she became pregnant quite fast, accidentally. I had to go and earn more money. At the beginning, the band thing wasn't being lucrative, bringing any money in, I ended up on building sites, but I needed to earn that money.

Bonehead How to describe Noel? We didn't call him the chief for nothing. He is a natural born leader. He's also got a real sense of humour that has got to be seen and heard to be believed. He is one of the funniest people you could possibly meet. That aside, don't step on his toes the wrong way or you will know about it; but then he won't hold a grudge.

Liam I didn't call Noel the chief. But I know people that get called chiefs and it's not a good thing.

Noel Liam? We wouldn't have been what we were without him, that's for sure. As important and as vital as those songs were and still are, I think the two elements that made Oasis was his thing and them songs. If it wasn't for him we might have been just another band. I couldn't imagine anybody else being the singer.

Bonehead Liam is Liam. I suppose everybody thinks they know Liam. Everybody knows Liam's walk, everyone knows Liam's clothes, everyone knows Liam's voice, everybody. Because of the press and the interviews whatever, you'd feel as if you knew him and you'd probably be three-quarters right because he is honest; he is a really, really honest person. Everybody's read a million interviews with Liam and that is the Liam you are going to meet, he doesn't lie. I love him to bits for that, his total honesty. But if Liam starts growing a beard, watch out: something is going to go wrong. The longer the beard gets the more you should worry.

> If it wasn't for him we might have been just another band.

Liam Me? Beautiful, mental, the best one out of the lot of them. I could have multiple personalities, but they are all fucking amazing. Whoever they are they are all fucking great. Every one of them is good.

Home from home

Bonehead There was a club in Manchester called the Boardwalk, it's gone now, sadly. It was a great venue round the corner from the Haçienda. Looked like an old church and it was a cool place, used to have good club nights at the weekends, great gigs during the week. Any band from around the country would roll into the Boardwalk and play at some point. It was a cool place to be, cool crowd, just people out, loving music. They had a big loading bay and these stairs down into the basement where a few Manchester bands used to rehearse. I think the Mondays used to rehearse in there, the Inspirals used to go in there ... We got this room that we actually could leave our gear – all the amps, the PA – in. We painted it, put pictures up and draped things on the walls. We made it our own.

Liam I painted that Union Jack on that wall, that's my work. Stuck a Beatles poster next to it. That was our home for a bit. I loved it. I wasn't into dance music and the whole fucking town, the whole city, was like just immersed in this fucking music that didn't make sense to me. Everyone was in the Haçienda popping pills. Everyone was fucking stood there fucking off their head, dancing like idiots. All me mates would be knocking on the door going, 'What you doing tonight? Going down to fucking ...? Come out, man, and fucking let's go out.'

'No, I'm not going out listening to that fucking stupid music. I'm staying down here and listening to the Faces. Fuck that, mate, you're only fucking dancing to it because you've got some drugs inside you. You try to tell me if you put that tune on there without nothing inside you, you'll be buzzing like you are now? That's bollocks.' I can listen to Led Zeppelin and I can listen to The Beatles, fucking clean as a whistle, and it still gets me off.

Bonehead There was always a fight when it got to 11 o'clock at night. Everyone would just leg it, get your guitar in the case and just run. Last one out of the door had to bring the key up and you knew you were going to get battered for rent. But the people who ran it were cool and we got away without paying rent for months in there, which was great.

Liam 'We'll give it you next week, come on, chill the fuck out, man, have a spliff.'

Noel We were always getting in trouble with the people from the Boardwalk: for smoking drugs, for any fucking wrong 'uns hanging out. If anything ever got stolen they said it was our fault, but it never was.

> If anything ever got stolen they said it was our fault, but it never was.

Bonehead We were pretty committed and dedicated to rehearsing. It didn't matter what night it was or who was doing what on what night. If we were rehearsing, we were rehearsing and that was it: 'Sorry, boys, we are not going there, we are not doing that.' People couldn't understand it, but that's how we developed our sound, playing his songs, singing his words, as that unit. Every night, you know? I was working, Guigs was working; Guigs had a great job, he worked for British Telecom with a pension, it was like, job for life. So, he would just finish work and walk straight down the Boardwalk. Every single night. We didn't go in there and just plug in and say, 'Alright, let's have an hour's jamming, like, give us a beat, Tony, let's come up with some ideas.' We actually went in there, get all the chat out of the way, laughs and jokes, plug in and away we go. We'd have a set list of songs that we'd play, again, and again, and again, night after night. We didn't dick about jamming and messing about. I don't think it was we've got to make this happen, it was, we're *going* to make this happen.

Playing as loud as fuck, playing guitar and working out bits, it's great.

Noel It would have been very easy to say, 'Me bird's getting on me case,' or, 'I'm fucking skint,' or whatever, you know what I mean? Then, when the music arrived, when you've got the songs, you don't need anything else. We were fucking dedicated if nothing else, and that is the thing we carried on right to the end really. For us, rehearsing was sacred, we would never go out on tour without two months of solid rehearsing. Day after day after day, because people are going to come and see you and you have got to blow them away.

Liam We never jammed, man, never, ever jammed. We weren't like Led Zeppelin or anything. Just rehearsed and rehearsed and worked it out.

Noel I fucking love rehearsing, what could be better than rehearsing in a room with no pressure on you. Playing as loud as fuck, playing guitar and working out bits, it's great.

Bonehead Coyley was always there. Coyley would bring a little four-track recorder and a microphone. He'd fix the mixer because: 'We need Liam louder, but it's feeding back.'

Coyley They were there all the time, they were very committed. At that time, they sounded very powerful, moody, belligerent, dark; it just had a devilish, filthy little sound to it and I was immediately drawn to that, I like that kind of thing, you know.

Bonehead I remember it being a great sound because, all of a sudden, there was two guitars. The noise we were making was outrageous. Everyone always says, 'Bonehead, how did you get that sound, the driving guitars?' I just turned the fucker up, every dial, turn it up, crank it. It didn't take long until that noise we were making, in that room, was going to do something. I knew it was going to reach out to people, I knew if we could bring that onto a stage and people would come and see us they would get it immediately. I never went into rehearsals thinking, 'Just rehearsals,' half-heartedly strumming. I was in, I was doing it, I was nailing it, I was getting it how it should be. I had to do it right every time. Had to. We got it just right where you could hear Liam, you could hear Noel, you could hear me, you could hear Guigs, you could hear drums . . . but massively loud. It sounded incredible in that room. We could all hear each other, Coyley had sorted that out for us, and it was like doing this massive gig every night and it got tighter and tighter. There came a real confidence after a time. You really start to believe that you are going to do something with this. We didn't do a lot of gigs, it was all rehearse, rehearse, rehearse. We played the Boardwalk more often than not, because it was a case of going upstairs and knocking on the office door. 'Can we play next Friday, is there a slot?' – 'Yeah, go on.' We'd do it that way.

Liam I think we just went in there and just made a fucking racket, you know what I mean, I think we were the loudest thing going.

Loud as fuck

Noel I was rehearsing with them and then Bonehead said, 'We've got a gig next Tuesday.' The first one – and it hadn't dawned on me until that moment that I'd never played guitar standing up. I was like, 'I haven't even got a strap for me guitar . . .' I had to borrow a strap from someone and stand in the bedroom – I should have done all this with the tennis racquet years ago – because it's a crucial thing, where you are going to hold that guitar and how long that strap's going to be. Too long and you're heading into punk-rock territory. Too high and it's a bit Haircut 100. Luckily for me the place where it felt most comfortable was the place where it fucking looked the best. But I have got to say it was a big thing learning to play that set of songs in about five days standing up. It's a really kind of innocuous thing, but it was like such a big deal for me.

Liam Bonehead had been in bands so he'd done fucking lots of gigs. He knew his way around the stage and venues and shit like that.

Clint Boon I remember seeing that gig at the Boardwalk, Noel's first gig with the band. There weren't many people there. It was like probably twenty of us and five of those were the Inspiral Carpets. It wasn't the Oasis that we came to know, and Liam was very much under the spell of Ian Brown, I think he was in his mind, thinking, I'll do it the way that Ian does it and that will get me by.

Liam I don't know if there was anyone in there. I mean there might have been a few, but I think it was just mainly our mates, just sort of going, 'What the fuck are they doing?' I don't know, I can't really remember. It didn't matter to me whether people liked it or not, that wasn't what we were doing it for. We were doing it just to fucking do it.

Tony Our friends, of course, would be supportive, but you know, you'd hear calls of 'Stone Roses', but we knew we were something different from The Stone Roses, without a doubt.

> It didn't matter to me whether people liked it or not, that wasn't what we were doing it for.

Bonehead Nobody clapped, it was just silence, it was like, fuck. Then you got the odd clap, it was like, shit, that went down a storm, didn't it?

Noel I've never really had stage fright or nerves because we rehearsed so much, we knew it backwards. We were very, very well-rehearsed and that went right through the whole thing with Oasis, the band were fucking on it, drilled, do you know what I mean? There was no stone left unturned as to make it the best that it could be.

Liam We were good live, I can tell you that, we were fucking shit hot. Individually we weren't great musicians or great singers or particularly great songwriters but we were great together.

Noel The Boardwalk was very small. From street level, there was two stairs, one leading down into the basement where the rehearsal rooms were and a staircase leading up to the door where they took the money. You walked in through the door and there was a bar to your left, then there was another bar to your right then there was the stage kind of in front of you. Small, but a pretty fucking good gig. We did it at least half a dozen times.

We were good live, I can tell you that, we were fucking shit hot.

Coyley Sharp as fuck, loud as fuck, you couldn't help but notice there was something very different and very special about this band. Not that there was a lot there, some of these early gigs are fucking half empty, most of them are half empty.

Liam At the time we weren't there for anyone else except for us. We'd walk off and we'd be, 'Fucking great, all we need now is a crowd and we'll be happy,' but in our heads we were just waiting for everyone else to catch up I guess.

Noel I was kind of awkward playing these things. I couldn't play the guitar stood up so I was really concentrating. That's when this 'stillism' became this thing that we'd invented.

Liam It felt natural for me to do nothing, it was like I never, ever broke into a sweat about should I be jumping around like Mick Jagger, should I be fucking wearing make-up like Bowie or should I be doing this or that? It just felt natural to do fuck all. Except for rip that mic apart and to sing as best as you can, as powerful as you can. And that was it. I thought, 'I can do that. Who needs make-up and fucking leather kecks and fucking Cuban heels. Just stand there and fucking have it. I can do that.'

Paul There would be no audience interaction, it would just be Liam going, 'This one's called . . .' and then just play it. Kind of cocky Manc arrogance, just go on stage, play your tunes and get off.

Liam I've tried dancing, done it in the mirror once and I looked like a fucking cock, so not happening, mate. I can stand still really good.

Noel The singer wasn't going, 'Fucking love me!' you know what I mean? Mick Jagger showmanship was fucking beneath us. We don't have to. You are going to come to us because these songs are brilliant.

Liam I've never really held a microphone, only in the early days, I guess. All the thought of taking that microphone off

Who needs make-up and fucking leather kecks and fucking Cuban heels. Just stand there and fucking have it.

and walking around like Ian Brown just didn't give me any power. I just don't know how people can fucking sing like that to be fair. I had to be right up on it, hands behind me back and just fucking pouring everything into it. The more people went on about it the more we played on it. Not that we could have done anything else because we are not dancers or anything like that. It was getting to the point where you'd kind of get fined if you moved, like James Brown would fine people for fucking a lyric up. It would be like that.

'Did I fucking see you move in the middle eight of "Supersonic"?'

'No.'

'Better not, bitch. Did I fucking see you tap your foot in the middle of fucking "Wonderwall"?'

'No, no.'

'Okay, must be seeing things. If I see any of that nonsense there will be a fine going down. Static.'

I can stand still really good. You're never going to outdo 'Jumping Jack Flash', you're never going to dance better than James Brown, so don't fucking bother. I don't know many other people that stand still on stage so we were owning that.

National Flat Cap Day

Noel Bonehead's brother must have worked for Granada Television and, as I'm thinking of it now, it is amazing. What on earth were we doing? Was it Red Nose Day? It definitely wasn't Children in Need. Children in Need is fucking massive. It must have been something, though. I've got a feeling it was a bit more local than that, it was like Save the Hot Pot or something; National Flat Cap Day or Where's Me Whippet?

> We went on after Alvin Stardust, *the* Alvin Stardust, and we mimed to one of our demos.

Tony We were told, you're going to be filmed, you're going to get exposure, TV exposure, this could be it, this could be the one we'd been waiting for.

Bonehead It was an all-day thing outdoors. Somehow my brother knew somebody who was involved in it so I was, 'Yeah, alright, cool, it's going to be on TV.' I don't know what it was all about. I think it was a bit of a shambles really, from what I remember. It was one of them gigs, what was the point of that? A couple of mums and dads and four-year-old kids in prams sat on the grass watching us . . .

Noel We went on after Alvin Stardust, *the* Alvin Stardust, and we mimed to one of our demos. It's like grannies, a Sunday-afternoon thing. The guy introduced us as a rave band, unbelievable. It was one of Liam's and Bonehead's songs called 'Take Me', which they steadfastly refused to record. Fucking great song and all, the *one* great song they wrote. How that footage has never come out is amazing. Obviously someone's flipped the off switch and gone, 'Fuck these cunts,' do you know what I mean?

Liam I remember we borrowed Alvin Stardust's drum kit. We'd done this tune with a sound of a big fucking air-raid siren going down, very strange, man. We sounded good I think, I don't think there was anyone there, it was like a village fête kind of thing, it was just pretty odd.

Tony Gutted, we were devastated.

All the things that I wanna be

Noel The way that I write songs is I have songs that are in cold storage for years and I know they are great. I know I am going to finish it one day, but I'm not going to rush it, it is going to fall out of the sky, I'm not going to just write it for the sake of it. That is why I have always got a backlog of forty-five slightly unfinished tunes that need a first verse or a middle eight, but they are essentially fully formed.

Liam I didn't really get involved in the music – I was like, 'That's your thing, you do that, I'll just be cool as fuck over there.'

Bonehead Me and Liam would often go round his flat and just strum acoustic guitars. Liam would sing, no microphone, nothing, just sit on the couch and we'd strum through Noel's songs. It was great to do it that way sometimes. But he'd bring them into the rehearsal room and then they would really come to life; there would be drums, bass, amplifier involved and Liam would be singing through a PA with the delay on his voice. For Noel to hear them like that, he must have thought 'wow'. To see them come alive in that way with a band, that's how you hear them in your head when you write them.

Noel The first real song I wrote was 'Live Forever'. The first real song that I completed that was good was 'Live

Forever'. Oasis was going for about maybe six months or a year before that song and we were kind of alright, we could all play a little bit. I remember one night being in a rehearsal room and we were one kind of band – like a shit indie band from Manchester – then the next night going down with 'Live Forever' and everything changed. I knew enough about music and about songs to know that that was a great song. Then one followed another and it's like this is happening now. Even if nobody else takes any notice of it, this is happening. Bonehead was saying, 'You've not just written that, there is no way that is your song.' He still to this day fucking debates whether I'd written it or not.

The first real song that I completed that was good was 'Live Forever'.

Bonehead I wouldn't believe it, you know? You heard songs like that on the radio and you didn't hear them coming from someone you know in the same room, claiming that they had wrote it. So, for someone to come in and just go, 'I'll play you one of my songs,' and play you 'Live Forever', fuck off. You didn't write that. He was like, 'Why didn't I?' Because listen to it, you know? Wow, what a song.

'You didn't write it.'

'Yeah, I did.'

'No, you didn't.'

We're still in denial now. He didn't write any of it in fact; in fact, he's bluffed it, he's winged it, someone's wrote it, wasn't him.

Liam I don't remember that one specifically. I know it's a great tune that, but all of them were good. It wasn't like a eureka moment, all of it was kind of like, 'Fucking hell, we've got some good tunes now, man. These are fucking great, this is it.' We'd got our sound, because that is the hardest thing about being a band. We'd just sounded like a really shit Stone Roses at the beginning, really shit.

Noel I kind of write without writing if you like. I'll be strumming three chords on a guitar. The opening chord sequence on 'Live Forever' I must have strummed that for weeks and weeks on the guitar until a melody came, the words come later, right at the end. So I will be strumming the chords that are saying something to me musically, but in its early stages I won't know what it is. Then a melody will arrive and so I'll have the music and the melody and then I'll arrange the whole song without any words. It will just be me singing whatever is coming into my head and then, over a period, little bits of words will stick. So the first line, I'll have that straight away, and then maybe another couple of lines after that and then I will get to a point where I will write down the bits that have fallen out of the sky and then I will try and fill in the gaps. That has never changed from the minute I started writing songs; it has always been about the melody and the music. I don't really put too much stock into the words if I am being honest.

Bonehead Every night he'd come in with something, he'd just go, 'Hang on a minute, I'll just play you this song,' and you'd just be all blubbering wrecks and he just kept churning them out. They weren't half formed, 'I've got this idea'. It was, 'Here's me latest song.' Done. I was doing a riff in rehearsals one night and he was, 'That's tops that, what is it? It sounds like "Taxman" or whatever.' He come in the next day and just went, 'Check this out.' And he played 'Up in the Sky' start to finish, done, arranged.

'What's that?'

'I did it last night after rehearsal, in bed.'

Liam The songs were uplifting, they were definitely escapism, but they were definitely real. For me, when I was singing them, they weren't like something that couldn't be attained, it was real fucking life. 'Rock 'n' Roll Star', that's me, and I've not even fucking done a gig yet. I can go with that.

Noel I like music to be up, I think it comes from listening to a lot of acid house music in the eighties, which was so uplifting; I always wanted my music to be euphoric. I was at the Haçienda when acid house was invented and that music is still really important to me. I never write words down particularly. I find that if I've written something it stays there and it can never be changed. But if I just let the words come, and if they are good enough, then you remember them, you don't need to write them down. I only used to ever write them down to give to Liam and then, as I'm writing them down, I would be thinking, 'What is this song about?' And you'd have to make up some meaning for Liam because he would get freaked about things like that.

> It felt like the songs weren't his and they weren't mine, they were ours.

Liam It felt like the songs weren't his and they weren't mine, they were ours. So it felt pretty natural, all the words he was singing, they weren't alien to me, it was like 'Yeah, I get this'. Coyley had some kind of recording equipment up in his bedroom, we'd go round there, everyone would be downstairs, smoking dope, talking about pyramids and fucking aliens and all that nonsense, like you do. We'd go up and we'd record some of these tunes with him. I think it was 'Married With Children', 'D'Yer Wanna be a Spaceman' and stuff like that. Then go back down, get stoned and walk home. They were good times, innocent times, not knowing what's going on; you are kind of just hoping that it takes off. Yeah, good times.

Noel We were just hanging out at Coyley's house, you know, he had a four-track in his bedroom, and that's where I met Phil Smith.

Phil We'd be up late, but Coyley, he'd be up all night, we used to call him 'The Prince of Darkness'. We just started hearing noise when we were going to bed, usually it was some mate's band, and they were crap. Tell him to go and turn it down. But I remember going up to bed and knocking on the door and asking, 'Who's that?' and he went, 'Oh, it's one of Noel's tunes,' and it was kind of like, 'Ah, well, that's pretty good.' And then a few days later, going to bed and it's a different tune, 'Oh, that's another one of Noel's.'

'Oh, right.' That's something else, that.

Liam I'd hear him playing his songs and I'd be thinking, 'I can't believe my brother's wrote them songs.' You just go, 'That's fucking cool, you make that all by yourself?' Writing songs, words and melodies and getting it to a guitar was, 'You're fucking amazing,' totally.

First demos

Liam It was serious and it was fucking intense, but it was never desperate. It was never, ever desperate. We just knew it would happen and we never licked arse and we never begged. We were never running around, banging people's doors down going, 'Please give us a deal,' or, 'Please listen to us.'

Noel The original demo tape, which is the one we gave to Alan McGee, we did that in the Real People's practice room. I was on tour with Inspiral Carpets and the Real People were supporting them, a band from the arse-end of the eighties who I really fucking love and still like to this day. Typical Scousers, two brothers, Tony and Chris Griffiths, headcases, brilliant, just talk shit all night, brilliant, brilliant bullshit all night. Me and Liam loved them. I got to know them on that tour and then when that tour finished the Real People came to Manchester and did a gig at the Boardwalk where we were rehearsing and we all went down to see them. Then we all went back to my flat in India House on Whitworth Street and there were guitars out and boozing and smoking weed and all that. They said that they had this eight-track recorder in their practice room in Liverpool. So off we went and recorded what became the famous demo with the Union Jack on the front – the demo tape that became sought after, the holy grail demo tape.

Liam Yeah, I can't remember much about that. There was acid involved, lots of weed, going back and forth. It was great. They were out there, man, they were top, top musicians definitely. They were miles better than us, they were great players and they were great songwriters.

Noel We had some great times. We were doing acid and just sitting up till all hours talking about music and they were happy days. We ended up driving over every few days to record 'Rock 'n' Roll Star', 'Columbia' and 'Bring It On Down' . . . we did about ten or twelve songs and we got to know them quite well. I loved them, I loved being there and hanging out in their rehearsal room. They had a real enthusiasm not only for music but for *our* music. We were doing 'Columbia' as an instrumental and I think either Tony or Chris said, 'That is a boss tune that, mate, why don't you write some words for it?' It is still a bone of contention to this day as to who wrote what. I definitely wrote most of the words, I think Liam wrote a line or two, but as we were all tripping the night we did it . . .

Liam We were up all night and I wouldn't like to say what it was like, but it was pretty out there. I remember everyone was playing and I remember waking up with fucking blisters on my fingers and I was going, 'What the fuck is all that?' I'd been on the drum kit all night, just tripping me head off. So I don't remember doing much of the singing, or recording it to be fair. Or the writing. But I knew who'd written it.

Noel We had ten copies pressed up and gave them all away to our friends, didn't send them to any record labels. We only went to one record label and that was Factory and we went to see Phil Sax who was head of A&R because we had this demo tape and that's what you do. It was shit, it wasn't any of the stuff that became the famous songs.

Bonehead So we go upstairs with the demo tape for him to have a listen and have a chat through it. Me, Noel and Liam, three of us. I had a copy of this tape obviously and I put it in my system at home and I would turn it up and it sounded pretty fucking good to me. He put it in his and I remember he had the bass turned right down to the left and he had the treble up there and he had the balance there and he played it sort of half-heartedly, dead quiet. He sort of skimmed through it. We were looking at each other going, 'He's got all the bass turned off there, turn the fucker up, have a listen!' I remember coming out and thinking, 'He didn't have a clue, man.' Didn't seem arsed. Thank God, eh?

Noel He said, 'We'll play it to Tony Wilson and see what Tony thinks,' and we never heard from them again. Fair enough.

Liam Maybe he just didn't get it and that's fucking cool, I listen to lots of shit that I don't get. He just didn't see it, which means, fair enough, we weren't meant to be on that label. McGee seen it and got it and the rest is history. I wasn't arsed whether he got it or not. The funny thing is that he turned round and said, 'You sound a bit too Manchester for my liking.' That's a bit fucking strange considering we are from Manchester, you lunatic . . . As opposed to what, being from Wakefield?

Noel I remember feeling if it's going to happen they are going to come to us, I'm not going to go to anybody else.

Bonehead There were a lot of people going, 'Why are you dicking about, man?' There were a lot of people questioning it. Why? I don't think I even bothered answering them. Because, that's why. It's like asking George Best, 'Why are you always kicking a football?' Because I'm George Best, I'll show you why. That's what we thought. We knew.

Noel We'd done this festival in Manchester called In The City where all the record labels come, it was an unsigned band night. We did two of those. Fuck all, nothing, not even a drink, nothing. No one even said we were shit. We were completely and utterly fucking ignored. I'd already written the first three albums. I'd already written the melody and the chords, I was only waiting on the words. To me that is a finished song because I would quite frankly just get fucking pissed and make the words up and freestyle it. A lot of *Morning Glory* was in my head as we were recording *Definitely Maybe* for sure. And I knew, for instance, that 'All Around The World' was going to be the last track on our third album before I had a record deal. Bonehead used to laugh and say, 'What third album? We've not even got a manager.' I truly believed that it would come to pass. I don't know where that belief came from.

Liam I weren't the best singer, Noel weren't the best guitar player, Bonehead weren't the best guitar player, but we had spirit, man, and that was lacking, massively, at that point in music. I kind of knew to be honest and I know people think you are being big headed, but I had a feeling it would happen, man. Just because, if you want something so much, you know, it happens. I fucking wanted it, man, and I wanted it for the right reasons. I actually fucking needed it. It was like, this shit has to happen. And I don't know what the consequences would have been without it happening, that's how much it had to happen. It needed to happen because if it didn't happen then the world would be black, that's how mad it was.

King Tut's

Noel No one in the outside world is taking a fucking blind bit of notice, we didn't have one single paragraph written about us, ever. Then we met McGee and of course this is the guy who signed Primal Scream, Jesus and Mary Chain, Teenage Fan Club and all that, and he's coming up to you and offering you a record deal saying, 'This is fucking great, you are fucking great.' It is like thank you very much, I know, I thought as much. We were sharing a rehearsal room with an all-girl band called Sister Lovers; there is no need to google it, they didn't go anywhere, I am not even sure whether they put any records out. Unbeknown to us, one of the girls in the band, Debbie Turner, God bless Debbie, was an ex-girlfriend of Alan McGee. We were asking them what they were up to and they are saying, 'We are going up to Glasgow to do this gig.' We'd never heard of King Tut's Wah Wah Hut – what a stupid name for a place anyway.

Debbie Turner I think I was probably being quite cocky actually, saying, 'Noel, we're playing in Glasgow.' For an unsigned band to get a gig outside of Manchester then was like playing Glastonbury.

Noel She said, 'Why don't you come with us – be on the bill?'

We were like, 'Yes – fucking Glasgow – let's do it.'

Liam 'How the fuck have you got a gig and not us?'

She said, 'Oh, we know this band, why don't you just gig along with it?'

We were thinking, 'We'll get there and they will tell us to fuck off.'

Coyley Noel decides we're going to do this the proper way, we're not driving up, we're going to get a fucking driver and a bus.

Noel We kind of got a few headcases together. If we all put in £25 we can hire a splitter van and get up there, kip in the van, do the gig, get back, fucking Friday night, yeah, let's do it. I remember it was a gold van, which I thought was amazing.

Liam Beautiful day, smoking weed, all the nonsense, drinking. One of them days where you just go, 'It's fucking going to be the day today.' Maybe it was the drugs or something.

Noel We get there really early of course and we go to the gig before anyone's turned up and said we were Oasis from Manchester, we'd come to play tonight. The guy said . . .

Liam 'Never fucking heard of you, you are not down.'

Noel We said, 'Yeah, yeah, it's alright, we're with Debbie,' and he's like . . .

Liam 'Fuck you, you're not fucking booked.'

Noel Turns out Debbie and Sister Lovers are supporting this band called 18 Wheeler that McGee had either signed or was about to sign, so it wasn't even their gig. Why the fuck they were even inviting us up is . . . well, who knows.

There is this story that we threatened to smash the gaff up and all that, that's bollocks. If anybody's fucking been to a nightclub in Glasgow, you don't go throwing your weight around up there and live to tell the tale.

Liam You would have got fucking rolled up in a little ball and fucking slung in the corner. There was none of that.

Noel We said to the guy, 'Come on, man, we come all the way from Manchester, all these guys here, our mates, we are alright.' Debbie's turned up and the rest of 18 Wheeler. 'Well, if you don't mind they can go on first.' In the middle of the afternoon or something.

Debbie Turner We said that if they're not playing then we're not going to play. We'll do a really short set, which wasn't hard because we only had five songs anyway. Then Oasis were allowed to play.

Noel So, we got to do four songs. We used to finish with 'I Am the Walrus' and we never really worked out an ending, so what Liam used to do is he would finish the 'coo, coo, cachoo' bit and he'd walk off. Then I would go round it maybe three or four times with the band and think, 'Fuck it, I don't know how to finish it,' so I would leave the guitar feeding back and I would walk off and leave. Then we would go and stand on the dance floor,

> There is this story that we threatened to smash the gaff up and all that, that's bollocks.

watch them and take the piss and, where circumstances would allow it, start slinging shit out of the dressing room like bags of crisps and oranges and apples. Some nights that song used to go on for ages because the three of them didn't have a clue how to fucking end it. People thought this was performance art going on but invariably it would be a shit ending. At King Tut's I think there was loads of feedback, a smattering of applause.

Coyley The set is very, very short, they squeezed us on. Very grateful, because all we want to do is go and play King Tut's, that's fucking big time at that level. King Tut's, a very famous little gig in its own right. So, the gig finishes, I walk over to the bar and order a drink and I swung me head to me right and fucking Alan McGee. So, we walk upstairs and I introduce them.

Bonehead I was well aware of who Alan McGee was, I loved the Mary Chain, loved Primals, was a big fan, so I knew who he was. Didn't know he was in the audience.

Alan McGee Debbie doesn't even know that I was coming up to that gig and being an evil twisted fucker, I thought I would just show up to put her on edge. I really do believe that some things are meant to fucking be. I'm standing there with my kid sister Susan. She immediately says, 'You should sign these.'

'Let's hear the second song.'

Then it was like, I am signing these; third song, I'm *definitely* signing these.

Noel I'm up by the mixing desk with Coyley, Alan McGee walks up and says, 'What's your band called?' and I said,

'Oasis,' and, these were his exact words, he said, 'Do you want a record deal?'

'Who with?'

'Creation Records.'

We kind of went back that night, I don't remember anybody high-fiving in the back of the van thinking, 'Yeah, this is it!' I don't remember us being nonchalant about it either. We were going back to Manchester and getting into where I was living at 6 o'clock in the morning. My then missus, Louise, was getting ready to go to work. I said, 'Creation Records have offered us a record deal,' and she started crying. I was like, fucking hell, I expected a bit more than that. She knew then that, you know, that was going to be the end of us.

I often think what would have happened if he'd have not been there that night.

Coyley For me, says it all about Alan McGee, he knew, immediately, there is no negotiation to be done, no fucking about and he just come and said, 'I want to sign you,' just like that.

Noel I often think what would have happened if he'd have not been there that night. The arrogant side of me thinks we would have definitely got a record deal and changed the fucking world and blah, blah, blah because the songs were too good. But really, if it had been someone else, I don't know.

Creation

Noel I phoned around a few people in Manchester who knew Alan McGee and said, 'Is he liable to be in any way fucking serious?' and they were saying, 'Run that back, what did he say?'

I said, 'He came up to me at a gig and he's offered me a record deal.'

They went, 'Well, he's, yeah . . . fucking hell, if that's what he said then yeah!'

It just felt a bit too good to be true, you know. You've got the head of the coolest record label in England saying, 'Do you want a record deal?' Not, 'Send us a demo and I'll speak to me boss.' Yes, please. 'Right, it's done.' It's a bit like, really? Fucking hell. I don't think he was that pissed. He did have white jeans on, though, so he obviously was taking something.

I guess I called Creation. 'Come down and you can meet everybody,' and I'm going, 'How we going to get there?'

'Go to window number five at Piccadilly Station, your tickets will be waiting for you.'

Fuck off; I'm not fucking having this, going to Piccadilly Station, 'Um, we've come to pick our tickets up . . .'

'What name is it?'

'Gallagher.'

'Here they are.'

Wow, train tickets, fucking hell, it's the real deal there.

Me, Bonehead and Liam getting on the train and going down there, getting to where the offices were in Hackney and being quite underwhelmed by this shithole office that we got to. I don't know what I was expecting, but I wasn't expecting it to be a fucking toilet. I'd been to Mute records, who Inspirals were signed for, and they were in West London and it looked like a record company's offices: it had a car park and a front door. This place was just a door on a fucking high street. It looked like a derelict shop and Bonehead was going, 'Are you sure this is the right place?'

Then Liam and Bonehead are saying to me, 'You do the talking because you know what you're fucking going on about.' I suppose I knew all the terminology; I could meet with a manager and not feel out of place. I guess the rest of the boys in the band left it all up to me.

Bonehead It was rough, it was horrible. Didn't like it. I think, in my mind anyway, a record company is going to be like this huge building, massive glass doors, with palm trees in reception and polished floors with efficient people running around, being busy record-company people, with a girl at reception like, 'Hello, Creation Records, how can I help you?' Like that, that's a record company. Fuck off. We opened these doors, and it was all these women, sewing and knitting and doing whatever, in a sweatshop. It was like, fuck, this isn't a record company. You know what, I thought we were being taken for a ride, I thought that guy had thought it well worth his while to shell out £120 of free train tickets, just to sit on a roof with a pair of binoculars, watching us, pissing himself, going, 'Dickheads.' But there was a staircase like that, and a little sign, you know, Creation, and we were like, 'It's got to be up there.'

Noel Inside the front door of Creation was scrawled on the wall, in big felt-pen letters, 'Northern Ignorance'. It was in massive letters, scrawled in felt pen and I thought it was fucking brilliant. As soon as I'd seen that I thought, I fucking love it here. I feel comfortable here already.

Liam There was loads of people, loads of like record-business types, but not like the knobs that are in it today, just cool people. I can't remember any of the names and that, but just cool people. Just doing the business.

Noel The first person that we bump into is Tim Abbott and he had a mullet and really strange clothes on. His brother Chris was running the dance music side of things for Creation, and Tim had his own little corner in the office. It was Tim that had written 'Northern Ignorance' on the wall. McGee had an office downstairs called the bunker and on his desk he had this sign that said 'President of Pop'. I remember it being very laid-back. Somebody sent out to the pub for some booze and we just sat in the office for quite a while, just talking about music.

Liam Who is this fucking dude, Willy Wonka of fucking Creation? He looked like Gene Wilder. He had a bit of a weird head, curly hair and ginger . . . Tim was like a David Essex lookalike. So there's fucking Willy Wonka and David Essex and I'm stoned out of me head and thinking, 'Yeah, let's fucking sign to these fuckers.'

Noel McGee just got it. What can you say when the head of the record label, the guy that owns it, is offering you a record deal and he's into it and you become friends and fucking drug buddies and all that. That's it, what more do you want out of life? There's nothing else a record company can give you. We didn't know it then, but he was the last of a dying breed in the music business. Never got involved in anything other than making sure you had everything you wanted to go and do the records. He would come down and say, 'This is fucking great.' Alan McGee was brilliant. He is up there, one of the most important people in my life that's made a fucking real difference. Being on Creation is as important as Oasis being from Manchester, I feel. Major record labels are now set up for commerce and not for the art. It's all about the numbers and hits on YouTube and all that.

> I would have signed to Creation for nothing you know, I gave them my word and that was it.

Liam I was impressed, not that I would have known what another label was like. McGee was top, really enthusiastic about music and about us and just buzzing off the vibes, you know what I mean?

Bonehead I think if we did go into the big glass building with the palm trees and the receptionist and the guy manning the lift and the fella behind the big leather chair, I'd have come out thinking, 'Fuck, do I really want to do this? I don't like this music business, record company, office thing.' But I came out of there and it was like, 'Really like them, cool people.' Absolutely. I do remember the feeling – what was a record deal? Do you want a record deal? Fucking right I do. What's one of them, what happens, what do you do next? Dunno. I'd never had one. I didn't have a clue what it was, it was just like, 'Yeah, fucking great.'

Noel That is what happened, it was that straightforward. There was no doing the dance and all that. In any case I would have signed to Creation for nothing, you know, I gave them my word and that was it. The fact that I never asked for a record deal or I never asked to be in this band, has served me well down the years, do you know what I mean? Because, hey man, you fucking asked me. When the shit was hitting the fan with Creation I would say, 'You asked me to be on your record label, not the other fucking way round.'

Peggie I remember the day Liam came back and told me he had the record deal with Alan McGee. They come up here and said, 'We got a record deal, Mam!' And of course I thought, this is great, they'll get a bit of money and maybe buy a house. I never really thought it would go the way it did go. All Liam wanted was new clothes. Then it went haywire. I never, ever thought that it was going to go like that, never. I found it very hard to deal with actually at the beginning.

Paul I remember Liam being excited he didn't have to go to work any more. He got paid to be Liam, which was sing a bit, smoke loads of weed, hang out with your mates, get drunk . . .

Liam The main thing was just getting a deal, that's the best thing. Better than Knebworth, better than the best . . . When people go, 'What's the best thing about Oasis?' it was just having someone have the faith in us and letting us show them what we could do, getting that chance to record our album, those songs. Because we knew we weren't going to fuck it up.

Peggie

Noel Me mam was fucking fearless.

Liam Mam was an angel, still is. Me mam's cool, she's the coolest woman that's ever walked this fucking planet, in my eyes. Me mam's an absolute diamond. I know a lot of people have fucking dickheads as mams, but my mam's cool as fuck, absolute cool as fuck. Everything that is good about me is definitely from her.

Peggie I'm one of eleven, there are seven girls and four boys. We were the poorest of the poor, you could say. We had nothing, but we were happy enough. School was about a mile, we used to go down across the fields. with no shoes on us, bare feet, in the summertime. And if we got a pair of wellingtons, we'd share, we couldn't all get them. We used to love them wellingtons. I suppose we all brought each other up, you know, a lot of fighting and arguing going on. I left school when I was thirteen and a half and went out to work. I was working all my life really. My dad was no good, he was always coming and going. He'd go, then he'd come back, she used to get pregnant again, then he'd go and then he'd come back. So, we never really knew him. Eventually, he just went off and never came back at all. I was nearly eighteen when

> Everything that is good about me is definitely from her.

I left. We were very naïve. What I thought was going to happen, I don't really know. We just came over here to Manchester because everybody else did, but I hated it when I came over here first. I must have cried for about six months. I used to think, I wish I could get on a train and go back home. It was a big shock, I'm telling you, to come to a big city out of a small village. Oh, it was massive, I couldn't get over the size of the buildings. The Carousel was a big Irish club that was just up the road, it used to be packed. I would go there, but I was never really one for going out all that much, I'd only go out maybe one night a week whereas my sisters would go out Friday, Saturday and Sunday. I used to think, 'I can't be bothered going out,' one night was enough. I used to go on the Saturday night and that's all we did. Go to church then go to the Carousel. You'd be there and you'd dance and jive and do all this old-time waltzing and all that. Never really let themselves go that much, if you know what I mean. It was after the New Year, I think it was 1963, I went to the Carousel and I met him there. Tommy Gallagher. It was lovely when I met him but he was always a dodgy one from day one, did exactly what he wanted. He was always disappearing as well. But anyways, we got married after about nine, ten months and that was it. People used to think he was lovely, 'But your husband would do anything for anyone, he'd be a true friend.' I said, 'Yeah, but you don't know what he's done in the house.' That's why I always said street angel and the house devil.

Liam Mam's not impressed by all this rock-and-roll business. She is proud and all that, but I guess there are some bits where she's completely and utterly just gone, 'You fucking knobheads,' cringed and rightly so. There is some shit that come out of our mouths that was just fucking ridiculous.

Peggie I remember the first time he'd come back and he walked in to the house and he said, 'I'm used to big hotels, Mam,' and I said, 'I don't care what you're used to, you're back here now. If you want a cup of tea, get out and put on the kettle and make it.'

Noel Thinking back on it now, as long as we were happy and out of her hair, she didn't really give a fuck.

Liam I wanted to make her proud, wanted to get her from having to do three jobs, I wanted her to put her feet up and have nice things.

Peggie I was cleaning five houses a day, me. I was forever on the bloody roads, walking, going from one house to the next. Then I worked in an old people's home for two years. I used to be shattered. I used to get up in the morning, clean, tidy up everything here, then go out and clean maybe two houses in the day then go on at night time and work all night.

Liam At this point we still weren't making any money, so she was like, 'You're still fucking scrounging off me, you little shit, I don't give a shit what band you're in. When are you going to start fucking pay me some rent?'

Peggie Do you know what, it never came into my mind that they would make it. I just thought, well, they are in a band, hopefully, they will go out and they will make money for themselves and they will have a better life. I was glad they were together in a band. I would not have wanted

Liam in a band without Noel and I wouldn't have wanted Noel in a band without Liam. I always thought when they started out, so long as the two of them are together I didn't need to worry as much. I thought Noel will look out for Liam so they are alright, but ... and they did look out for each other for years like, but they grew up.

Liam Then I bought her a house round the corner up in Eaton, beautiful, 120 grand, which is a lot around that time. I said, 'There is your keys, I'm out of here,' and she says, 'I don't fucking want it.'

I was like, 'I've bought it now, you can have it.'

She was adamant, 'No, I don't want it.' She didn't want her life to change; 'What do I want to live in a big posh house for when all my mates are down here? Your life's changing and good luck to you, but mine's staying the same. Get me a garden gate if you want.' So that was basically it, she's a cheap date. I bought her a garden gate, I think Noel bought her a fence, and she's not asked for anything ever since.

Peggie I did worry, I've done nothing but worry about them. When they'd be away I'd worry about them. I spend my whole life worrying about them.

Liam I guess she thought, 'One of them is going to end up dead or one of them is going to end up with a big

> She could hear in my voice that I wasn't turning into a fucking idiot . . .

drug habit.' There's been a few scrapes but we're still here, man, I've still got my fucking head screwed completely on. I'm not a casualty and I never will be. There are a lot of dickheads out there going, 'Oh yeah, I'm going to get fucked up in the first year.' Well, good luck to you, mate. I was fucked up at fifteen before I even heard a note of music. I didn't join a band to be a casualty. I speak to me mam three or four times a day. So I'd be always reassuring her. She could hear in my voice that I wasn't turning into a fucking idiot, she'd get it. I think she's just going, 'Jesus, I wished they've never joined that bloody band,' because of the shit. But she's well fucking into it. She fucking loves it.

Peggie Never in a million years did I think that they were going to be as big as what they were.

Enter Marcus

Noel Alan had handed me a list of managers that he knew and at the top of that list was Marcus Russell. Funnily enough I'd just become friends with Johnny Marr and he was Johnny's manager; I didn't know any of this. Johnny just said, 'He's a straight-up guy and fucking great.' That was it.

Liam When we met Marcus, I was impressed. With every other person that we'd met, they were a bit fucking tin pot, fucking two bob, you know what I mean? This geezer had a Beemer – I was impressed with his car. So I thought, if he's got a fucking motor like that and he manages Johnny Marr, he's got to know what he's doing.

Noel When we got back to Manchester and I was speaking to Marcus I told him we'd already got an offer of a record deal. I think he initially said, 'Hang on a minute, you don't just take the fucking first record deal that you can get.' But I had already given McGee my word and I wanted to be on Creation, not because of Creation records, but because of Alan. The way that they loved us and they loved our music and they got it – and they got us. Where the businessman thing came from is fucking beyond me. I sat back into a life of chemicals and fucking expensive champagne after that, thank you very much.

Liam I never really got involved with what we were signed for and whatever. You don't think like that, do you? I was thinking about the bigger picture, man. I mean a

I never really got involved with what we were signed for and whatever.

contract didn't mean jack shit. If you are thinking about contracts at nineteen, then there is something fucking wrong with you. I don't think I ever signed a contract with anyone. It was like 'Look, you fuck me over and I'll burn your fucking house down' and I still will to this day, that contract still fucking stands.

Bonehead There was no contracts, no lawyers, no nothing from Marcus, that is the way Marcus worked which was old school, it was really cool. Probably stupid, you would be advised not to, but just, 'Yeah, right, I will be your manager,' spit on his hand, shake your hand. It was done on a handshake. Cool by us.

Noel There has been this misconception that I'm some character walking round with a clipboard, with a graph, a pie chart, fucking spreadsheets while Liam is this caged panther. Our *Bo Selecta* puppets summed it up perfectly: Liam was this dribbling 'duh, duh' and I was this posh guy going, 'Oh hello, fucking hell, dreadful, what's the merch score? How much did we take on the merchandise?' I haven't got a fucking clue about anything, for all I know I've been ripped off fucking left, right and centre for the last twenty fucking years, I really don't know. As long as there's money in the hole in the wall when I go there I couldn't give a fuck really, you know what I mean?

Good evening, Great Britain

Bonehead Not long after signing we did our first radio broadcast, *Hit the North*. It was a big deal but I don't think we got mad excited; I think we were pretty calm about it actually. I remember Peter Hook being on it and Liam made some comment about Hooky's leather trousers. He was like, 'Are you wearing them leather trousers up there, you dick?' Or something to that effect.

Noel The story goes that it was Mark Radcliffe's show and he fucking hated us, like most people in Manchester did. He was away for a week so Peter Hook stood in for him with Mark Riley; they liked us so they got us on while he was away. The reason it sounds a bit odd is because there was only one vocal mic in the studio, which Liam was using, but he wouldn't speak to them. They came in and said, 'Right, we are going to do a little tune and we are going to do a little chat,' and Liam was, 'I'm not fucking speaking.' He couldn't get his head around an interview, so he said to me, 'We'll do the song and you come and do

> It was a big deal but I don't think we got mad excited; I think we were pretty calm about it actually.

the talking.' So we had to quickly swap. Peter Hook was having a little pop. Him in leather trousers. Fucking hell, mate, come on, it's the nineties.

Liam Being on the radio, it was fucking good, yeah. It was like, 'We are fucking on the radio, who wants it?' I remember telling him, putting him in his place, yeah. He was saying something about 'You're banned from my club,' and it was like, 'Look, I don't fucking go in it anyway.' He obviously thought that everyone in Manchester was in his club and I'm sure they were, but I wasn't.

Bonehead We played a blinder. We did 'Bring It On Down', I can't remember if we played anything else. I remember it sounding great.

Noel Afterwards me, Coyley and Phil all bowled into a van and went up to the moors because Halley's Comet was passing. We all sat on the top of this van smoking weed, going, 'Hey man, cosmic shit, man.'

Growing up

Noel Liam, I would suggest, needs an audience. He is an ideal frontman.

Peggie Always very quiet, Noel. He would go upstairs and bury himself, always strumming a guitar.

Liam Mam was an angel, still is. She's the coolest woman that ever walked this fucking planet.

© Tom Sheehan

Noel The Inspirals were a fucking good laugh, really were. Clint Boon and Graham Lambert, they used to make me belly laugh all the time, we always had a good laugh with them.

Liam It didn't matter to me whether people liked it or not – that wasn't what we were doing it for. We were doing it just to fucking do it.

Liam I've tried dancing, done it in the mirror once and I looked like a fucking cock, so not happening, mate. I can stand still really good.

Coyley Sharp as fuck, loud as fuck, you couldn't help but notice there was something very different and very special about this band.

KING TUT'S WAH WAH HUT

GLASGOW !!!

GREAT

Alan McGee
I'm standing there with my kid sister Susan. She immediately says, 'You should sign these.'

×MANCHESTE

Glasgow

Manchester

© Jill Furmanovsky

Maggie It's quite difficult to crack the music industry as a female and there were not many female tour managers at that time because the touring world is even more male-dominated than any other part of the industry. Luckily these five guys were actually quite nice to me.

Noel If anybody was a sixth member of that band, it was Mark. We were roadies together with Inspiral Carpets; the first or second batch of demos I ever did were at his house, 'Married With Children' was recorded in his bedroom.

Fifty quid on the door

Bonehead Going out on stage, we just gave it our all. In rehearsals we gave it our all, we didn't do it by halves, it didn't matter who we were playing to. We did a gig in Leeds to two people.

Noel We had a gig booked at one of the nights of In The City and maybe two nights before that we did a warm-up for it in Leeds at the Duchess of York. We soundchecked in the afternoon, the guy came in and said, 'How much do you want to charge for this gig tonight?'

Liam We were like, 'What are you on about?' and he's going, 'How much do you want to put outside?' Fucking joking we said, 'Fifty quid to come and see us.'

Noel So we played the gig to a barman who was just cleaning glasses. I think towards the end a boy and a girl might have come in and were just fucking snogging on one of the benches as we were bravely going through 'Live Forever'.

Bonehead The only applause we were getting were off the bar staff who were just sat there, chewing their nails, watching us.

Liam Between songs you could hear the bar lady just squeaking the fucking glasses. But we were mega, man, every gig we did at that time was like we were fucking steaming it, man. A couple of months later I guess, we were selling places out.

Bonehead I remember breaking a string on 'Rock 'n' Roll Star' and fixing it dead quick as if there was a crowd there. There was nobody, but we played a blinder, we played it like we meant it, you know, top gig as well, it was brilliant, one of the best.

Noel We went back there six months later to play, couldn't even get onto the street, it was fucking bedlam.

Bonehead It was like, 'Oh God, we're going back to that venue again, we're doing Duchess of York again.' I remember we did the soundcheck sitting in the dressing room looking out the window and it was just like 'Fucking hell!' The door was directly below and there was just a queue of people coming out of the front, turning left, going right down the street and round the corner.

Feeling supersonic

Noel Creation were only really aware that we had about six songs; I knew I had about thirty-six. At this point they'd never heard 'Slide Away', never heard 'Married with Children', they had never heard 'Shakermaker'. I'm not the kind of person that would sit in a dressing room and sing fucking fifty songs in a row, that's fucking boring to me, let's wait till we record them. So they never knew what *Definitely Maybe* would eventually sound like even though I did.

Liam He always had more, he always had tunes coming, but they were like planes, you've got to wait for the fucker to land. My vision was like when those planes go round and round above Heathrow Airport, you've got to land one of them first for the others to land. Otherwise it all just becomes silly, you can't land them all at once.

> I remember thinking, we can't be in a studio for three days and go back with nothing.

Noel When somebody at Creation said they were going to put out 'Columbia' as a one-sided 12-inch white label, great. Then Radio 1 put it on the playlist and I remember being a little bit horrified thinking, 'Oh no, that is the first thing anyone's going to associate us with.' It sounded a bit tinny, there is no bass on it, and it was clearly fucking recorded on an eight-track. At the same time, thinking, 'Wow, we are on the radio, they've said the name Oasis from Manchester.'

Noel So we've got to the point where we've signed the record deal, 'Columbia' has been played on the radio, it's now time to record a single. This is what's great about Creation Records, they just gave us some money, they didn't give us a producer or anything, they just booked us a studio. We thought we would do it in Liverpool because if we are in Manchester it will be fucking chaos at the studio. So we'll do it in Liverpool, at a place called The Pink Museum. McGee suggested that 'Bring It On Down' should be our first single and I was like, 'Great, I fucking love that song, it's like the Pistols, like the Stooges, that will do for me.'

McGee 'Bring It On Down', for me, it's just punk; 'You're the outcast, you're the under-class, but you don't care, because you're living fast.' I just loved it.

Liam That's a tune, mate, that was what Oasis was about before they got caught up in this Beatle web. We were rocking, steaming, it was like the Pistols with melodies.

Coyley We were all very inexperienced and I think we booked in for two days. The first day is just horrible and it gets worse and worse, and the session starts degenerating.

Noel We couldn't get it right, whatever we had in our rehearsal room and on stage wasn't translating into the studio.

Liam I don't remember not being happy . . . it certainly wasn't my vocals, they were rocking.

Noel It would become apparent that session didn't work because our drummer wasn't the most consistent from one fucking bar to the next, never mind one day to the next.

Tony 'Bring It On Down' just wasn't coming together, the tempo, the speed, I don't know what the fuck was wrong with it like. I can't say that I understood why it was chosen, it was out of my hands really.

Noel I remember thinking, we can't be in a studio for three days and go back with nothing. What if they tell us to fuck off? It was either Tony or Chris Griffiths, who were with us in the studio, who said, 'Well, if it's not happening, just do something else.'

Coyley Noel's got a riff, but that's all he's got, so they're just kind of knocking this little thing around, which all bands do, a little riff.

Noel Why I chose to write a new song as opposed to record any of the others off *Definitely Maybe*, is still a little bit of a mystery. Because it's quite a mad thing to do. I remember someone sent out for Chinese or fish and chips or Chinese fish and chips, and I went in the back room and, as bizarre as it sounds, wrote 'Supersonic' in about however long it takes six other fucking guys to eat a Chinese meal. It was a brilliant moment in time because I would never be able to do that again.

Bonehead Noel's just sat there with the guitar and he just wrote the music, that will do, and then he wrote the words, any old fucking words and he came back in the room with us, with his guitar and he said, 'Look, I've just written another song.' He started singing it and we nailed it and mixed it that night, rapid, because that's what we'd been doing every night in the Boardwalk, you know, and it sounded massive, absolutely massive.

Noel We all stood in the same room and it was like, 'Well, this is how it goes.' It's really slow because we are all in the same room looking at each other, nodding for the changes. We could never get it that slow playing it live. We recorded it and mixed it in that night and I've got to say, listening to it on the way home on the cassette deck in Mark Coyle's Renault, I thought it was fucking brilliant. As good as 'Bring It On Down' and 'Columbia' – I thought it was fucking great.

Tony It just unfolded, within minutes maybe, done. Some of the greatest things that have ever been recorded, just happen like this, bang, there it is. Eat that.

Noel What really set it apart was Tony Griffiths had come up with those backing vocals – the 'aahs' in the bridge – and it was just a fucking brilliant moment in time. It showcased everybody's talent: Liam singing is fucking brilliant, the drumming's great, Bonehead's bits are great, Guigsy's bits are great, the guitar solo was great – even though everyone thinks it's ripped off something or other – but it was all good. Lyrics are fucking bananas . . .

Liam The producer had this big fucking Rottweiler called Elsa, and she would be there all the time sniffing shit and getting off her tits. I think Noel just wrote lyrics about her.

Noel The way I generally write is the first few lines will form a story and then it kind of gets confused and muddled up a little bit. Then you might have a line that might be true, in the sense that that's what might have happened, but it doesn't work in a song. So you have got to fill in the gaps . . . but it's the overall thing that matters. It's why, when I'm asked about my songwriting I find it quite difficult to talk about because 90 per cent of every line I've ever written has got some kind of meaning to me, but then you are kind of just filling in gaps with lines that are quite vague but get you to the next place. I'm a songwriter at the end of the day, I'm not writing novels here, I am not writing reportage; they are pop songs and a great deal of pop lyrics are fucking nonsense. It's all about the tune, but you do have hit songs from time to time that really get to sum up an experience that you had.

Liam Didn't care what they meant, still don't care what they mean. They mean something different to everyone, don't they, so . . .

Noel One night a girl came up to me and asked if 'Supersonic' was about prostitution . . . I don't think I've been speechless many times in my life, but that was one.

'The whole thing about Elsa doing it with the doctor in a helicopter . . .'

Elsa's a fucking Rottweiler, it is a fat stinky dog. She was convinced it was about prostitution and I told her she was right as well. I would never spoil it for anybody. It's usually lyricists that will tell you that the words are fucking everything. They are not, the words don't mean shit to anybody. It's the melody is what you remember. We all whistle tunes; it's always about the melody, and that's what I do. Roger Waters for instance is very fucking willing to tell you what every single line of his songs mean. When I first heard *The Wall* I was gone ... and then you find out it was all about his dad. Don't fucking tell me that, I'm not fucking interested. I thought it was all about

> There was
> something
> magical
> going on,
> and still is,
> in those
> tunes ...

me. I like to think that all my favourite songs are somehow about me. Which is why you love them all. I leave it up to people to interpret those songs. When journalists come after the meaning I always dismiss it and say they don't mean anything. I don't want anybody to know about me and my life, my songs. A great deal of odd lines and even half sentences have real proper relevance to my life and growing up but it is not something I'm interested in telling you or anyone else because then it spoils it. That is why Oasis was so brilliant because they were so inclusive. They weren't about anybody on the stage, they were about – if anybody – the people in the crowd. And I think that is why it was so immense because it appealed to so many people, right across the board: the middle classes, the working classes, the toffs; the older generation, the sixties generation and still kids to this day. There was something magical going on, and still is, in those tunes, I don't know what it is.

Liam I've never spoke to our kid about what any of them mean because they mean the world to me, but I don't know what. I could ramble on, but I would never do them injustice by just saying something flippant. I could never go, 'It means this,' because they just mean everything. I don't want to know what they are about. That's the beauty of it.

Coyley I'm not a big word man, me, I don't really listen to the words, but it's how they make me feel and if I can feel it, it turns me on, I don't give a fuck what the singer's saying. I'm on it, I'm with you, Noel, I didn't understand what 'feeling supersonic' meant, but whatever it is, I'm fucking there. I'd die for you right now. That's how I felt about Oasis.

Noel 'Supersonic' was never even remixed. The mix that's on *Definitely Maybe* is the rough mix from that night. A brilliant moment in time and if push comes to shove it's probably still my favourite ever recording because of the flash of inspiration; something was going on that night, bang and it was there.

Bonehead I remember going down to Maida Vale and doing a BBC session straight after and McGee turning up.

McGee Noel came in and said in true Noel fashion, 'The recording session was rubbish, it never worked out, but I've written a smash.'

Bonehead Noel put this cassette in, McGee was expecting to hear 'Bring It On Down' and instead 'Supersonic' comes fucking blurting out of the speakers. Blew his head off. Blew mine off.

Noel We played it and he went fucking mental, he loved it.

McGee But I was nuts, I was fucking nuts. I mean, most people would have gone, wait a minute, but I was on my own trip. Then they gave me a line of coke and four or five seconds into a line of cocaine, fucking everything seems like a fucking great idea. I did wake up the next day going, 'What the fuck happened, how did they do that?'

Coyley It just showed the potential that was just bubbling underneath at that time. The explosion was just imminent, this is going to happen any second and here is a little taster of how it's going to be.

Monnow Valley

Liam Beautiful studio, Monnow Valley.

Phil Everyone used to go and do a debut album there. It's an old farmhouse with a barn attached to it that's been converted into a studio. You're just holed up in the country, windswept and rainy, with a massive log fire.

Noel It's not even the best studio in Monmouth, Rockfield is four minutes up the road; The Stone Roses were there recording *The Second Coming*.

Liam We met them on the high street. I was star-struck by them. Ian Brown had a big beard, he looked like Jesus, he looked cool as fuck.

Tony God, it was a massive adventure, a holiday we'd never had. I just didn't know what to expect. A fantastic place but quite daunting and nerve-wracking. It's not a demo, we're recording for real, paying thousands of pounds to be here.

Noel It wasn't the most glamorous place to be, but it was nice. I'd been in recording sessions with Inspiral Carpets – I've loaded gear in and out of studios and sat in on their sessions for years – so I am already a bit underwhelmed by it all. I'm not running around like, 'Yay, we are in the studio! Fucking hell, look at all these teabags. It's unbelievable. Crisps!' I just wanted to get cracking.

Liam I'm not having that. He'd set up an amplifier, that's about it . . .

Bonehead We had never been in a recording studio in our lives. People were putting a lot of faith and money into us so we just strolled in there like we knew what we were doing. Did we fuck, didn't have a clue. Everyone was pretty green, but that probably helped it work. No one came in with preconceived ideas, no one came in lording it: 'I've done this before; I know what I'm doing.' Everyone was winging it to an extent.

Noel Johnny Marr sent down some guitars because I only had one guitar and Bonehead had one guitar.

Bonehead We didn't have that much in the way of equipment. Because Marcus was managing Johnny Marr, Johnny was really good. I remember going up to Johnny's house in Cheshire, with Noel, and we went downstairs – he had a studio in the basement – and he had a whole collection of guitars. He was just like, 'Take your pick.'

Noel He sent down this Les Paul and I took it out of the case and immediately wrote 'Slide Away' on it.

Liam Obviously I get a decent room, but they're all playing tricks, going, 'Oh look, it's fucking haunted.'

Bonehead One day, one of the staff casually mentioned, 'So, who's sleeping in room number three?'
    Liam says, 'That's me that, I'm in room number three.'
    'Alright, you got the haunted one then.'

We were just like, 'Whoa! What are you on about? A ghost?'

And she was like, 'Yeah, real ghosts; some dark figure's been seen.'

So Liam, of course, is just shitting it.

Liam I go to bed one night, wake up in the morning, all the furniture is moved round. I've gone downstairs going, 'Look, it must be fucking haunted, I've got to change room.'

Bonehead The next night I'm thinking about this ghost thing. By the front door there are a load of fishing rods with hooks and fishing line so, if you're into that sort of thing, you can go fishing by the river that goes through Monnow Valley when you've got a break. I got a load of fishing line off one of these rods and looped it through a little hole in the corner of the *Daily Mirror*, right in the top right-hand corner. Put a bit of fishing line through the laces of somebody's pair of trainers as well.

Phil The line went along the picture rail, round the back of the chairs, all around this massive living room, round the back of the TV.

Bonehead Everyone else knew about it, but Liam didn't. We're all watching football or something on TV and I just started pulling this line.

Liam So we are sitting that night round the fire, there was lots of fucking about, and the chandelier tilts and then a paper goes over.

Bonehead I'm doing the newspaper; I just started pulling it so the page started curling open, held it vertical and then let the line go so it dropped.

'Did you fucking see that – did you see that?'

And we were like, 'See what?'

And he's like, 'That fucking newspaper just opened and shut.'

I say, 'I'm sure it did, it's the wind.'

And he's saying, 'No, it did, it did.'

'It can't have done.' But you could see him watching it so I did it again.

He's like, 'It fucking moved again!'

Then I really tugged it so the whole newspaper just went fuck off across the table. So, of course, we all jumped up like, 'Wow!' Liam was shitting it, because he didn't know anything about it. So he really jumped up. Someone tugged the trainer so, as he headed for the door, a pair of Adidas trainers, just scooted across the floor, chasing him. He was done. He was off, down the fields. See you later, Liam.

Noel Liam is a great believer. For a man that actually has no spiritual content whatsoever, he is a great believer in the spirit world, which I find fascinating.

Liam I don't remember doing much recording, just shitting me pants because it was haunted.

Noel This guy called Dave Batchelor got to produce the first incarnation; that was all my fault. He was the Skids sound engineer and he'd done a festival run with Inspiral Carpets four or five years before. I remember travelling around Europe with him talking about music and punk rock and all that. I thought he was a fucking cool guy, I used to like the Skids and blah, blah, blah . . . When it came to, 'Who do you want to produce your first album?', it was like, 'I want this guy to do it.'

Everybody went, 'What? He's not done anything for fucking . . . what are you talking about?'

I was like, 'No, this guy is going to do it.'

McGee Noel was a real road dog, he loved going out on tour. He'd bonded with the guy and he promised him he could do his album. Because he'd promised it, I gave Dave a chance and it was fucking wrong.

Noel I remember it becoming frustrating, but I don't remember entering into it with any sense of trepidation. I remember being pretty relaxed; all we have to do is play. It's fucking easy. I've written all the songs, I've come up with all the parts for everybody, fucking hell what else do you want me to do, make the tea? We had a producer in the room, it's his job to make it sound good. I know what I'm doing. If everyone else knows what they're doing, what could possibly go wrong?

> I don't remember doing much recording, just shitting me pants because it was haunted.

Bonehead I presumed that we were going to get in and someone was going to say, 'Right, okay, we're recording,

The idea of the song diminishes a little bit in the studio because you can never recreate what is in your head …

one, two, three, four, away we go.' But it wasn't like that, it was take, after take, after take.

Noel We were all in separate booths and it just wasn't fucking happening.

Liam I didn't like that, that did my head in. Felt like you were on the naughty step all the time. We were a good band, we played a lot of gigs and we were tight. I don't think all that doing it separately worked. It should have been done all at the same time. I think that captures the vibe, that's the glue. If you're doing it separately you're taking away all the glue …

Noel This is where the thing with Tony started. He was good live and all that but at that very moment of trying to record a fucking album, it was a pain in the fucking arse because he was very inconsistent.

Tony That wasn't a comfortable session, we quickly recognised that this isn't the right guy for us.

Bonehead We would go in the control room and listen back, and Dave just wasn't getting it. At some points it would get pretty tense.

Noel We did one version of the album which we mixed a fucking thousand times. Trying to replicate the sound that you have is the ongoing battle you have as an artist anyway. The idea of the song diminishes a little bit in the studio because you can never recreate what is in your head – my fucking head space is massive and the speakers are this big. Every time I go into the studio I'm trying to get something out that is in my head and it can become like a dog chasing its tail.

Coyley They all knew it was no good.

Noel We went away on tour, and the tapes were sent off to be mixed somewhere by someone. You are getting ready to go on stage in a fucking pub in Southampton, you're expecting your manager to turn up with a cassette of the album and it's like, 'It's fucking awful.' The feedback coming back is, 'Sounds shit.'

That to me is always the worst thing anyone can ever say about anything: 'It's shit.'

'Why?'

'Don't know, it just is.'

That doesn't mean fuck all to me. If you can't articulate what's wrong with it, how are you supposed to put it right next time? It would be great if somebody said, 'It sounds shit because of this, and this is what we've got to do to put it right.'

Then you'd just go, 'Right, well, let's do it then.'

Liam I'm sure it wasn't quite right, but when you start picking at these things you can fucking twist your head. I guess Noel carried the weight of the band. I was definitely not stressed; I was fucking having the time of my life.

Definitely plan B

Noel This is when the discussion about the sound started: 'It doesn't sound like you lot live.' I would be thinking, I don't know what anybody's going on about here because it fucking sounds like me when I'm stood beside my amp. Every time we would do a track and you'd think, well, it kind of sounds alright to me, McGee or Marcus or Coyley would say, 'Doesn't sound like you lot live.'

And I would be like, 'What do we fucking sound like live? I don't know, I'm on stage?'

'It just doesn't sound like you lot live.'

'Who *does* it fucking sound like? Spandau Ballet?'

McGee I knew what Oasis should sound like because I'd seen it live and I just knew the performances were wrong. I was at the point of going, 'Let's put the fucking demos out.' The demos were brilliant – better than the fucking recordings. We wouldn't have been as big, but on an indie level, we'd have got really big.

Noel We only came to the conclusion that Mark Coyle should go in with the band and record it live by drunken accident one night. If what you lot want is a live sound, who does the live sound? Mark does. So why doesn't Mark do the record?

'Fucking hell, that's a good idea!'

And I am sitting there thinking, is this how easy this shit is?

'Man, you are a fucking genius.'

'I know, thank you.'

Fuck me, if he doesn't know what it's supposed to sound like we are fucked.

Coyley Time for plan B on *Definitely Maybe*. I would be interested to know why they took that risk, because it's some risk, putting me in charge of that, no track record whatsoever. But somebody recognised a situation the band were comfortable with and just said, you do it.

Bonehead It's like, 'Right, we're going to redo it, we're going to take it down a studio in Cornwall, Sawmills Studio. We're going to get Coyley in.' Thank God for that, because we all knew that Coyley understood us, he got us.

Noel Thank God for McGee, you know. He's just like, 'Here's some more money, let's do it again, let's get it right.'

Liam People go, 'It weren't quite right.' Well, I'm fucking having it was that good, we did it again.

Noel I remember it taking forever to get there. We drove down, it took fucking ninety hours . . . And no one had told us that Sawmills was only accessible by a fucking canoe and if you missed the tide you had to walk up the train tracks. So we get to wherever it is in Cornwall and they say, 'We've got to load the gear onto this boat and then you've got to sail to this studio.' It was fucking freezing. We were like, 'What fucking studio is this?'

Bonehead It's mad really. We threw the amps on and drums and guitars and that sails over, and then they come back and get the band. There is no way out of that studio, once the tide disappears, you're stuck.

Coyley It's just idyllic, it was beautiful. We spent the week having chips and egg.

Bonehead Coyley used to have a little DAT player and a microphone, and he would go recording crickets, or bumblebees buzzing, so he could sample them on music at home. I caught him one day by the river and he was just recording the river rippling, you know, just being a weirdo. So, I sneaked up and stood behind a tree. I was making weird noises, hid behind this tree, and you could see him thinking, 'Oh man, I've just captured the sound of the greater crested woodpecker, this is going to be incredible when I put it on a dance record.' The dick's just sat there, you know, being Coyley. Then I started giving it all that and you could see him thinking, 'That sounded like "fuck off".' And you've got to own up, haven't you, so I stuck me head round the tree. I was like, 'Got you there, didn't I, Coyley?' He got really angry, absolutely lost the plot. He chased me all over the place, the guy was purple, he was going to kill me. Hippies, man.

Liam You've got to get a boat or walk through the woods and along a railway track to the one pub. Coming back was pretty funny some nights, just having a laugh, man. It was like fucking camping, it was great.

Coyley We started recording *Definitely Maybe* and we got results immediately. It was the easiest thing that any of us ever did.

Noel We hit upon this system where we would start in the morning when everybody had had breakfast and cigs and got their shit together. We all stood in the same room with no headphones, just like a rehearsal and just went through it. We would do three takes of each song and then move on. No going into the control room listening back to anything. Three versions of 'Rock 'n' Roll Star', tune up, three versions of 'Live Forever', tune up . . . That's how we used to rehearse. So the vibe was like it used to be in the Boardwalk. At night we would sit and listen and say, 'I like that version.' We would work on that, put some overdubs on and that would be it. It was really enjoyable as I remember. Liam was on top form, everybody was good.

> It was really enjoyable as I remember. Liam was on top form, everybody was good.

Coyley I think there is a lot of nonsense written and spoken about making records. You can take your technical bumph and your know-how and your knowledge and you can shove it right up your arse, because I made *Definitely Maybe*, where a technically minded man couldn't do it. So, it must be about the musician just feeling good and feeling comfortable and feeling confident. It was so relaxed, it was the way it should have been the first time round. I would have thought that album was recorded in three days, maximum.

Noel I remember mixing it with Mark and Anjali Dutt in Olympic Studios and struggling with it, a lot. I don't know why. The lesson it taught me is that I am not a studio technician; I shouldn't have to fucking know about stuff like that. Have you looked at a mixing desk? It's a thousand fucking knobs. Do they all do something? Fuck that. I write the songs, I play the guitar, I'll even do some backing vocals, I'm not getting involved in all that, I'm not interested.

Coyley Me and Anjali were there for a couple of weeks. It didn't really sound very good. I'd never mixed a record before, I think I was just a little out of me depth. I wish that I'd had more experience because I could have truly made that my own record, but I think the bottom line is that I just didn't know what I was doing.

Bonehead But it was there, it was all played right, that much was obvious. It sounded good, but it didn't sound great.

Noel It turns out even then it was shit so I don't fucking know what was going on.

Enter Owen

Noel You are talking to these people who make records for a living and they are telling you it is not right, but they can't articulate why. I don't know what I was supposed to do about it. I remember taking a cassette of a mix that we did to McGee's flat and sensing that he was completely underwhelmed by it. Me thinking, 'Fuck it, I give up. I really give up.' I couldn't understand why 'Supersonic' sounded so amazing and everyone thought these songs sounded so flat. Maybe it's because 'Supersonic' was written that night and these other songs had been on the verge of being three years old.

> We were never put under pressure by Creation, ever ...

McGee At one point, Noel was so frustrated with the whole thing, he went, 'Look, why don't we just put it out and we'll get it right on the second album,' and I went, 'You'll never get to the second album, we've got to get it right on the first album.'

Coyley That record had to be made, whatever cost it was going to be, it would have been made three times. Alan McGee knew there was a good record there.

Noel We were never put under pressure by Creation, ever, once, ever. Alan was such a fucking dude; that record label was never started for commercial reasons, it was for the love of music. I knew we'd spent everything, we'd definitely spent the money that we were given to do it, that was gone. As I remember it Alan had to go to Sony to get some more money and, because I was signing a publishing deal at the time, I paid for some of it with some of the advance.

Bonehead Alan McGee . . . a believer, I suppose; an absolute belief in what he does. A visionary. He is the type of person who, if he believes in something, will go out and do it and he won't stop. He will get that thing and he will take it to wherever it goes. He doesn't care if it just goes to there and falls. He'll still believe in it and still love it.

McGee Marcus announces that he's going to get Owen Morris to do a mix on spec and I'm thinking, 'Why?' I don't get it. He did one mix – I think it was 'Rock 'n' Roll Star' – and we went, 'Right, he's doing the album.' So, it was Marcus's relationship with Owen that was the final element in the whole jigsaw puzzle.

Owen Morris I was kind of angry and pissed off at music and the music business, so it was a relief to be given free rein of Oasis. I thought, this is my one crack: they've got a deal, said in the *NME* they are on the fucking go, Radio 1 all over them. I might get some more work off this. And they let me do exactly what I wanted.

Liam Mental Welshman; biggest laugh in the world. I loved him. He was fucking off his head, completely off his head. He is trouble, but he was great, because I'd be going, 'I'll do some shit and blame it on him,' and vice versa. Owen come along and just turned everything fucking up. He kept it simple whereas maybe other people were trying to get a bit flash with it. But Owen come along and went, 'Right, you lot just need to turn the fucking thing up,' and that's basically what he did. He was always setting fire to shit and things were always blowing up because he had it too loud, which was great, it was fucking great. With Owen, those recordings are the nearest it got to the gigs.

Noel Owen would get really excited and start throwing beer over everyone. He used to get very, very boisterous.

Tim Abbott The thing is with Owen, he's got a wall of sound with guitars but he can isolate the lead vocal. That's his trick. I think Coyley could do that on a sound desk, but he could never do it on a recording desk.

Noel Me and Liam were always arguing about the mixes, always, always, always. This went on all the time: 'The vocals should be louder.' My thinking is the vocals shouldn't be louder than anything else, it's all about the soup. The great records don't have loud vocals. He was always, always trying to get the vocals up. I can understand it if you've written these great lyrics and you're a singer and you need them to be heard. He didn't write a thing, not a fucking thing. He didn't even write the gaps in between the singing. Even I wrote those. So why he was wanting the vocals to be loud I don't know.

Owen Marcus sent me cassettes of the mixes they had so far, and he said, 'What do you think we should do with it?' Oasis were touring then, and Marcus was like, 'Fucking sort it out.' So I had a listen and pretty much said, 'We'd better re-record every vocal.' We went down to Loco in Wales for a weekend, to try me out and to try a couple of mixes. That's when I met Liam, I had already been briefed that he was a John Lennon freak and all that so recording Liam was really easy: I told him he sounded like John Lennon and he was like, 'Fucking . . . you got it.'

There was no vocal on 'Rock 'n' Roll Star', so that's the first thing we did, Noel just left me and Liam to it. Liam's lead vocal fucking blasted through it. Piece of piss.

Liam I loved the way Owen recorded. It was very simple to me and I think that is the way it should be done. A lot of musos will sit there and go, 'Blah, blah . . .' Well, I tell you fucking what, you go back to twiddling with your guitar over there, and your bass and all that nonsense. Your record sounds naff compared to ours because you've got the rule book out and you are on page sixty-two and your music sounds shite. Listen to ours, we are not on any page, we have not even got the book out. Ours will eat yours alive, and your mate's and your other mate's. So that is what I liked about it, it was just straightforward, simple and that is what our band was about. It was just solid rock and roll with great songs and great melody. There was no Slash doing his diddly dee, there was no drum fills, there was none of that. I would never go in there and sing it light. I found it hard singing less. I always had to give it 120 per cent. No one would ever have to ask me, 'Look, can you give it a bit more fucking bollocks?' I would just go in and just fucking rip the arse out of it and people would go, 'Stop singing it so hard, you are not at a gig now, back off a bit.'

I remember one fucking producer going, 'Can you get into a role?'

I was, 'Get to fuck, mate, I ain't playing a role, I'm going to sing it.'

I'm going to belt it out and fucking turn me down.

Owen They were good, the mixes were good, really fucking good actually. Noel comes in and was like, 'That sounds great, that'll do.'

Noel I don't like to spend too much time fucking about in studios, they are kind of in and out, put the kettle on, that's me done, let's go and do something else. If you've not got it in the third take you've not got it. That's still one of my golden rules to this day. If I'm doing a song and I haven't got it the third time I will go and do something else. I'm not one for sitting around all day fannying about, moving a mic an eighth of an inch.

> If you've not got it in the third take you've not got it. That's still one of my golden rules to this day.

Liam We'd do two takes and just go, 'Right, let's go to the fucking pub.' Take hundred is going to be absolutely fucking shit. End of. Take five is going to be fucking utter shit as well. Who gives a fuck about take seven? If it's not done in three takes, then you shouldn't be in a fucking band or you need to go and have a word with yourself.

Owen They went away, and everyone liked it. I think a cassette went to Noel, he listened on the tour bus. And that's when they said to finish the rest. I mastered it at Johnny Marr's studio. Noel came over and I just got on with it. There was this new box that could make things twice as loud without distortion. So, I thought, if I make it twice as loud as everything else, that will mask the fact that my mixes are not technically very fucking good. My theory was quantity, rather than quality, at the time really. When it went out, it was brilliant – in every fucking jukebox in the country you could go in and put Oasis on and it would be twice as loud. As funny as fuck, man.

Noel We mixed fucking shitloads of times and then Owen got hold of it and we all went, 'Fucking hell, at last.' I don't know what he did to it, but fucking hell that's what you hear today.

The Dam

Noel We were doing this gig with The Verve in Amsterdam. What the fuck for, who knows why? It is not even a tour, it is one gig. It was going to be our first international gig, which even saying it like that sounds ridiculous. Of course it soon descends into chaos. We didn't have any roadies at this point, so we get rounded up in Manchester and this guy picked us up in a van – Jason Rhodes – he's going to be our roadie. He knew Marcus because he worked for New Order and he'd done Bernard's guitars.

Jason Rhodes Marcus got in touch: 'I've got these three bands. I've got Oasis, I've got Push, I've got this, I've got that.' I know Noel because he's a roadie, I've met him through Inspirals, so I'll go with them. 'Right,' he says, 'do you want to go to Amsterdam?'

I went, 'Yeah.'

Liam The first time I met Jason Rhodes, he picks us up at me mam's house in this fucking van and he looked mental. He looked like a fucking psycho killer.

Noel I got in the van, 'Jason, nice to meet you' and all that, 'Did they give you a float? You need to give that to me.'

And he's saying, 'No, no, no, that is for petrol.'

I said, 'Never mind petrol,' and we took the float off him and then spent about an hour driving around Manchester getting drugs.

Bonehead I think we did a pit stop, straight out of Manchester and stocked up on beer and vodka and whatever you do, you know, and away we went.

Liam We stop off at some Spar or 7-Eleven, get a load of booze. We get on the ferry, I don't know how we got on the ferry because we are pissed, but we get on this ferry and we are all fucking about drinking.

Jason By the time we got to Harwich there was nothing, they'd drank pretty much everything. Five bottles of spirit, which is kind of going some.

Bonehead And then it just went downhill rapidly.

Phil The Thursday-night ferry to the Dam is obviously full of nuisances. Who goes to Amsterdam on the ferry for the weekend? What kind of clientele?

Noel As fate would have it, West Ham were on a pre-season tour of Holland and there was a load of West Ham fans on this overnight ferry. It's got a casino on it and a fucking nightclub.

Bonehead A disco boat and there were actually people dancing. We were just, Jesus, man, that's not right, you don't dance on a boat, do you? You sit in the bar, yes, or you go to bed if you've got a bed. You don't have a disco on a boat. We really didn't have any money at that point. A bottle of champagne appeared at the table and it was like, 'Where's that come from?' Another bottle appeared and these bottles kept appearing . . . So everyone got drunker and drunker. Liam was going for it and Guigs, weirdly, was going for it. Unlike Guigs, going for it in the bar, but he was up for a bit of fun.

Coyley In my memory, the drink of choice for a few hours before all the excitement started was champagne and Jack Daniel's slammers. So we're having a wonderful little time in the bar and the next thing there is sporadic fighting breaking out all around us. Liam is very excited by the prospect of a lot of chaos going on. He's *very, very* excited at this, so he goes and joins in.

Liam Guigs has come back with someone who's collared him saying that we were forging £50 notes. I was like, 'They are real, you daft cunt.' Then a fight broke out. All I remember was it was a bit Benny Hill, the police chasing us around the fucking ferry.

Coyley I keep seeing Liam running, through the windows, along the deck, he's having a great time, he looks like he's in a school playground, chasing leaves.

Phil I know Liam at one point said they ran through a casino and he flung all the roulette shit off the table, as he was running past.

> All I remember was it was a bit Benny Hill, the police chasing us around the fucking ferry.

Coyley The next time I see him, he's still running, but he's got policemen running after him.

Bonehead I just remember seeing Guigs getting hurled down the stairs from one deck to another. I was thinking, 'Oh my God, what's going on?'

Coyley I come to the bottom of a stairwell and Liam is on the floor with three or four coppers tying him up. Next to him on the floor is Guigsy. What Liam's done is he's swung for somebody, but completely missed. He's thrown a great punch, but he's not made contact with anybody so he's spun round and ended up on the floor. As soon as he went on the floor, the police have got him as well.

Liam Someone's punched someone, someone's kicked someone, someone's got nicked and then we are handcuffed, me and him.

Bonehead I don't know where Noel went, I think he was being a professional. He must have got his head down, he must have gone to bed or something.

Noel Everybody gets nicked except me. I don't know why I never got nicked. I somehow managed to wangle my way out of it.

Liam Our kid's been fucking reading Shakespeare again, he gets away with it. We get to Amsterdam, straight off the boat and we're nicked. We're sent down to the bottom of the boat into this fucking cell and we had to stay there, little mattress each. We'd been drinking all day so we were pissing in this bucket and it was going everywhere, it was horrible.

Bonehead I got back to me room, me passport was gone, me shoes have gone, everything had gone. So, I reported it and the security are like, 'Yeah, we know your passport has gone, we've taken your passport.'
'Why have you done that?'

'Because you're not going into Amsterdam, you're going to get off this boat and you're going straight home, mate.'

'Why, what have I done?'

'You're with them two, downstairs.'

Jason So, I went round and spoke to the customs or the cops and said, 'Look, I'm kind of missing four people, do you know where they are?'

They went, 'Oh yes, yes, yes, they'll all be getting deported, be getting sent back on the next boat.'

I'm thinking, shit, that's four out of five I've lost, we've not even got to bloody Holland yet. I said, 'Look, I need to give them some train fare at least.'

So he brought them down to this doorway and I gave them £20. 'Okay, say goodbye to your friends.' And this big shutter door came rolling down – I remember seeing everybody bending down looking underneath it getting lower and lower, till you could just see their feet and then they had gone.

Noel I went to see them in these cell things, it was fucking brilliant. I was saying, 'Don't worry about it, I'll call Marcus when I get to Amsterdam. By the way have you got anything left of that float?' Someone had £100, I said, 'Give us that float,' and they said, 'Why, where are you going?'

I said, 'I am going to Amsterdam for the weekend, fuck you lot.'

We went to Amsterdam and turned up at the gig, The Verve played and we got royally shit-faced.

Jason I can remember getting to the hotel and having to ring Marcus and Alan and they're going, 'You fucking what?

You what? Are you joking?' Wasn't my fault. What did you want me to do? Fucking slap them on the wrists? 'It's 10 o'clock, get to bed, boys.' A hell of a start that, isn't it? That's a great first day at work that, isn't it? Love it.

Bonehead We just sat in stunned silence. It was just like, 'What the fuck is going on, what are we going to do?' Panic. We were heading back to England, no money, no nothing, no mobile phones. I think Tony had a fiver, so we ate crisps all the way. We didn't even laugh. It was horrible, horrible.

Liam Ended up at Kings Cross with Marcus. There was a load of Americans coming over to see us and he said, 'You've fucking blown it, you've blown it.' He was going, 'You shouldn't be fucking behaving like that.' Who the fuck are you, my fucking dad? This is what happened and we were in the right. They fucking stitched us up. End of. You weren't there. Don't be fucking telling us what it was like and what we should have been doing, we didn't do anything wrong, we were just doing what we were doing. We were trying to just get on with our business.

Bonehead You should have seen the state of us, we looked like you couldn't describe, we were just a mess. I think it was more Marcus panicking about the Japanese record company and the American record company, because they haven't got a sense of humour. None of these people are going to find this funny so he was not happy with us. Everyone's nudging me, 'Bonehead, ask him if could he borrow us an extra £20 so we can get some food.'

I was like, 'You can fuck right off, no, you ask him.' So Liam had to ask him, 'Could you borrow us £20 for some food as well?'

Liam This is called life. It happens, people get into scrapes. We didn't plan it like that. Obviously we would have preferred to get on the boat, have a drink and not be fucking accused of having dodgy £50 notes. Then we would have got there and done the gig and blown everyone to pieces, but it didn't happen like that. It happened like this, so that's life. Them fuckers didn't even turn round and go, 'How are you?' or anything, they were just, 'You ruined the fucking . . .'

That's how I'd want my rock-and-roll stars to act. Stick up for themselves, get in a bit of shenanigans and that's it.

Fuck off, you knobheads, I've been sat in the fucking bottom of a boat, handcuffed, with piss running around for the however long it takes to get to Amsterdam and back. You've been sat in your fucking BMW.

Bonehead Marcus was pissed off. McGee, being McGee, thought it was great. He saw that he could say, 'You know what, this is publicity, this is rock and roll.' He was buzzing off it.

Noel This is another reason why I love McGee: I called him and got put through to his office and he said, 'Noel, man, how's it going?'

I said, 'Are you sitting down? I've got some news.'

He went, 'What is it?'

I said, 'Everybody's been arrested on the fucking boat on the way out last night.'

And the only word he said was, 'Brilliant.' I think within twelve hours he had a photographer from the *NME* out there and made a massive deal of it. It was a funny old night.

Liam I know Noel hated it because he wanted to do his thing, but I didn't think it was a bad thing. I thought, for one, we didn't do anything wrong, for two, they were fucking trying it on and three, we stood up for ourselves and that's it. Certainly wasn't going to roll over. That's how I'd want my rock-and-roll stars to act. Stick up for themselves, get in a bit of shenanigans and that's it.

Coyley I think Noel was a bit angry, but a bit excited at the same time. I don't think he quite knew what he should be feeling. In retrospect, I think it should have just been taken for exactly what it was, which is a great little rock-and-roll night out.

Back home

Noel Before 'Supersonic' came out we'd done gigs and there were people coming along because they'd read about us in the press, but nobody knew any of the songs. So we were supporting other bands, always playing to this void of an empty dance floor and people stood at the bar. Then on the day that 'Supersonic' came out – bang! The crowd are right there singing those lyrics that you have nonsensically written down at fucking 3 o'clock in the morning about a Rottweiler. We'd had two hard-core fucking years of being in that rehearsal room, rehearsing five nights a week, fucking going nowhere and yet all still believing in it. So by the time we got to be presented to the fucking public . . . they couldn't tell us anything about us we didn't know. People were saying you're great and we were like, of course we are, we're fucking brilliant, we've been great for the last two years.

> I didn't like TV . . . all the fakeness. I see through all the bullshit. I'm a right cynical bastard.

Liam I didn't like TV . . . all the fakeness. I see through all the bullshit. I'm a right cynical bastard. All the, 'Do this rehearsal, look into this camera, can you do it again, can you stop, can you start.' Telling the audience to move here, all this fussing about . . . It was a bit like, 'I don't want to see that side of it.' It was all a bit fucking poncey, 'Do you want to do make-up?'

Noel We never went into a make-up room for years, we were like, make-up? Fucking hell. Beneath us.

Liam When you are on the outside looking in you think it's great, but when you're there it's a bit disheartening. I'd rather just do a load of gigs than do these fucking shitty TV shows where it's all a bit smoke and mirrors. Just get us back to the fucking gigs, man. When we were playing live we were obviously not faking it, so everything just felt good. The minute you had to play the game I found it hard.

Noel *The Word* was quite a big thing. I'd bought this second-hand Super 8 camera because it looked great and I said to Liam, 'When we're doing the musical breaks, pretend you're filming the crowd.' When you see it, he's filming while he is singing and it looks fucking mental.

Liam I can't remember that. I think it just looked good and it was something to do. I don't think I had a tambourine at that time so I thought, have this . . .

Bonehead I remember Marcus saying, 'Look, guys, you are going to have to sign off the dole, man, and Guigs, you've got to leave your job.' Not that we were making money, I think we paid ourselves £100 a week into our bank accounts. But I couldn't get a bank account because I had a County Court judgement against my name, so I was like, 'I can't sign off.'

'Bonehead, sign off, you're in a band, you signed a record deal!'

Noel I remember being in the dole office and, in a glorious moment of fucking symmetry, as I was signing off, Phil Sax, who was the head of A&R at Factory Records, who told us we were too baggy, was signing on. Factory had just collapsed and I was like, 'Ah, how ironic.'

Liam The dole office had been saying, 'Look, you need to get a fucking job, have you looked over there?'

'There's nothing in there that I want to do.'

'Well, do you think I like doing my job?'

'I don't give a fuck about your job, if you don't like doing it, don't fucking do it, but I'm in a band and it's going well.'

Anyway, that time I went in and said, 'Look, I've got a new job and so I'm signing off.'

'What job have you got?'

I said, 'I'm in a fucking band, rock and roll,' and he started laughing. I said, 'Tune in on Thursday, you fucker. Oasis. Number thirty-one.'

Noel We were going to meet this tour manager, a twenty-year-old girl from Queens in New York, and we thought, 'We will fucking make mincemeat of this woman.' But the genius of it was, women were the only fucking people that we weren't insulting at that time, because we were all brought up by our mums. And Maggie was great.

Maggie Mouzakitis Marcus just rang me up out of the blue and said, 'I've got this band, quite small, they're from Manchester. They need somebody to look after them. They've kind of been doing it on their own, but they're getting into a bit of trouble. Would you be interested?' Bonehead was actually managing them on the road as much as he could. He was driving everyone around. He still drove us around, actually, for the first few months of the tour. We didn't have the money to have a driver and he was the only one of the band who had a licence.

Jason I can remember the gig at the Old Trout in Windsor. Maggie came along to that and that was her first gig, I believe.

Maggie This is the nineties we're talking about, and I was going in as a tour manager. It's quite difficult to crack the music industry as a female and there were not many female tour managers at that time because the touring world is even more male-dominated than any other part of the industry. Luckily these five guys were actually quite nice to me.

Noel About five minutes after we met Maggie, the dressing room erupted in a massive fight, chairs being slung and all sorts. It spilled out into the street in front of fans and everything. Proper fighting between me and Liam about, I don't know, what was the best crisps: Quavers or Squares? It's clearly Squares, but he wasn't having it. I remember saying to Marcus, 'I think Maggie might be quitting,' before she had even done anything, but, bless her, she stuck it out for fifteen years.

Maggie They were having fun. They had nobody to check and balance them; they were all boys and quite young. Can you imagine going with your best mates on a tour bus and not having anybody to tell you what to do? You'd just kind of go, 'Yes! I've got 800 quid from this gig – let's go spend it in the bar!'

Noel We were always spending the float on fucking coke and drugs and booze. Always going back to fans' houses, or going back to the hotel, and shit getting damaged. I don't just mean once a week, every fucking night there was something. It was a good laugh and all that, but it was becoming a bit tedious.

Liam It's called having fun and not thinking too much about the future. Living in the moment. That is surely what rock and roll is about. It can't just be all about writing a fucking great middle eight. I'm feeling supersonic, I'm going to bed at half nine. Give me gin and tonic, get my head down about half ten. Fuck off, mate.

> Give me gin and tonic, get my head down about half ten? Fuck off, mate.

Noel We are Irish, me and Liam, pretty much. There is no English blood in us, and anybody who knows that will know there is drinking and then there is Irish drinking. Irish drinking can be endless.

Bonehead Yeah, we were known for partying and sitting up and drinking and doing whatever, but you know, we didn't, as a rule, get on stage pissed up, we just didn't.

Liam We'd turn up stone-cold sober and everyone thinks we are fucking off our tits. It was like, 'Excuse me, I've had fucking eight hours' sleep if you don't fucking mind.' There would be people in the crowd shouting 'You fucking cunt!'

There is no English blood in us, and anybody who knows that will know there is drinking and then there is Irish drinking.

just to get your attention. Then there would be people going, 'Do you want a line?' I'm like, 'I'm fucking busy here.' They would be going, 'Do you want me to chop you one out?' 'I'm fucking on stage singing, you fucking maniac.' I would see them physically doing drugs in the gig, getting bounced about, crazy bastards. The fans were a lot worse than us. We weren't fucking raging cokeheads and we weren't Mötley fucking Crüe. It wasn't like, 'Hey man, d'you want a fucking line?' 'Okay, I'm just having me breakfast.' It was never like that. We need to get that cleared up. We were never having a line and going in and doing the gear. When we were working it was always work, work, work. We definitely put the hours in and then we'd get on it, we rarely did anything when we were off our heads. We'd put the work in first and then go mental. At night time the lines would come out and I guess that's when it would all turn to shit. Going on stage pissed was shit, it was like hell, the gigs would be four hours long and if your voice weren't up to scratch it was like, 'This ain't happening again.' You'd learn pretty quick to get your shit together.

Noel There is certainly no drug that I've ever tried that has given me the same fucking 'whoosh' as walking on a stage and playing your songs to these people.

Liam When you did it sober, the gigs were much better and you'd get a pure fucking clean hit. Then you come off and then you'd get wankered.

Noel We were ironing out a lot of drugs on nights in and nights out, and a lot of drink. By today's standards it was insane, even by standards back then it was pretty fucking hard-core. But it was all functioning. Nobody was doing smack and not turning up for shit, let's put it that way. We might have been pissed all the time and McGee might have been pissed all the time, me and Liam and all the people that surrounded it, but shit was getting done. It wasn't tragic in any way.

Noel There was a lot of drugs taken making records. As a rule, me personally, I don't do them during the day anyway. Anything that we ever recorded while we were out of it, we would always end up re-doing it the next day anyway because it was shit. So there's a little tip for you kids. Only when it goes dark; it is a bit more normal when it goes dark, I think. That used to be my mantra anyway: wait till the lights go out, wait till the street lamps come on.

Liam When we started, we were smoking joints on stage but then when it went into arenas it was a bit like, 'These lot have paid quite a bit of money for this, better fucking keep it together.' Obviously there would be days when you'd fall off the rails and shit would happen, but it was to be expected. I thought we kept it together pretty much.

Jason Definitely Noel was more the quiet, silent type and he would sip his drinks whereas Liam and myself and Bonehead were lashing down pints and shots and whatever.

Liam Noel obviously wanted to go to bed and read fucking books on Morrissey, I wanted to go to the bar. That's just the way it is. It wasn't like I was going to the bar to get in the papers. It just makes more sense to me to go to the bar and have a drink, than to go to bed and read a book.

Noel I'm of the opinion that – for want of a better word – partying, and all that shit, that's what time off is for, holidays. When you get to push the button, it is like 'Right, we are getting the show back on the road,' I'm all about the graft then.

Liam He was just as bad as us, without a doubt. There is footage where Bonehead and Guigs and Tony are still playing and we've come off and we've gone back to the dressing room, launching apples and pears and sandwiches and pizzas on their heads. If anyone was taking it fucking seriously it was Bonehead, Guigs and Tony McCarroll. Our kid was right up for the shenanigans as well, but he seems to have forgotten about that.

Jason It just got more chaotic a lot faster than it ever did with most other people.

Leathered at the Riverside

Noel There was a full section of a tour, maybe a full tour, when it was just going off every night, and that's when we had to get security guards. I felt that people were turning up to cause trouble and it was getting me down, if I'm being honest. I remember Liam thinking it was great, but I was saying, 'Hang on a minute, as I fucking recall the rock-and-roll mythology, aren't there supposed to be loads of birds everywhere, never mind fat, fucking dicks in Fred Perry shirts trying to offer us out. Where's the blonde birds with the big tits? Where's that?'

'It's great, it's chaos.'

I am like, 'Fuck chaos, sex is what we need. Women. Fuck fat dudes.'

Liam We always had a bit of trouble that followed us around, but I didn't mind it. We had security guards, we're not soft, so fuck it.

Bonehead Anybody will tell you: your reputation follows you. We weren't a bunch of lunatics, you know. Maybe people came to the gigs, trying to get a reaction from us and some gigs did get pretty tense.

> I felt that people were turning up to cause trouble and it was getting me down, if I'm being honest.

Maggie Some of those gigs were quite hectic. I remember me and Phil Smith had to go and hold up the PA stacks at one of them, because they were literally going to fall down on the audience. The audience was bouncing up and down so much that the floor was moving.

Liam People would chuck stuff and it was like, 'I ain't fucking about, we're out of here. I ain't walking on this stage with two eyes and walking off with one because fucking Dermott down the front from Hastings doesn't like our music. Fucking stone missed my eye by about that much, fuck you.' I ain't going blind for rock and roll. A lot of dickheads would stay on but it's not fucking panto.

Coyley Obviously, once you get that reputation, there is always someone who's going to go, 'I'll show him.' If he had never been in the paper having a ruck, that probably wouldn't have happened.

Jason I don't think there was a day went by without something. Right or wrong, you became immune to it. It was like, 'Never mind, everybody got all their fingers? Jolly good, let's get on with it, jump in the van, come on, let's go.'

Liam I should have got a fucking pay rise for them days. It's hard work taking shit off people.

Noel We went on tour with The Verve and this American band called Ace Tone or Acetone, we could never understand what the fuck they were called, but they were great. We were first on the bill playing the Riverside in Newcastle.

Jason We'd parked the van outside and luckily taken the flight cases out. Then I went back out and the van had been nicked. It had me new boots in and a bag of me clothes, I were right pissed off at that.

Maggie It was just like a bad luck show from the start.

Bonehead Newcastle is always a rowdy one. You do a gig up there and they are mad, they are just fucking psychos, man. Place is mad. But great, great gigs. The Riverside gig, I think it was going live on Radio 1.

> Of course there is a fight, loads of people jump in, and I hit somebody on the head with my guitar.

Noel I don't know what happened but in the middle of 'Bring It On Down' somebody got on stage and fucking smacked me right in the eyeball . . . At that point we didn't have a light show, it was just strobe lights. You know what strobe lights are like, when they flick fast, you don't really know what the fucking hell is going on. Of course there is a fight and loads of people jump in and I hit somebody on the head with my guitar.

Jason Noel leathered this guy with it, proper 'Boing!'

Bonehead Liam's trying to hit this guy with the mic stand, and Noel's trying to hit him with a guitar like, 'Fuck off our stage.'

Noel We kind of did that thing where we decided to fan the flames of the fight instead of getting out of there.

Bonehead The crew were trying to protect the amps because people were throwing bottles of lager. It started getting a bit out of control. We could hear it get really hostile. There was lots of feet banging and hands clapping and a real big murmur in the crowd. The next thing was, 'Pull the plug, the gig's off. It's getting fucking scary out there, there's bottles flying, all sorts of shit. Just get in the minibus and fuck off back to the hotel.'

Coyley We get out and as we started getting in the van, there's a few different gangs of people, pointing, 'There they are, there's the fuckers.' We get in the van and we can't get out, there's a car right in front of us and a car right behind us, so we're kind of stuck.

Liam I remember it being fucking moody, they were rocking the fucking van, they mashed the van up to pieces.

Tony The only way the driver could get out was to put it in reverse and shunt the cars out the way, which he did. He didn't give a fuck. Got himself a space and turned and got us back to the hotel.

Noel To leave the venue we had to drive up an alleyway and past the front door. There are people throwing fucking bricks and shit at the van. All very exciting.

Coyley Why they'd want to do something like that, and why that guy got on stage and hit Noel, who would know,

NG: If we're gonna get rid of Phil Collins and Sting... junk-food music, McDonald's music...
We've got to get in the charts and stamp them out.

I want the severed head of Phil Collins in my fridge by the end of this decade.

And if I haven't...I'll be a failure.

I could never understand
hotel rooms being smashed up.
That's like *hard work*.

LC: If you're feeling a bit of a geezer...

Right, whoever threw the fucking bottle, let's have you up here and I'll slap you in front of the crowd.

I'm not here to get fucking things thrown at me. Fucking coconut stall.

Give me gin and tonic, get my head down about half ten. Fuck off mate.

KODAK 5053 TMY   15   KODAK 5C

滞在日程表

アーティスト名	OASIS		予定滞在日程 1994年 9月12日～9月20日	
日程	出演先	出演内容	スケジュール	宿泊先
第1日目 9月12日 (月)			来日	大本木プリンスホテル 港区大本木3-2-7 03-3587-1111
第2日目 9月13日 (火)			オフ	同上
第3日目 9月14日 (水)	渋谷クラブクアトロ 渋谷区宇田川町32-B 03-3477-8750	コンサート 前売￥5500 (550P)	開場18:00/開演19:00 主催：(株)スマッシュ 企画制作："パルコ 後援：エピックソニーレコード	同上
第4日目 9月15日 (木)				同上
第5日目 9月16日 (金)				同上
第6日目 9月17日 (土)				大阪グランドホテル 大阪市北区中之島2-3-18 06-202-1212
第7日目 9月18日 (日)	心斎橋クラブクアトロ 大阪市中央区心斎橋 9-1 06-281-8181	コンサート 前売￥5500 (700P)	開場18:00/開演19:00 主催：(株)スマッシュ 企画制作：スマッシュ/パルコ 後援：エピックソニーレコード	同上
第8日目 9月19日 (月)	名古屋クラブクアトロ 名古屋市中区栄3-ストト10 052-264-8211	コンサート 前売￥5500 (550P)	開場18:00/開演19:00 主催：(株)スマッシュ 企画制作：スマッシュ/パルコ 後援：エピックソニーレコード	名古屋クレストンホテル 名古屋市中区栄3-29-1 052-264-8000
第9日目 9月20日 (火)			離日	
第10日目 月 日 ( )				

1994年 8月 9日

招聘社　株式会社スマッシュ
所在地　東京都港区南
TEL　(03) 34
代表取締役　　　日

JAPAN TOUR
Sept 1994

Noel When you are seeing massive fucking billboards of yourself in Tokyo, honestly it is unbelievable. It might have been the one time in my life where I thought, 'Fucking hell, wow.'

Liam I loved going to Japan, it was fucking great, man. They give you presents and stuff and chased you down the road.

but I think the perception is that they are a bunch of thugs from a council estate in Manchester so let's go and fucking have a bit of a do with them, you know.

Noel I ended up with a massive black eye, and had to wear fucking shades for about six weeks, on stage. The other brilliant thing was the guitar had got smashed so Johnny Marr sent me another one, a black Les Paul which he played on *The Queen Is Dead* and I never gave it him back. He claims he borrowed it me, I'm sticking to it to this day that he fucking gave it me. You are not getting it back now, Johnny.

Johnny Marr Yeah, that guitar I bought in early 1986 from John Entwistle and it had been Pete Townshend's guitar, it was a 1960 Les Paul, which buzzed me up. It's on quite a lot of Smiths records that. We never discussed any kind of passing of the baton, I used to tell this story of how we met on a grassy knoll under a full moon, the two of us were there in our shades and I said, 'Here, Noel of Burnage, taketh this Les Paul, ex of The Who and The Smiths and lay down some licks,' and then we drank the blood of a groupie. That was my story. But there is a tradition in rock-and-roll music of giving someone a guitar when you respect them. I did it because I liked him really, I thought he was going to be great.

Noel It's a fucking great guitar and it's got a lot of history, but that just sums up Johnny as a dude really, he's a very fucking generous dude and he is into passing on the light sabres of rock and roll and that kind of thing. I can't believe I just said that.

Jason Johnny sent him a little note, something like: 'This guitar has got a bit more weight to it, you will get a better swing next time.'

Liam I enjoyed that night to be fair. He jumps on stage, gives our kid a crack, he got a beating. I know he probably got a bit sore and that, but that geezer got a beating, man. I guess in hindsight it was a bit fucking scary, but I loved it. I'd rather a bit of chaos any fucking time than people just walking off and going, 'That was a fucking splendid gig. Eleven songs and they were all fantastic. All in time, sounded like the bloody record.' Fuck it, man, it's what it's about, innit? It's good looking back. Shitting it at the time, though, thinking, 'Fuck, we are going to get fucking battered.' But like you say, you go down fighting, don't you. I like shit like that. No one really got fucking hurt. Our kid's had worse. Have a bit of fucking chaos, come on, it would be boring being great all the time, being perfect.

Noel We were getting the reputation as these bad boys of rock and roll, which was alright, but can we talk about the music first? Because that is what is going to stand the test of time, if you don't have the songs, you don't have anything. But it was the other thing was getting spoke about first.

> I think any band worth their salt is not just about the music.

Liam Well, it wasn't just about the music, was it? Our band was not just about the music and I think any band worth their salt is not just about the music. You need good tunes to accept that kind of behaviour, but if you haven't got that kind of behaviour and you've just got great tunes, then you are pretty boring as far as I'm concerned. It's about both.

The Richard Madeley moment

Noel There was a festival in Sweden and Motörhead, Primal Scream, Verve and Oasis all managed to book into the same hotel. Unbelievable. More unbelievable is that the barman shut the bar at something ridiculous like midnight. We went off the rails that night.

> Yeah, they were good days. You're young; you've got no fear, have you?

Maggie It started on the way in. It was the first time we'd had a bus. The buses have got these hatches on the upper level and Liam kept on opening up the hatch and coming out. The bus driver was getting really annoyed. He was like, 'Tell him to come in, he can't do that, it's really dangerous!' I was like, 'You fucking tell him that.'

Liam I remember getting on top of the bus a few times, fucking about. I can't see it being that dangerous. I remember jumping off a bus once and breaking my ankle and then hobbling on to do a gig. It was one of them double-deckers. I didn't think it was a double-decker, I thought it was a single one, it took me about half an hour to fucking hit the deck. Yeah, they were good days. You're young; you've got no fear, have you?

Jason Chaos again. It seemed to be just chaos all the time . . . chaos, chaos, chaos.

Liam The hotel was in the middle of nowhere, a little postcard village. They shouldn't have fucking put us there; put us in the city where things are open.

They've gone, 'There is no more booze.'

'There is fucking loads behind that bar, fuck off, give it us.' And they didn't.

Noel We basically robbed the hotel bar, told the manager to fuck right off and took all the booze. When that ran out it was like 5 or 6 o'clock in the morning. There was a church across the road from the hotel, I don't know who come up with the idea but it was like, 'The church must have some wine in it.'

Bonehead We were in a church in the middle of Sweden with Primal Scream, fucking weird. Morally is this right? Should we be doing this? You've had a few beers, you're like, 'Fuck, it's rock and roll . . . but should I be doing this shit? You know what, I'm going to go back and say me prayers and ask God for forgiveness, I shouldn't have done that.'

Liam I was still at the bar having an argument and then they come back with some wine, they all had Russian hats on and shit, it was funny, man. We just smashed the gaff up, it was good. I remember some geezer screaming, 'I thought John Bonham was dead.' TVs coming out the window, but fuck it. We were getting the money so we paid the fine. Fuck it.

Noel The next time we're in Sweden, Liam gets nicked for shoplifting.

Liam My moment of madness. That was my Richard Madeley moment. I don't know what the fuck it was. I bought a pair of trainers and on the way out I just thought, 'I'm fucking having them razor blades.' I had them and I put them in my pocket, next minute I got collared. That was it; I don't know why the fuck I did it. You'd think I'd have grabbed more than fucking razor blades, bottle of whisky or something or even robbed the trainers that I'd just forked out £40 for. I think they just give me a fine. I was always getting fined for shit, that's where all my money's gone. Fined here, fined there, just fined. I think they just went, 'Look, what are you doing robbing razor blades, you're a millionaire?'

I just went, 'I don't know, really sorry.' Then they give me a fine and I got back on the bus. Got a bit of grief off the squares and then we carried on.

Noel Just fucking ridiculous. A rock star getting caught for shoplifting.

Jason Fucking razor blades of all things. He could barely grow a fucking beard, what are you nicking razor blades for? Silly fucker.

Noel Liam got arrested and the hotel got destroyed. I wasn't there, I was off cementing international relations with Swedish women, which is what you should be fucking doing. Never mind slinging video recorders around the fucking hotel foyer, that's bollocks. I could never understand hotel rooms being smashed up. That's like *hard work*, you get a sweat on, do you know what I mean? I remember the hotel manager coming into my room and telling me, 'Get out of bed, you're leaving, you're being thrown out.'

As he was in the room, fucking screaming and shouting, he was stood against the window. I couldn't understand what was going on until I seen a fucking telephone and a bedside cabinet come flying out of the room above; I was thinking, 'Oh fuck.' I walked past Liam's room and the door was open, I've never seen such destruction. He fucking demolished this room. The Swedish press referred to us as animals.

I could never understand hotel rooms being smashed up. That's like *hard work.*

Jason I think the headline was 'The death of a hotel room' or something like that, and it just showed this mess of a hotel room.

Maggie They're showing this room that's completely trashed, and we're looking at it ... I was like, that's not even the hotel room. That's not the hotel room! That's another hotel!

Liam Back then you are just thinking, 'Fuck it.' You just get pissed and you look at something and go, 'Bit fucking boring in here, isn't it?' Before you know it you are out on your fucking arse on the street. Lovely. But I guess that's what you do when you're daft and you're young and you feel invincible.

Maggie It did cause us problems with other hotels down the line though.

Liam We were getting kicked out of shit hotels; we were thinking if we get kicked out of this shit one they might put us in a decent one for a fucking change.

Jason Bonehead was very minimalist, he used to like taking a little bit of furniture out of his hotel room and making it a little more spacious. There was one time, I think it was in Newport, I knocked on the door and they opened it. I went in and had a look and there is nothing in the bedroom, there is just Bonehead and Tony sat there on the floor. I looked and thought, 'What's wrong with this?' You don't realise there is no furniture at first and then I see the curtains blowing a bit. 'Alright, lads, how you doing, bit of a night, was it?' I can remember leaning out and looking out the window and seeing a bus driving round the debris on the road. Okay, so you've had a good evening. 'You better get the hell out of here quickish.'

Noel We were getting barred from everywhere at one point. We were barred from a full chain of hotels all over England. We were barred from the Columbia in London and we couldn't afford any other hotels.

Maggie I think that might have been orchestrated purposely, that one. Nobody wanted to stay at the Columbia Hotel any more; I think we all kind of had a little hand in that one. That was probably one of the best things they did, actually, banishing us . . .

Noel I wasn't there because I was living in London by this point, but everyone else was staying in hotels in London. We recorded 'Whatever' in Maison Rouge in Fulham or Chelsea. I remember the band turned up, bags and everything. Been barred for life from the Columbia, police were called and all sorts. Somebody fucking smashed up the hotel manager's car.

Liam Even to this day I am fucking banned. Great hotel, man, great hotel. You would get there and there would be about 900 beds in your room. There was never one bed. 'Have I got guests or something?' It was like being in the nick. I can't remember what happened but I guess there were glasses being thrown and shit being thrown out windows and the usual shenanigans.

Jason I think it was Bonehead just doing a little interior decorating again. He was really good at it actually.

Liam We were never rude to anyone, that is the thing, we were never like, 'Oi, get us a fucking drink!' We just got a bit carried away, having a laugh. Going through the corridor, going for a piss, and you see a nice vase – or a shit one in the Columbia – and you go, 'That would look lovely on Bonehead's head.'

Noel We were fucked at one point, no one would take us anywhere. Trouble seemed to find us at any given point. A lot of it was exaggerated by the press because they were desperate for something. We'd done a gig in Portsmouth and got back to a hotel which had a swimming pool in the bar, or the bar was in the swimming pool, whatever. East 17, who were the One Direction of the day, were also staying there, so there is a lot of screaming schoolgirls. I remember Guigs trying to tip a vending machine into the swimming pool. Why? I don't know. We used to regularly clean bars out in the hotels we were staying in, but tipping stuff into swimming pools, that's fucking slightly mad, now when I think of it. I remember East 17's lot being horrified. I think they checked out. It was a right palaver anyway, a bit of damage, a bit of thievery, a lot of drugs. Yes, Liam copping off with loads of birds, all that kind of shit.

Bonehead Chaos! It followed us, couldn't stop it. Some nights you used to have to sneak out, 'Don't tell Noel.' We'd go out, but something would go off, paparazzi would catch us and we'll have it in rehearsals tomorrow. He will batter us.

I remember Guigs trying to tip a vending machine into the swimming pool. Why? I don't know.

Noel At that point it was always going off at gigs and being banned from this and being fucking banned from that, police being involved here and fucking gigs getting cancelled. It was kind of becoming a bit of a pain in the arse, to be honest.

Liam People were still buying the records. You don't buy a scene, do you, you don't buy a scrap, when we put the singles out they were still buying them and going home and getting turned on by them. So the music wasn't getting lost.

Noel The press were loving it. You've got a load of journalists who were vaguely the same age as me, maybe ten years older, they'd never seen this, they'd only read about this before, but it is happening right in front of them.

Liam My main thing was singing and being cool as fuck. I knew my place: my place was singing the songs and I loved that. Second to the singing, was being the ultimate rock-and-roll star. While you are fucking farting about trying to get a guitar sound, I'm going to go to the pub and cause some fucking chaos, or I'd go and have a drink and things would follow me. While they were all trying to be Jimi Hendrix, better guitar players and all that, which is great, I was going, 'That's what you are doing, I'm going to be the face, the geezer who wears the clothes, and I'm going to be the ultimate number-one rock star in this country.' And that is what I was, by doing fuck all and just being cool. I know for a fact when all this ends, at least I'd done what we said on the tin. Bless these bands today, they haven't lived. It ain't big and it ain't brave but it fucking feels good.

Definitely Maybe

Noel The first album is really the purist representation of what we were then, because it was conceived live in a rehearsal room and it was played live in a studio. We'd been playing that for two years before we recorded it. It is perfect, that album. It is fucking ten out of ten, perfect. Thinking about it now, I don't think I would change a single note or a single inflection of any lyric or anything.

Noel The cover was fucking haphazardly thrown together on the day. All of Brian Cannon's covers are, then Brian would invent a concept four weeks later and say it's about this or that. It was great to have Brian on board and Brian was one of us, he was the same age as us, wore the same clothes, was into football and all that kind of thing. Brian was one of those guys who came from the Peter Saville school of artwork, which is the artwork is more important than the record. 'The record just sits inside my fucking sleeve.' For a while that was mildly amusing.

Liam Brian Cannon was doing The Verve stuff. We met him and he was a little bit left-field or whatever it is. He just went, 'Let's try it like this.' We never questioned it, we just went, 'Why fucking not?'

Noel I remember the day being long and kind of, 'You lie there; no, you sit there; no, you do that and I'll do that.' We were going to shoot it in somebody's front room, I don't know why. Why is it in Bonehead's front room? I have no idea. I don't know what the concept is of that, 'At home with

Bonehead'. All the props came from Phil Smith's bedroom. Bonehead's house, clearly, didn't look exciting enough, didn't have many cool things in it, bar a spider. There is a picture of George Best and of Rodney Marsh, which depict City and United; there's a video still from *The Good, the Bad and the Ugly* – may I point out the worst fucking still, it's not even fucking Clint Eastwood, you would have to watch that film a million times to go, 'Oh yeah, it's that bit' – the globe and the Burt Bacharach picture. I remember saying, 'Get the Burt Bacharach picture,' because the Burt Bacharach influence had already started to

> It is perfect that album. It is fucking ten out of ten, perfect.

take shape in the songwriting. I've always admired his songwriting and particularly that song 'This Guy's in Love With You', which for years – as I'm sat in my flat in Whitworth Street in Manchester, fucking stoned – thought was called 'The Sky's in Love With You'. I thought that was so cosmic; wow, the sky's in love with you, fucking right it is. What? Oh, it's a fella. Okay, still a good tune, but it's a love song. Not psychedelic.

Liam Obviously he's great and all that, but when they all started listening it was like, 'Fuck's going on here?' But as you dip your toes more into that kind of music you go, 'Ah right, he wrote that, fucking hell, cool, yeah, very smooth.'

Noel The cover is iconic because the album is iconic. If *Definitely Maybe* was the cover of some shit album, it doesn't mean anything. It's given credence because of the music really.

Liam We looked at it and went, 'That will fucking do, can we go to the pub now?' It was just all fucking very odd, but good odd. We always liked the covers.

Noel I can only speak for myself, I felt I knew it would get to number one. I knew all this shit was going to happen. It was just destiny. I don't remember being immensely proud, I remember thinking, 'Right, okay, there is work to be done then.'

Coyley The reaction from our entourage was really quite muted. There wasn't 'Hurrah!' A cheer didn't go up because, well, why shouldn't they be number one.

Liam Job done, we made it, people are into us and we did a great record, we've won the fucking war. We've banished all these cunts out of the way by being us, regardless of all the smashing hotel rooms; that's obviously what people want.

Maggie Those songs, for Noel particularly, had been in his repertoire for a long time, he finally got them on an album and people loved them. That is a huge achievement for five guys back in Manchester who were on the cusp of not making it. You know, something in that period, in 1994, made it possible for them to break through.

Noel It is a funny thing, people are kind of embarrassed about fame and fortune. I've always been of the opinion if you earn it, fuck 'em. None of us got given it, we didn't win the pools, we didn't have a trust fund, it was fucking ours. Let's spend it and make some more.

Liam Without a doubt, nothing to be ashamed about, we wanted it. A lot of bands around at that time say they didn't want it – they were just fucking scared, to be honest with you. We were just fucking having it, we were having the lot. We were having fun with it and keeping it real as far as I am concerned.

Johnny Marr *Definitely Maybe* sounded like it had always been there. It's interesting when music or a film does that, just makes sense straight away. So, it has a kind of familiarity about it, but a kind of necessity too. It was just of the moment, without it necessarily relating to any of the bands that were around. Noel's lyrics definitely had a sense of optimism in there, forward thinking and forward motion. However he's expressing himself, he's certainly expressing something that is aspirational. Not necessarily economically aspirational, or socially aspirational, just personally aspirational, you know. Get me out of this feeling, or, I'm going to feel better any minute, but this ain't too bad either.

> Without a doubt, nothing to be ashamed about, we wanted it.

Noel *Definitely Maybe* came out and then we didn't see Alan for a couple of years.

Liam One minute he was there, then he weren't there. Obviously it was to do with fucking drugs or something. I don't know, he just wasn't there and it was like, 'Where the fucking hell is McGee? Come on, join the party, what's going down here?' Then he just stopped hanging about and coming out. That's what happens when you play with fire. It is what it is. People, if they are not well, they've got to go and get their head sorted. The show must go on, as they say.

Noel I was quite shocked because I was like, 'What? Really? Fucking hell, I didn't know he was that bad.' Goes to show you how much of a fucking haze we were all in. I didn't truly understand what was going on with him. 'Well, fucking hell, so you've had a line, so what?' I've never had a nervous breakdown and I've never been to see a psychiatrist so I don't know, I just couldn't understand it.

Liam I didn't go and see him in hospital. The last thing anyone needs to see when they are in hospital is my fucking head marching through the door.

Gunchester

Noel At the start of the nineties Madchester turns into Gunchester. If there's anybody making a few quid there will be someone turning up with a fucking shotgun trying to take it off you. Luckily we don't get involved in all that hairy fucking shit, you know what I mean, but Manchester gigs will always be stressful events.

Liam I remember playing the Haçienda, that was good. I went out for a cig or a beer down the road, come back and one of the bouncers is going, 'What are you doing?'

I was like, 'I'm going in there to do the fucking soundcheck,' and they were getting all fucking lairy like, 'You're not allowed in.'

I was going, 'Come on, I'm in the fucking band.'

That's what it was like back then. But I got in and done the gig.

Noel At the Haçienda, one of our mates was doing the merchandise. It was a fairly small-time operation at that point. He comes back at the end of the night with the take and it's all £50 notes. Surprise, surprise, they are all fake £50 notes. 'I didn't know they were all fake.' What planet are you living on – people are coming to a fucking gig paying with £50? Okay, take one maybe, but not eleven.

Maggie Homecoming gigs are really hard for any band, I think. The crazies came out, the ones that they'd never heard from for years. You know, 'Hey, remember me? We went to school . . .'

A fucking pain in the arse playing up there sometimes.

Noel It's great when you get on stage, playing in front of your home town and all that, but it can be quite stressful because of the guest list and all that. You've got your family and your connected family and all their mates and everybody trying to get in. It's just a fucking hassle for a week before, trying to get everyone in and then a week after for all the people that you couldn't get in and it's just mither. A fucking pain in the arse playing up there sometimes.

Liam I found it hard playing in Manchester. It's easier playing away. Playing at home, I found it a bit uncomfortable. The crowd would be full of people you knew. Your mates that you went to school with jumping up and down at the front, waving at you. Too fucking weird, just weirded me out.

Peggie I thought, 'These young ones, Christ, they're mad.' They were just in there jumping. I thought, 'What the hell are they jumping up and down for?' I couldn't get over it the first time I went.

Liam I didn't like me mam coming to gigs, it done me fucking head in, to be fair, even right up to the big gigs. I would be, 'Don't come.' I'd be stressed out with all the fucking commotion, worried about me mam. Everyone's going fucking nuts and I'd be going, 'Is she alright up there?' Not a good look, is it, when you are trying to rock the joint. I was always on edge; I could never relax with me mam at gigs. Plus, I wanted to get off my fucking box.

Peggie I used to get mesmerised with Liam. I used to look at Liam and think, 'He's got some face, he stands there and just stares the crowd out.'

Fuss in Japan

Bonehead Next thing you know, we were going to Japan. What do you expect? I've never been to Japan. Noel and Coyley had been so they were the old hands. They were like, 'It's mental, Japan, it's really fast and busy and lights and this and that.' So you think, 'Alright, I'm prepared, they told me.' No, nothing ever on this planet was going to prepare me for what we got. It was the other side of the world; I might as well have been doing a gig on Mars.

> You felt like a superstar. You couldn't go anywhere.

Noel It was a wild tour, it was fucking great. You felt like a superstar. You couldn't go anywhere.

Jason That was when it actually hit home to them how big they were actually getting. It was very Beatlemania-esque.

Noel We fly into Japan; Guigsy meets a girl on the plane that he ends up marrying, still married to her to this day. That's how weird he is. We were a successful band in England, we were the big noise, but when we got to Tokyo we were met at the airport by fucking thousands of screaming fans. It was like, 'Whoa, fucking hell!' They followed us everywhere, outside hotels, in the fucking foyer, outside your room, in your fucking room, everywhere you went.

Liam I loved going to Japan, it was fucking great, man. They give you presents and stuff and chased you down the road. They speak in a different language, which is perfect when you don't want to really communicate.

Bonehead It was like, 'Oh, Bonehead, Bonehead! Liam! Noel! Guigs! Tony!' and it was just like, fuck off, this is Japan, but they know me name! Yeah, of course they do. How did that happen? How? Tell me, I don't know.

Liam Just hearing that word 'Bonehead' screamed by Japanese people, it's just mental, innit? Bonehead! I loved that.

Bonehead We got to the hotel, go upstairs and every door on the floor that we were on opened and all these heads come out: 'Oasis!' They had pre-booked the fucking hotel. It got me and I loved it, I loved every last minute of it. You'd go out and have a look around the shops and within seconds you were being followed by a lot of fans, and I mean a lot. You turn round and they all stop; you move two steps, they move two steps; you start running, they start running. It was a bit like a *Carry On* film. It was mental, but good mental, it wasn't threatening, I really loved it. They were never going to run up and jump on you, or attack you, they followed you, with presents – they had little dolls they'd made that looked like me.

Noel You couldn't leave the hotel, you just got mobbed everywhere. These little girls follow you with tiny little gifts and dare you not to fucking take it off them. You get back to the hotel with loads of tiny little bags and you open them and there is a really heartfelt letter about some shit or other. Then you open this thing with more wrapping paper on than is legal, eventually inside this box, inside a box, inside a box, is a biscuit.

Liam I absolutely love Japan. Guigs wasn't too keen on it. He was, 'This is fucking too much fussing over nothing, I don't know what they are fussing about.'

I'm like, 'Me, you fucking lunatic, that's what the fuss is about . . .' It was exactly what we signed up for and it was amazing. It was fucking living the dream. It's mad how you want something so much and it happens. It was fucking mayhem, man, I loved it. I loved the chaos, loved the mania. I loved it, man. That's what it was about, that's what I joined the band for.

> I loved the chaos, loved the mania. I loved it, man.

Noel When you are seeing massive fucking billboards of yourself in Tokyo, honestly it is unbelievable. It might have been the one time in my life where I thought, 'Fucking hell, wow.' Because how has it, whatever *it* is, how has *it* landed here? Why are all these people, who don't speak English, obsessed with it already, before we've even fucking plugged in and played?

Phil I think your first trip to Japan as a band should be nuts, because it is nuts. It's through the looking glass. You go over doing club gigs like you do back home and you're treated like The Beatles, even though you're only playing to 500 people. In Britain, at that level, you're lucky if you get a tray of sandwiches and some crisps. Whereas there, they take you out for meals and take you to clubs and pay for everything.

Maggie We weren't really culturally on the food thing, so we went to McDonald's a lot.

Noel There is this club called Abbey Road and this Beatles tribute band called The Parrots. Fucking great. We went to see them one night and they asked me to get up on stage. Everyone was like, 'Whoa!' I got up and I had Japanese people saying, 'Do you realise what's just happened?'

I was like, 'Yeah, just done a shit version of a Beatles tune.'

They said, 'No, they never ask anyone up on stage, the only two people they've ever asked up are Jon Bon Jovi and Bruce Springsteen.'

'Well, fuck me. Am I at that fucking elite level already? Thank you very much.'

Coyley Bonkers, it's like going into outer space going to Tokyo, just bizarre. Never seen such enthusiasm for bands.

Johnny Hopkins[*] To me, that was the best of times, there was something magical and other-worldly about it. They were driving through the streets in a popemobile – they can stand up in it. I don't know how that came about, but it happened.

Jason They were chasing the van all through the streets and trying to do shortcuts. People on scooters just trying

[*] Head of Press for Creation Records.

to slow the van down, getting in the way so that the people could catch up.

Noel It's the opposite of America. It's hard work being in Japan; there is a lot of hard work involved, but the people are great to work with. In America there is a lot of hard work involved but the people are not great to work with, they are very serious and everybody's set in their ways. The Japanese seem to be a bit more loose.

Maggie They were really good shows, the audience really loved them, definitely much more reserved than in the U.K., but really into the music.

Bonehead When you ask me about some of the best gigs we did, probably it's that Japanese tour. We did encores – and we were too cool for encores.

'Great gig that, could you do an encore?'

'Fuck off, we're Oasis, we don't do encores.'

There we were in Japan: 'Got to do an encore? Yeah, yeah, no problem, we'll do an encore, how many do you want?' Kept doing encores because we loved it and they loved us.

Noel The only reason we started doing encores was because in Japan you were contracted to play for a certain amount of time and Marcus, in his wisdom, had signed off on us playing for an hour. We didn't have an hour's worth of material so we used to drag these fucking shows out. We'd go on at ten past nine and really labour it between the songs. Then it was, 'Why don't we do a couple of acoustic tunes.' We would really labour the point for ages and then we would still go off with twenty minutes left. We'd have to come back on and do 'I Am the Walrus'.

Liam I don't think there was any need for that acoustic bit. I like a couple of acoustic songs and that, but going out on the road it was like, 'Come on, let's get the guitars out and fucking have it.' When you've got people stood in front of us, it's a bit of a war, let's fucking blow their heads off. You ain't blowing no one's head off with an acoustic guitar I don't think.

Noel We developed an acoustic bit in the middle of the set in Japan to save Liam's voice. He is resting his voice whilst standing on the side of the stage heckling, smoking and drinking, which is a wonderful remedy for any vocalists out there. Shouting.

Liam There were two reasons for it. I'd say resting the voice would be one. Two, because he fucking wanted to sing songs. I put that one up at the top. He wanted a bit of the fucking action, testing the water for his solo career twenty years later. Maybe my voice was getting a bit tired, I always found it hard singing out in Japan, it was harder, I always had to struggle out there.

Johnny Hopkins There were no drugs on that tour, so the band were completely drug free. That sort of gave it an extra dimension, you know. There was a sense of purity about it. I was going to use the word innocence, but there definitely wasn't any innocence there. It was madness, but at the same time, it was really, really calm.

Noel The usual: we got barred from the Roppongi Prince Hotel. We are still barred, forever. I was upstairs entertaining – socialising is what I like to say. But I did write 'The Masterplan' that night – I found the lyrics on Roppongi

Prince headed notepaper. So while everyone was having a good time I was fucking keeping shop. Like a square.

Liam I like being in a band, I like that gang mentality. I like hanging out with the lads. I'm not one of them that would do a gig and then go, 'I'm off to me room.' I definitely sit down in the bar and have a crack, have a laugh and probably stay up a little bit too late. It's the way it is. Rock and roll to me should have no rules. At some point the rule book comes out and then you are always going to fight against the rules. It is what it is.

> I like being in a band, I like that gang mentality.

Daniela Soave I was writing for a 'nancy boy's' magazine as far as they were concerned. I knew that I was ten years older than them, I was female, I was a mum and it was all blokes – so I just thought, 'Right, I'm going to stay up later than you, I'm going to drink more than you, I'm going to behave more badly than you,' because I wasn't going to get this story otherwise. The first night in Japan, we'd all been out; it would have been about 3 o'clock in the morning, my head had just hit the pillow, and the phone rang. 'Who's calling me?' So I picked up the phone and it was Liam. 'Get down here now!' So I walked down the corridor back to his room and, honestly, it was like he was shimmering.

He said to me, 'Do you believe in God? Do you think there's a God?'

I looked at him and said, 'How did we get on to this one?'

He said, 'Because. I don't believe there's a God because all that wouldn't have happened.'

And I said, 'What wouldn't have happened?' I didn't know what he was on about. There was all this pent-up, simmering rage.

Liam I think I was getting a bit heavy and a bit deep round them times because all that stuff was happening. There was change going on with the band – this fame and all that stuff. My thing was about me mam going to church; she was going to church every fucking Sunday and then when she got divorced from me dad, she wasn't allowed to take the body of Christ. And I was going, 'That can fuck right off, what's that all about?' She's got to sit in the back and I think that's a bit shit, so I might have been having a bit of a rant about that. You think to yourself, know what, maybe there isn't a fucking God and it's just life and it's just the way it is. I was definitely angry with life, I guess, the shit with my dad and all the other crap, just life in general fucking just pissed me off. I was an angry young man. Singing those songs sort of released it. Released all my shit onto other people but in a good way. It was like everything, all the shit that I had during the day or last week or a month before, just got released, turning it into a good thing. All that fucking angst and all that energy would go through the mixer and come out in a better way. Hopefully people would like it and jump around and get into it. I used to come off stage and be floored for ages, it was like a fucking exorcism or whatever the word is. It was big and powerful and it was great.

Grim up north and all that

Noel My old fella was violent towards me and me mam, that's a fact, but if I could sum him up I would just say he was a shit dad. That's pretty much what it boils down to. A shit dad.

Peggie I have always said that he was jealous of them because they were lads and they were starting to grow up. He thought they should go to bed at 8 o'clock at night; they would be working and coming in with their wages and he'd be, 'Get up to bed.' He was terrible to Paul, he really was. Paul worked with him longer than Noel. Noel got wise to it, Noel couldn't be doing with him. Paul would work from 7 o'clock, because he always worked on the building sites. It could be 11 o'clock before they'd come home. Then Paul would go for his wages on the Friday and he'd say, 'I haven't got them. I haven't got them ready yet.' He'd make Paul beg for his money. Noel wouldn't be bothered, Noel would think, 'I don't want it anyways, I'll get it off me mam.' I would rather give it to them than see them beg. Noel was the one that got it the most because he always thought Noel was out up to no good. I said, 'He is only down the road with the rest of the lads his age.' Fifteen, sixteen, they were standing on corners. Tommy would always come back and say, 'The police are after that lot down the road there.' I said, 'Don't be so stupid.' Then I'd say to Noel, 'What were you doing down Burnage Lane, Noel?' He'd say, 'Doing nothing, I was in somebody's house.' I really think there was something wrong with him. I don't know what it was, whether he had a guilty conscience himself and he was taking it out on them.

Liam He used to knock her about. He never touched me, he used to knock Noel and Paul about a bit, but I never got it. People go, 'You never got a crack,' but you'd seen it. Sometimes you'd want the crack instead of having to witness it. If you're getting booted across the room it has an effect on you. Whether you're getting a kicking or not, you're still watching it. Seeing it and feeling it, they're both shit. They'd be rucking in the morning about something and you'd go to school thinking, 'Fucking hell, this is going to be shit.' You get through school and come home and go, 'I hope the cunt's gone out,' and then you come round the corner and his car would be there and you'd be thinking, 'Fucking hell, here we go.' You get in and then they'd be rucking. So then you'd be going, 'Fucking hell, I hope he goes out with his bird,' or whatever he was doing, because when he'd go out it would be chilled. But then he'd come back a couple of days later, not good. It was shit. It was shit for my mam and it was shit for us and there you go. It was shit, but I guess two fucking doors down it was happening to them as well.

Peggie I remember Noel once saying, 'If you don't get out of here, Mam, and leave him I'm going to kill him.' I thought, 'Oh Jesus, you can't be doing time for the likes of him.'

Liam I remember me mam packing all the gear up and then leaving. My dad had hurt his back at work, I think, and he was on a mattress downstairs – she left him the mattress. I think my mam's brothers come over, stacked the van up and then off we went to this new house, which was alright. I mean, we had no money, but it was just good me mam not getting a kicking.

Peggie When Liam was eleven, nearly twelve, I thought, 'This is it; I can't be doing with this any more.'

Paul We only went down the road a couple of miles, he never once came after us and knocked on the door. Wouldn't dare.

Noel To get a new council house when you've already got one, in the eighties, is virtually impossible . . . I remember going with her on endless trips down to the council offices. She finally managed to get one and then she had to do it.

Peggie I left him a knife and a fork and a spoon, and I think I left him too much. Of course it affected them, it definitely affected them. They got very bitter. They never really talk about him.

Liam I just wanted my mam to be alright, that was basically it. I didn't give a shit about me, it was like, 'Look, if that fucker starts again, he's going to get it.' If he continually fucking starts, the older we get, the more he's going to get a proper fucking beating or whatever. I wasn't bothered about us, it was just making sure my mam was happy and safe. Once she's happy, I don't give a shit about him. It was mainly about getting her away. She thought it was best to get us out of that shit scene. We wanted her to get out of it.

Noel Life didn't change that much apart from fucking idiot Dad wasn't fucking getting on your case all the time about shit. The main thing I liked about at the new house was there was no shouting or slamming of doors. If I am being honest, I don't know many of my mates' dads at that time who were any better. To me everybody's dad was like that. Dads were just twats then because of unemployment and them being men in the seventies, do you know what I mean? Housewives were housewives and kids were kids and the dog got a kick in the arse. Your dad hit your mam, your mam hit the eldest, he hit the middle and eventually the dog got a kick in the bollocks. We never had a dog, though, so the goldfish used to get a flick round the gills. Not that we had a goldfish either, we used to do it to next door's goldfish, the fucking orange bastard. It never made it into my songs, any of it, at any point ever. I don't really look at the songs that I wrote then as a reaction to a childhood; that really has been overplayed a lot. Why

I wanted to be rich. I was driven because I was working class and poor.

would I want to write about that? I wouldn't want to be playing Knebworth singing a load of songs about domestic violence, trust me. I don't pick the scabs of my childhood at all. We had a shitty upbringing, but it was normal to everybody else of our age, it wasn't like we were locked in a cupboard for thirteen hours a day. It was hard work being working class then and we dug ourselves out of it because we had talent and we chased it and that was it. What drove me on was not the fact that we come from a dysfunctional family, what drove me on was I wanted to be rich. I was driven because I was working class and poor. I wasn't arsed about the fame, I didn't want to go through life being fucking poor. Joining Liam's band was when the light bulb finally came on. It was like, fucking right, this is it. You can't let that kind of thing affect you because then you're carrying that weight all the way through life. I've relieved myself of all that weight a long, long time ago. I know other people's perceptions of it must be vastly different to mine... My missus thinks my old fella beat the talent into me. There, what a guy. If I wanted to take revenge on my dad I'd put a fucking baseball bat on his head. I am not that poetic to have done it through the art of song.

Going Val Doonican

Liam He'd always wanted to be the singer, without a doubt.

Noel I always used to think that it's really difficult to be a singer, but now I am a singer, I know that if you are not in the mood, you know what you do? You get in the fucking mood. If you are not going to be in the mood at ten to nine, then fucking get in the mood, sharpish, because there are people out there and they've paid to come and see you. They don't particularly care whether you are fucking brilliant; have the decency to walk on stage and give a little bit of a shit.

> If anything I done gigs when I shouldn't have done gigs ...

Liam I never, ever squirmed out of any fucking gig, man. If anything I done gigs when I shouldn't have done gigs, which fucked up my voice along the way. Yeah, drinking, smoking, staying up all night, I can own that shit, but also doing gigs when you shouldn't be fucking doing gigs, when you are fucking gigged out, when we should have had a bit of time off basically.

Noel All the acts on Creation and some of the acts that inspired them were going to do like an answer to MTV's

Unplugged: Creation Undrugged. We were doing two or three acoustic songs. Liam developed a phobia of the acoustic guitar.

Liam I'm not into all that acoustic nonsense, fuck off, mate. That was when it all started getting a bit silly, doing acoustic bits. It's like, come on, mate; we're the Pistols here, now we've gone all fucking Val Doonican. No, not for me.

Noel Liam did that thing that Liam always does: there is an offer to do this thinig, shall we do it? Yes, fucking great, it will be fucking brilliant. Get to the soundcheck, everything's great. Five minutes before you are due on stage: 'I've got a sore throat, I can't go on.' Which basically, in Liam Speak, is, 'I'm fucking shitting it so I'm not going on.'

Liam The only time he'd ever do any of them kind of songs would be if my voice was fucked then he'd take over. I'm sure he was slipping shit in my drink so he could do it. I'm sure that fucker was spiking my drinks with fucking gravel or something or some shit.

Noel Singing is hard on the brain, it is hard to get up there and do it. It is even harder if you are staying up till 7 o'clock in the morning drinking and smoking. That's the bottom line, because I fucking said so.

Liam You can't ask a twenty-one-year-old or nineteen-year-old lad to be professional. Can you be more professional? Fuck off. I don't even understand that word, what you on about? It's like trying to take your rawness away.

Noel You can't have it both ways. If you want to do that, great, but something is going to suffer. You can't be on tour and have a great social life. Socialising is for your spare time, it's as simple as that. If a kid is gracious enough to queue up to buy a ticket, you are duty bound to fucking show up. I don't give a fuck if you've got a sore throat, or a sore cat, or a fucking dodgy knee. If they've paid, you play, and if you don't, get a fucking doctor's note.

Liam He was wanting to sing more songs for whatever reason, but you just know where that's going to end, don't you? He'll want to do another one and another one and another one; he was basically after my job. He is within his rights, he writes the songs, but get the fuck out of the band if that's the case. I'm the fucking singer and I should be singing all the songs so if you want to go and do that, then go fucking solo, mate.

Noel Of course, it never dawned on me to be a singer until I actually had to be one. Until he started walking off stage in the middle of gigs and it's, 'Fucking hell, we've got another forty minutes left here, someone better do something.'

Liam He's a great fucking songwriter and always will be, but singing is my gig. If you are going to write the fucking song, at least let me sing it because if you are going to start singing the fucking songs as well as writing them, what am I doing, making the fucking tea? All the coming off and, 'I'm doing this tune,' I was like a fucking yo-yo half the time. On for one song, off for one song, on for one song, off – leave it out, you're taking the piss, mate. Here he comes, here he goes, here he comes . . .

Noel He never rehearsed, he couldn't be arsed, so you didn't really know what anything was going to sound like until you walked out on stage. Which is alright when you are playing the Forum or some fucking pub somewhere in fucking Aldershot. It can be a bit hairy when you are playing a stadium, to 70,000 people, and you think, 'I wonder if he knows the words . . .'

Singing them songs the way I sing them is like being in a boxing match . . .

Liam We had a little argument, the fucking amplifier fed back and hurt your fucking ears, the set list got put out wrong, or someone had a fucking bit too much to drink that night. Fuck off. We're in a fucking rock-and-roll band here and everyone's, 'Oh God, he turned up pissed' or, 'He missed the fucking gig.' Fuck off, mate, are you taking the piss? If that's the formula these days, no wonder rock and roll is over.

Noel He was always complaining about monitors, always fucking complaining about the sound on stage. 'Well, why don't you fucking soundcheck like everybody else does?'

Liam The reason I didn't do soundchecks is because I'd be singing in the soundcheck and my voice would go. So I just keep it chilled until the time of the gig. It's fine if you are playing guitar, but even getting up and doing a couple of tunes would fuck my voice up, so I would just wait until 9 o'clock and then hope for the best. I didn't gargle with honey and all that because it wasn't the way I sing. Singing them songs the way I sing them is like being in a boxing match, it's hard work. It takes its wear and tear. I ain't moaning about it, but that's just the way it is.

Noel I remember Barrowlands well. He didn't have a sore throat; the usual shit, out all night the night before, not bothering to soundcheck. Turns up at the gig, within fifteen minutes he is out of puff. We are halfway through one song, he stops singing, walks off stage. It's Glasgow, they are going fucking mental. The song stops and there is a bit of confusion as to what's happened. You go off stage and say, 'What's happening?' Not only has he left the stage, he's left the building, he's fucking gone. So you are there, fifteen minutes into a gig, what are you going to do? You are either going to try and save the night or there is going to be a riot. As luck would have it on this night it was both.

Maggie You don't walk off a Glasgow Barrowlands stage, you know what I mean? That could be quite seriously not good health and safety-wise, or security-wise. You go on there and you finish that gig, because they're quite a rowdy bunch in Glasgow.

Liam If your voice goes it's like the end of the fucking world and there's nothing . . . It's horrible for a singer. It's like a guitarist getting his hands chopped off.

Noel Our security guard came over and said, 'Liam's not coming back. The cars are running so we should leave before there's a riot.' He said it a bit too close to the mic, it went out over the PA thus instigating a fucking riot. Shit started getting thrown everywhere and then we had to fucking leave. Then you go back to the hotel and Liam would show no remorse, he would just be like, 'Fuck 'em.'

Liam I've never walked off because I weren't into it, are you fucking kidding? There is no fucking way. You've got your fans in front of you going mental, the last place I want to be is sat backstage freaking out. I want to be in there getting amongst it. All that nonsense about, 'He didn't give a fuck,' or, 'He walked off,' I never, ever walked off stage because I had a headache or I'd broken a fucking nail or I couldn't be arsed with the gig. Are you kidding? It's because I can't physically fucking sing. A lot of the reason my voice is fucked is because I probably should have walked off. The amount of gigs I stayed on and fucking battled through it because of the shit you get or whatever . . .

Maggie Legally, they have every right not to pay us, so we have to finish the gig. We need to get paid, so get up there and work it. Not finishing the gig was not really something that we could entertain.

Noel I don't mind cancelling a gig before it takes place, if the singer has got a sore throat, I don't mind that. Walking off stage during the second or third song and when there's 15,000, 25,000 people there, that is unforgivable, because how do you get out of that? What happened, nine times out of ten, was I'd take over. And the more I would take over or finish the gig, the more that it became acceptable. So what happened is I really enabled him to behave like that. Nobody wanted to fucking hear me sing lesser versions of 'Live Forever' or

'Supersonic'. Those songs were written for Liam. That kind of thing started to become really regular: Liam just walking off stage, not turning up, turning up and then leaving, or turning up and then sitting in the crowd and basically being a fucking lightweight about it all. Not turning up for stuff, saying you are going to do stuff and then not doing it . . . If you are going to wind me up, that is one fucking way to do it for sure. That went on forever, not turning up at *Jools Holland*, not turning up at *MTV Unplugged*, walking off stage halfway through countless fucking gigs because he'd been on a bender. My whole attitude towards all of this is: that's great, we all love going on benders, I fucking love it, but if I've got shit to do the next day . . . You have got to make a decision, haven't you? I'd rather be on the telly with my band, smashing it, than sitting maudlin in a hotel

Nobody wanted to fucking hear me sing lesser versions of 'Live Forever' or 'Supersonic'.

room at 3 o'clock in the morning, smoking cigs listening to fucking 'Strawberry Fields'. You are not a rock star sitting in a hotel room at 4 o'clock in the morning, listening to fucking 'Bungalow Bill' again, you are just a fucking lad on the piss. When I would be arguing with Liam about shit like this, I would always go back to us in 1991 and say, 'Why were we doing this in the first place? It was to be on MTV.' We used to watch *MTV Unplugged* and think, 'Fucking smash the arse out of that when we do it.' That's what we wanted. What's changed in four years? Why are you now not arsed about going on *Jools Holland*? Why are you now not arsed about fucking turning up for video shoots? When we were starting off we used to laugh at people like Kurt Cobain. He was in the biggest band in the world and was moaning about it all the time, moaning about selling loads of records. We would sit there laughing; 'You fucking knobhead, you cheeky cunt, we are slumming it here at the Boardwalk, damp, shit, fucking awful, playing to six people. I'll take your place any day of the week, give it to me now.' I always used to say, 'We are living someone else's dream.' Think of all the bands who are playing in pubs tonight who are trying to make it, who'd give anything to be on *MTV Unplugged*. Why rehearse five nights a week if you don't want to make it? Why do all those local band nights, to like eleven people, nine of them being your mates and two inquisitive punters, why do all that? In one ear and out the other.

Liam I had problems with my throat, just probably caning it too much, just fucking screaming and shouting, I don't know. Oasis was a loud band, having to sing on top of them songs was hard, your voice would pack up and that was it. I never, ever, could not be arsed getting on that stage. I take massive offence at that. There is no way I'm having people going I can't be arsed, that is bollocks. Not having that.

Noel Certainly by the time we get to Knebworth, Liam is not the same frontman as he is eighteen months previous. The more money you get, the more fame, the fucking chicks and the booze and the drugs and all that . . . The entire world is staring at you. I know how I would have felt. You know, you have not even got a guitar to defend yourself with. You are kind of stood there with your balls hanging out singing somebody else's songs. It must be fucking difficult. I am not sure I could do it.

Shitholes USA

Noel Arriving in New York for the first time, I can look back now and think how it must have been annoying for the rest of the band, because I was like, 'I've fucking seen Times Square, so I'm going to fucking stay in this room and get through this massive bag of psychedelics. See you at the soundcheck.' The Inspirals prepared me because I'd been on stage, even if it was only handing a guitar to somebody, you've kind of been out there in front of a big crowd. And I'd done tours, I'd been on tour buses, I'd been through customs, I knew what it fucking was. American customs fucking blow Liam's mind.

> I'm a fucking rock star. I'm here to steal your soul.

'What is the purpose of your visit?'

'You what?'

'Purpose of your visit.'

'What fucking visit, I'm not visiting, mate, I'm a fucking rock star. I'm here to steal your soul.'

'Okay, you can follow me now, sir, you're coming this way.'

Liam Never been to America, man, never been. Never been anywhere, so it was fucking great. It was mega. You could smoke on the planes then and everything. The roads were massive, and the food. I was always, 'Can I get a cheese-and-ham,' then the sandwich come and I'm just sitting there getting rid of twenty layers, launching half of this food into a bin, and then going, 'That's fucking more like it.'

Noel I meet the video director. This guy is talking director bullshit and he said to me, 'I was thinking at the end we should bury the drum kit.' I said, for a laugh, drunk, 'Why don't we bury the drummer?' and he went, 'Great. That's amazing, wow, fucking hell that is amazing.' I remember looking at him thinking, is that how easy this shit is? You just suggest shite randomly? While we're at it, why don't we throw the singer off the Brooklyn Bridge? Fucking hell. Fucking dreadful video. I will tell you what's good about that video, there is a bit where Liam's strapped to a chair, halfway up a wall. Never get him to do that now.

Liam I'd been out all night partying somewhere and I remember getting down to wherever it was on the docks, and there was this chair there. I hadn't had any sleep and I was thinking, 'Bastards are going to put me in that.' It was stupid. I was fucking singing and lip syncing and I could just hear it creaking. I think that sealed the deal for me with videos. Who fucking screws a chair to a fucking brick wall? That's not cool, is it. The last thing you fucking want is to be stuck on a wall, you want to be on your sofa or in bed.

Jason We did the Wetlands, a great little gig downtown, proper classic New York club, it's great. Once you get the gig out the way, it's head out into New York. It's always a great city is New York, it's got that certain something, a certain energy. I think that night we bumped into the 'rock chicks'.

Noel 'Have you met the "rock chicks"?'

'No. What, are they a band or something?'

They were quite famous for their after-show parties and seemingly every band in the world would end up back at their apartment. One of them, Christine, would end up working for us at one point. She has remained a very dear friend of mine. There were lots of people at these parties, but they weren't wild. Americans are like, 'Fucking hell, a wild party . . . we've got twelve beers and half a joint!' I was like, holy shit, honestly I've had better parties on a fucking Wednesday afternoon.

Liam The beers were always shit until we found a decent Irish bar. Them light beers, how do you get drunk on this shit? There was one in New York, I can't remember what road it was off, but it was just called The Irish Pub and it was amazing. It had the best jukebox, we would go in and stay there till five in the morning. The geezer'd come over and go, 'Right, lads, I've got to have a clean up and you've got to get out, we will be open at eight.' So we'd go back to the hotel, hit the mini bar for two or three hours, then we'd come back into The Irish Pub and stay there again and do the same fucking thing. It was a good crack, man.

Noel So by the time Oasis had kind of come to do the American tour I was very focused and I was going to drive it.

Liam I went over there with a chip on my shoulder, but a good chip. It was like, 'Look, we're going to fucking have you and we're going to do it our way, the same as in England. You won't be moulding us to be one of your own. I wasn't mithered whether we made it in the States. Obviously we would give it a good crack, but it would have to be on our terms. It was never about changing your style – trying to turn a fucking grape into a diamond – to sell a few records because I would have been off. If you like us, great, if you don't, give a shit. My main thing was to make an album and be fucking great where I lived. To be the best band in my country. In America it was, if it happens it happens. I knew we were the best band in the world, regardless whether they did or not.

I knew we were the best band in the world, regardless whether they did or not.

Noel The contrast of getting on a plane from England, where the mania was just starting, and going to Japan, where the mania was like fucking 'blam', then getting on a plane and going to America, where nobody had heard of us, it was huge. That didn't freak me out, I was ready for that. I don't know if anybody else felt it was beneath them to be playing tiny little fucking nightclubs, but I was ready for that.

Jason The venues were really, really tiny on that first American bit and you couldn't even fit the equipment on the stage. We just got on with it. It was a new thing: we are in America, we are going out, we are doing gigs, it's getting well received, it's got plenty of people, plenty of interest and the more that we went out, the more gigs we did, more word got out and more people would turn up. I think it served its purpose. When you start off in any place you've got to do the smaller venues and then work your way up. You can't just go play Wembley from doing a Saturday afternoon at the pub, can you?

Maggie They were quite small gigs, proper little shitholes where literally you'd have a pillar down the middle of the stage and you'd have to put Liam on the side. It was the toilets of the world.

Noel I thought the gigs were great – apart from the one in the Whisky, which was fucking appalling. The crowd reaction was mixed. You've got a few people down the front – and I mean a few people – not necessarily British, but anglophiles who are into it, if I'm being honest, just a little bit too into it, do you know what I mean? Then you've got a group of people in the middle who are completely perplexed, 'Who the fuck are this lot?' And then you've got the people at the back who are just not interested at all. You would be playing to a thousand people a night; 750 had heard of you and the rest had come along to see what all the fuss was about. But there was a thousand leaving who were into it. So that, to me, is what it is all about. I remember enjoying it all, but I've heard it said that junior was a bit perplexed about going from a nice tour bus to a fucking van, but there you go.

Liam So we went over there behaving the way we were behaving in England, and it just didn't happen. They were like, 'Get to fuck, no way.' The way we were on stage wasn't a polished thing. They like things a bit more refined and stuff. They want to be told how great they are, don't they?

Are you having a good fucking time? Clap your hands together. They want the big fucking thing, don't they? Not into any of that nonsense. I never felt the pressure to move or get a little dance routine together or anything like that. Or speak to the crowd, or even acknowledge the fucking crowd. Are they here to hear us talk about our day? They are here to hear the tunes, aren't they, surely? Once you get into that world of, 'This song is about this and blah, blah, blah,' you open a can of worms because you are expected to tell some funky little story. It's not a fucking comedy show and we are not up there for a laugh, we are up there to fucking sing and play music, I ain't saying fuck all. They were confused when there would be no chatting or banter in between the songs. It would just go silent – sometimes people get awkward around silences, where I thrive on it. My vibe was get your head down and get on with it, blast their souls into a good place with your music. We'll have a chat later in the bar.

They were confused when there would be no chatting or banter in between the songs.

Noel I've never been one that actually gave a shit about what the audience felt. I've done plenty of gigs where you are looking out at the audience and thinking, 'I wonder if they are getting it?' Particularly in America where they're blankly looking at you. But I don't give a fuck whether they are getting it or not, as long as they are there, I don't give a shit.

Liam I haven't begged you to come here, you're going to get it how we want to give it you and, if you don't like it, you don't have to come back. I wasn't doing it for them, I was doing it for us. They just didn't get it, and so be it. Fair play to them. They weren't budging and neither were we, at least there are people with a bit of integrity.

> They just didn't get it, and so be it. Fair play to them.

Noel We were winning over a lot of sceptics. We were doing a gig, in Washington or New York; we did 'Cigarettes & Alcohol' in the soundcheck and it was fucking great. I remember there are lots of crew putting a PA up and all that – generic crew in Black Sabbath T-shirts, shorts, key chains and the long hair – and when we finished the whole place just started clapping.

There is a lot of shit you have to do in America. For instance, on that trip, me and Liam got taken off to a recording studio and given a sheet of paper with all these one-liners for radio stations. We had never done this before, I was never aware of it when I was a roadie, this is fucking news to me. So we were looking at each other and going, 'What do you want us to do? Read these out? There are like blank spaces.'

'Yes, well, put your name in the blank spaces and read it out.'

So there's me and Liam round one mic going, 'Hey! This is Noel and Liam from Oasis and you're listening to WX9 fucking blah, blah, blah the only place to listen to modern rock in the whole of the fucking universe.'

I think it might have lasted to about the third one and we are like, 'No, this is not going to fucking happen.' And that kind of set the tone for our relationship with Epic records in America.

Liam I had gone in to do some interviews in a Sony Music building. This guy was sat there, throwing this American football up in the air.

'You the guy from Oasis, man? I'm such and such, head of . . . You must think yourself really lucky in the position you're in.'

'Why is that then?'

'Being signed to Sony Music.'

'You're lucky that you've got a band like us on your fucking label.'

Some fucking big knobhead who doesn't even know who you are and doesn't care, telling you how fucking lucky you are to be on his label. Fuck off, knobhead; you're lucky to have us. You're lucky there's a band like us that give a shit. Now put your cigar down, put my beer down and get the fuck out of me room, fatty.

Noel You don't realise until you get there, the amount of fucking bullshit you have to do. You're expected to go and meet the guy who runs the biggest record shop in that state. Not only the guy that runs the record fucking shop, but the guy's wife and their kids. To me that's all fucking bullshit. That was a thing that went on for years in America. It was like, 'We're not playing a game here to be contrary or to be cool; I don't want to go and sit in a fucking meeting with a load of radio people. I don't want to do it.' I feel uncomfortable. When they talk, it's like they are talking about somebody else. There was this dinner thing and I said to this guy I would go, but I don't want anybody to talk to me, I've got nothing to say. This guy stands up and announces, 'He's coming here, but he doesn't want to speak to anyone.' Everybody started clapping. So fucking cool. I was really embarrassed, I remember sweating, thinking get me out of here. We famously went to a thing in L.A. before a gig and we were taken by the head of somebody to meet some sales team in a fucking room. The guy was such a fucking bell-end he introduced us as Leyland and Norton. Liam said, 'What? One of us named after a fucking car firm, the other one's a motorbike.'

Liam It wasn't like, 'Either get us or we're going home!' We definitely went back for more in America, but not to the point of selling our souls. It wasn't if you don't get us after one gig – you should do because we are fucking great – we're going home. We knew it would be a long process and we definitely grafted over there as much as we did over here, it just didn't happen as big as what people thought it might have.

Coyley There is all this pressure on bands to break America, you know, everybody sees it as so important. But breaking America quite often breaks the fucking band, because they're that concerned about it. It's that vast, fuck me, man, you could tour forever. You have a good time and all that, but I tell you what, when you get home, your carpet doesn't look the same. That was always a sign for me, you don't recognise your own fucking stuff when you get home. That means you've been somewhere too long; you need grounding again.

Liam He lived in Liverpool, his carpet probably wasn't the fucking same. Someone had probably been in and had it.

Noel We would get subtitled on MTV, which I found fucking hilarious. People would say, 'Does that offend you in any way?' I would be, 'No, I think it's fucking brilliant.' Life should be subtitled.

Liam I had a feeling they'd never take to us. I just wanted to go home, to be fair. Can we just go back to England where we are fucking massive and everything is great. People get us and we don't need subtitles and people call me Liam instead of Leyton? I know a load of big bands that have been great in the world, but I know they've been bent over and fucked up the arse to get to that status. I'm quite happy where I am. I can sit down and my bum doesn't hurt. So I am quite happy with that.

Noel The American thing exhausted me a little bit. I never got two minutes to sit and have a cig and stare out the window. 'Got to come and see Marty. Marty's in town, you'll fucking love this guy!' Who the fuck's Marty, you know what I mean? I was glad when it passed if I am being honest. I guess I was beginning, at that point, to see my own limitations and I didn't like it.

Liam In England people kind of got what we were about more. Abroad it was like 'Who the fuck are these fuckers?' and I guess the standing still and the staring people out or not saying much, people thought that we were trying to cause shit, but we weren't, we just didn't have fuck all to say. We were there to sing music. I think people just wanted to have a pop and all that, but some days you'd walk on stage and go, 'Right, this is going to be a bit of a battle.'

Noel The funny thing is, in the States we made it because we weren't English. There was no English blood in anybody in that band. Blur's tunes were about the quirkiness of English life and English things; that won't come as a surprise to anyone, them being English and very English. Pulp's songs were witty and northern; that won't come as any surprise. My songs weren't either of those things, my songs were quite universal, the words were kind of inclusive. I wasn't picking any scabs off my heroin-riddled arm. We are all about having a good time – as *Spinal Tap* as that sounds. You don't sell out Madison Square Garden singing songs about Walkers crisps and the delights of an Eccles cake; you don't do the Hollywood Bowl raving about Vimto, I'll fucking tell you that for nowt. And 'Cigarettes & Alcohol' means the same to the lad from Burnage who wrote it as it did ten years later to the kid in Brooklyn listening to it. So I didn't think we were going to struggle over there. We struggled over there because of our personalities. We were on a massive corporate record label and we are not corporate people, at all. Professionalism meant nothing to us, it was beneath us. I'll turn up for interviews and all that; I am not spending eight hours on a photo shoot for *Rolling Stone*, they can kiss my arse. In the end we fucking

In the end we fucking smashed the arse out of it in America.

smashed the arse out of it in America. For a brief period we were selling more albums in America than we were in England. It was only six months, but we were the biggest band in the world. I know what it feels like to be in the biggest band in the world . . . even if it was only while U2 were having a cig somewhere. We still did it, and I can tell you it is fucking hard work and we treated it with the contempt it deserved.

Ninja speed on the Strip

Liam Didn't really get on with L.A. I found it a bit weird. It was either mental and dark and full of heroin or it was either full of fucking rye bread and sparkling water. There was no in between, I always felt. You would either fucking die there or you'd end up fucking doing squats in the corner and yoga and shit. I can't remember anywhere really in America that we hung out. Just probably at the hotels or at the gig. We'd never go to clubs or anything like that, or hang out in these hot spots. I know it sounds boring, but we never did. The crew did, they were always off gallivanting in these nightclubs, but we'd be, 'Fuck that, where's the nearest Irish bar?'

Michael Spencer Jones[*] They barely got off the plane, I'm checking into my hotel, I walk in to Liam's room and there is a bag of cocaine – or whatever it was – the size of which you have never seen in your life, it was just like a bag of flour on the table. It was unbelievable. I'm thinking, 'Wow, you've only been here about twenty minutes.' What is remarkable is that whatever it was, it was consumed within about seventy-two hours. It was astonishing, it could have kept the Bolivian army going for about twelve months, what was on that table.

Noel The Whisky a Go Go on Sunset Strip . . . It's the most famous club in L.A. The Doors got signed there apparently and all that kind of thing. Wow, fucking hell.

[*] *Photographer responsible for Oasis's early album and single covers.*

Coyley I think the perception was that the Whisky a Go Go was one of those moments: if you get it right here, it will set us up for this tour, you know. A couple of days before was the Bottom of the Hill gig, not a good fucking place, it's a bar not a club. It was so loud that day. So, I said to Noel, 'You're too loud, I can't keep up with it.' And he told me to fuck off. I think I just got pissed that night and just thought, 'I can't do anything here tonight, all I can hear is his guitar, can't hear a voice or anything.'

He would not turn it down: 'Don't fucking tell me turn it down!'

That was the lead up to the Whisky.

Maggie The Whisky a Go Go was supposed to be an industry gig, a record label thing. It is quite strategic that leading up to L.A. we've got Seattle, Portland, San Fran, Sacramento to warm them up. Trying to get them into the gig mode, you know what I mean?

Liam Everyone sits there and goes, 'Oh, you know, they're doing their first gig in L.A. and it's going to be fucking the best thing ever. The boys are here and it's going to be like this, and it's going to be like that.' Life doesn't work like that, you know what I mean? Just shut the fuck up and let us do our gig. If you've got these big expectations all the time, they're not going to happen. So, don't fucking hype it, let's just do what we do.

Noel Someone had discovered the joys of crystal meth, which is effectively like ninja speed. It's not even fun, it's a fucking horrible drug.

Coyley Everybody had a dig at it, the only problem with that is that you couldn't get to sleep. I don't mind having a dig at anything, as long as, you know, about half ten at night, cup of tea and go to bed.

Maggie The only one who didn't really overdo it was Noel, actually.

Noel I don't know why, but I wasn't partaking in crystal meth, I really don't know why.

Liam Crystal fucking whatever it was, I don't know the name of it, but it was horrible. We all thought it was coke and we were doing big fucking lines of it and it just fucking kept us up for days.

Maggie Record label decide to put on a party for them, a little bit worrying.

Noel A party on the roof of the Hyatt . . . there's a party on the roof of the Hyatt in *Spinal Tap* and I thought fucking hell, how amazing is this? This is real, this shit fucking happens, you know. I remember that being great, but those things, they don't mean a great deal to me. 'Blah, blah, blah, you guys are amazing.' Yeah, I know. To me it's when the lights go down and you go on stage, that's when it matters. All the bullshit that surrounds the band at the time is great, but it doesn't mean anything, if the gigs are shit, the party means nothing to me.

> To me it's when the lights go down and you go on stage, that's when it matters.

Michael Spencer Jones It was one of these really shallow, pretentious showbiz meet-and-greets that Oasis really did not have any time for at all. Whilst I was there, I was taking some pictures of Noel, sat down at the table, signing autographs, you know. I sensed that Noel wasn't there really, he was somewhere else; he just looked really, really stressed out and under a lot of pressure. You can see that he's got the entire world on his shoulders.

Bonehead Everybody was there, you know. I think it was on the roof of our fucking hotel. Free beer and this, that and the other, it wasn't terribly exciting I don't think. Great view, because we're on a roof looking at Sunset Boulevard.

Noel We get to the soundcheck, everybody's been up all night and looked like it.

Phil Soundcheck was alright, gig wasn't. Obviously, the record company is there, and they are the ones who had put the money up in L.A. This is important and so when it goes wrong, it's even more of a fuck-up.

Bonehead Starts off alright, good gig. I remember it going steadily downhill.

Noel Phil Smith was responsible for putting the set lists out, would write loads out at the beginning of the tour and we would do the same set every night. For some reason my set list was different to everybody else's. Mine was from the previous U.K. tour so I was starting songs and the rest of the band were kind of looking at the set list, or they were starting songs and I was, 'Oh, we're not doing it.' It was all a bit like that.

Jason It sounded like they were all playing different songs at the same time and it were like, whoa, what's going on here?

Bonehead I could see Liam going behind one of the amps throughout the gig, man, and he was just snorting lines of crystal meth on stage. That's going to go tit's up, innit, and it just went fucking chaotic.

Liam I remember it being alright . . . I remember I might have had a line halfway through it, and then I think I went a bit fucking mad.

Coyley The whole thing just fell apart, it was like the fucking roof fell in or something, the band stopped and couldn't restart. I thought, maybe a guitar amp has gone off, I just couldn't really tell what was going on. I'd never seen it with this band before, it just seemed to tumble in on itself. It took them a long time to restart. I'm on Noel's side, so I can see him, and I see that boy is really rattled. I'm just looking and thinking, fucking hell, he will kick off tonight.

Bonehead Liam was just fucking about singing whatever, you know, any old words will do.

Noel Just making up stupid words to 'Live Forever' and stuff like that and I could feel it was a bit of a catastrophe. I was in a fury. I was like, 'What the fucking hell are you doing?'

Liam Every now and again I'd fucking change the lyrics just for the crack and Noel'd do the same. I guess it's got to be whatever day suits him. If he's not in a fun mood, he was the one that would come and turn the vibe switch down.

Jason I think there were a lot of tensions on stage, a lot of gesturing between Noel and Liam, well, more from Liam to Noel, then the tambourine came flying.

Liam He said something and I fucking launched the tambourine at him. He was lucky I didn't launch a fucking monitor at him or something, or a fucking drummer.

Noel The tambourine. Yeah. Not like the Bruce Lee throwing star or a fucking light sabre, it was a tambourine that hit me on the shoulder. Went 'tsh' – out of time, I might add.

Liam I think we were just knackered, or maybe just maybe burning the candle at both ends a bit too much. Or Noel being a pompous little fucker who was trying to fucking put everyone in their boxes: 'You are having too much fun,' and me going, 'Fuck you, I've not had enough.' Fun, fun, fun.

> He was lucky I didn't launch a fucking monitor at him or something, or a fucking drummer.

Noel There is the legend that Ringo Starr was there and walked out. I was fucking pissed off.

Liam It weren't that bad or I'd have fucking thrown Ringo at him. Here you are, cop for Ringo, you fucking knobhead.

Phil We'd just got hold of the wrong type of drugs and it wasn't good for me personally, that's all I can say. I might plead the fifth on the rest of it.

Liam I don't think it was a triumphant gig, I might have been singing really bad or I might have been just pissed and off me tits. The gig might have been shit but you're allowed them every now and again, aren't you? We've done one bad gig, it's all over. We got the set list wrong, fuck. It just wasn't our night that night, but the next night probably was.

Bonehead It's one of them gigs that you want to just push out of your memory, you know what I mean, fucking ground swallow me up, man.

Noel I felt we could have smashed it in America, I really felt we could have been bigger than anyone that had gone before us because the timing was right, but I also knew that you've got to be able to play when you go there. You won't get anywhere on attitude in the States, you've got to be able to play.

Liam I don't think we were dicking about, I think we were just probably having one of them days. Can't be great all the fucking time. Obviously in Noel's eyes you can, but you just can't. However long we'd been on the road, we had been on the road, I imagine we'd done a lot of gigs and that's just the way it is, everyone just needs to cool out. That's just the way it was, mate. I'm sure they've seen worse than a set list being wrong and a tambourine being thrown at the guitarist. Haven't they had Guns N' Roses and all them other weird fuckers. Jim Morrison played that gig, didn't he?

Coyley I don't know what happened to the band at that point, something changed. The band was never the same. In some respects, that was the night it finished. That was it.

Noel I remember going upstairs to the dressing room and there being a huge argument. Shit got thrown around the dressing room and of course fucking half of the people are on crystal meth so they are not in the best of moods.

Bonehead There was a massive hoo-hah, big screaming match and he said this and he said that. Noel's like, 'You're off your fucking head,' and I was like, 'No, whoa, whoa, no, I'm not, man. No, I'm not.' A fucking raging, serious hangover, do you know what I mean, but no . . .

Noel I might have overreacted a little bit, because it was only one show. In the grand scheme of things it's fuck all.

Liam Maybe it got a bit dramatic, but fuck it, who gives a fuck. We're meant to be a rock-and-roll band, not fucking Boyzone or whatever.

Noel It was a funny old night, but it kind of set the tone for the rest of the nineties because it made me think, actually, you know what, these lot really don't give a fuck.

Liam We were so super real we were never going to keep it together 24/7 twelve months a year. That was never going to

In some respects, that was the night it finished. That was it.

happen. Whatever band he was in, it must have been a real fucking shock to him to find out that he was actually in a band full of real people that didn't take themselves too seriously. It must be really fucking hard for him, but a couple of shitty gigs here, there and everywhere didn't freak me out because we'd make up for it along the way.

Noel Why would you put all that at risk? Three years previously, this is the same bunch of people who were rehearsing every night of the week in a dirty fucking rehearsal room in Manchester, going nowhere. But the only reason we were rehearsing every night is to get to this place: L.A. Paid to be there. Fucking hell, it's going to happen and you are going to fuck it up? I was thinking, 'You fucking wankers.'

Liam I didn't worry about it at the time. Water off a duck's back. Tomorrow is another city, another gig. Good night's kip, head down, here we go again.

Noel I don't recall at the time thinking, 'This is it now, the band's finished and I'm going to go fucking solo and be bigger than Cliff Richard.' I don't recall thinking that. I may have been trying to teach somebody a lesson. It failed miserably.

Liam We had a lot of madness around Oasis. We were playing with fire most of the time and that's what it needed. So when shit happened you just had to fucking deal with it because you knew that the good would come and sort it out. I don't know what it is, it's nothing to do with us as individuals, it's the spirit man of Oasis. I truly believe that there was another force out there that was bigger than me and Noel and the band. I know it sounds hippy and shit, but when that fucker had something to say he would say it.

Noel I remember going back to the hotel and seeing Maggie; I think I took the float off her and went to San Francisco.

Maggie Noel was quite upset by it. He came to my hotel room and he said, 'I'm leaving. Can you give me money?'

'What do you want?'

'Well, enough money to go back home.'

I had more money on me, but I said I'd got $700, enough money that he could probably whiz around the States, but not further than that. He said, 'Can I have my passport?' so I gave him the passport. At that point I thought, this isn't really good. He left the room, I remember ringing up Marcus saying he's going to leave, 'No, no, no, he'll be fine, he's going to sleep it off, he'll be fine, he'll be fine.' I don't think so.

Bonehead Noel just got off, you know. Do you blame him? It was one of them, 'Alright, he's got off, he'll be back, he'll be back later, on we go, it's happened before.' No. He didn't come back, he was gone, that was it.

Noel I went to San Francisco from L.A. You know, when I think about it now, that's insane. I left a big bag of charlie in the fucking taxi as well, on the way to the airport. I thought, I better not take that, put it down the back of the seat.

Maggie So, I woke up in the morning and I found a note underneath my hotel-room door. I opened it up, it said, 'I'm leaving.' Bollocks, I knew it. So, I rang up Marcus and told him, so he came over.

Liam I remember some fucking soppy note coming through the door saying, 'How can we go on like brothers when we do this?' It was like, fuck right off. So that got rolled up and then another line of crystal meth went up the old fucking tubular bells.

Noel I don't remember leaving a note. No, that's way too fucking pretentious for me.

Bonehead So, it was like, what do we do? No one knew where he was, he could have been two doors down for all we knew. You know, you have a little bust up, something happens, it goes wrong at a gig, band member storms off, band member comes back, and it's all forgot. So, it was like, alright, we'll just stay put. I really didn't think he'd be gone on a plane, out of it, no way.

Maggie I came up with this idea. We didn't have mobile phones then, so I went down to the hotel and said, 'I'd like to check out Mr Gallagher in room blah, blah, blah,' and they're like, 'Okay.' So I checked him out, I got his bill, and then I traced all the last numbers he rang. The last couple of numbers were U.K. numbers, so he must have been calling his mum or somebody back there. Then I noticed there was one number: 415. I thought, San Francisco? We've just been to San Francisco, and I knew that he had some little fling over there with some girl. So I thought, 'Hmm, he's got to be there.' Me and Marcus were both going, 'He's got to be there.' Marcus is like, 'I know what I'm going to do, I'm going to ring the number, just going to speak to the girl

and see what she says, you know, he might not be there.'
So, he gets her on the phone, he said to her, 'You know, we're not saying anything, but obviously, you know, legally, if he's missing for another twelve hours, we have to report him as a missing person, you know. We're going to have to get the police involved. We need to find him.' The minute he hung up the phone, he said, 'He's there, I could just tell by the stuff she was saying, he is there.'

Noel I met this girl, I don't know where I met her, it has to have been either at an Inspiral Carpets gig or at an Oasis gig, fuck knows. I must have phoned her and said, 'It's fucked up here, I'm going to come and stay with you for a few days.' I don't know what the fuck I thought I was doing. I was just going to disappear, fake my own disappearance or something. It was quite a traumatic time because you are, at this point, you are the biggest band in England. Thank God you don't have a mobile phone or a computer so you don't realise what the fallout is. I was hanging out there for a couple of days and probably doing too many fucking drugs and blah, blah, blah, not eating and being a bit fucking mad. She was saying, 'You are going to leave and that's it? What are you going to do?'

> I just needed a bit of time out, I guess, and a bit of perspective.

I guess at that point I'm thinking, 'Actually that is a fucking good point, what am I going to do?' I can't sing, I wasn't a singer then, I'm no frontman. It wasn't like this girl saved me from myself; I just needed a bit of time out, I guess, and a bit of perspective. I wasn't going to burn the house down to prove a point, a few gigs got blown out, what can I say, I had a good time.

Coyley You meet them people in America, you don't meet them anywhere else in the world, I've met a few like that. They take you under their wing, they're not drawn to normal people, they're spiritual people is what they are, they're not rock-and-roll fans. She was one of them. He didn't come to us, he went to her, and when he come back, he was different. Does she even exist? She probably just turned into a wisp of smoke.

Maggie Marcus's idea was to get Tim Abbott over, because he was quite friendly with them, and get him to go up to San Francisco, find Noel and literally talk him back.

Tim Noel phoned me, about 4 a.m., and I went, 'Alright, Noel, what do you want, you alright?'

'Yeah, I'm alright. What you doing the weekend?'

I said, 'What's it got to do with you, haven't thought that far.'

He said, 'I might be back.'

'What do you mean, you might be back?'

He said, 'Look, can you get Marcus to get me guitars back for me.'

'Hang on, I'll call you back.'

I literally put the phone down and Marcus phoned. He went, 'Boyo, have you heard, Noel's left the band? He's gone AWOL, we don't know where he is.'

'Really,' I said, 'that's funny, he's just fucking phoned me.'

'Has he?'

So, I said, 'Well, get off the line, he's going to call me back.'

So then he calls back and says, 'Oh fuck it, I've had enough of those cunts blah, blah, blah. I'll see you next week. Can you tell Marcus to get me guitars back, and say sorry for everything, sorry but that's it. I'll see you next week, we'll go out.'

Then Marcus called again, 'Have you heard, have you heard? They've all done meth, they are all off their tits, there's been a massive row, he's took the tour money and he's fucked off.' Right, he didn't say that.

I said, 'Seriously, do you want me over there?'

So, I literally flew out and arrived in L.A., jet-lagged, the day after. Marcus and me sat down, and Bonehead came and joined us and went, 'We fucked it.' Liam was just like, 'Fuck it, another day in the office, what's up with him, he'll be back, won't he?'

Bonehead We found out he was in San Francisco and then his next port of call might be home . . . Uh oh, this is serious, you know? We come out of Marcus's room and we all look at each other and go, shit, there's the songwriter gone, there's the chief, I think it's really over, innit? No, we didn't want it to end, why would you, do you know what I mean?

Phil We stayed in L.A. another night, which I presume was just in case he came back. It transpires that he is at this place, but he's not speaking to anybody on the tour: band, crew, Marcus. And if he's not talking to Marcus, then you know it's kind of serious, he's not even going to have a chat. Then we set off on the bus and start driving round America. We just followed the route of the gigs because hotels were booked, where else are we going to go?

Maggie We thought, by the time we get to Texas, hopefully Tim will have done his magic.

Noel Clearly it's not a normal thing to have taken the tour float and a big bag of fucking drugs and run off and left the tour. Clearly that is quite a bizarre thing to do, but I don't remember thinking, 'This is the end', or feeling suicidal or anything like that, at all. That is not the way I am. I kind of sat in this girl's flat, drinking, skinning up whatever, watching fucking American football, I don't know what I'm doing, can't remember. Then a doorbell goes and the girl says, 'There is someone here to see you.'

I was like, 'Wow, fucking hell,' and in walks Tim Abbott.
'Alright, Tim, what you doing here?'
'I've come to find you.'
'How the fucking hell did you find me?'

Then me and Tim went to Las Vegas. I don't remember saying goodbye or thanks. She had a job and all that, I'm sure she was probably glad to see the back of us.

Tim I felt quite happy that he was okay, to be honest. I definitely wasn't that arsed about the agenda of the band or the record label or whatever, as long as he was okay, and he seemed fine. And I felt quite cool, like *The Fugitive*, the one-armed man, you know, you've travelled 7,500-plus miles and nailed your man.

Noel The next gig that hadn't been pulled was in Texas, which gave us a few days. I don't even know why we went to Las Vegas. When I think about it now that is insane.

I don't know what I was thinking . . . What a weird place to go while you are in some deep kind of fucking cocaine psychosis. I just remember it being a laugh. I remember we were on the 58-thousandth floor of the Luxor – a nice relaxing few days in a fucking giant jet-black pyramid in the middle of the desert with a boy dressed as a pharaoh bringing you a club sandwich. Mmm. This is going to be fun. I remember going to turn the tap on in the bathroom and the water coming out like a shower and having a fucking serious conversation with Tim, saying, 'This is fucking amazing, I live in a flat in Manchester which is two fucking floors above a canal and my water fucking comes out of the tap pathetically.' And we had a fucking good hour-long conversation about water pressure. At that point I might have thought, 'You know what, it might be time to get back on tour here.'

Liam I wasn't worried for his state of mind at all, he wasn't the one on crystal meth. He weren't in that bad of a state of mind if he turns round and fucking gets his tour manager to take all the money and book a nice little flight off to Las Vegas. He's got on a flight and hit the hot spots. Not worried about his state of mind at all. I was more worried about the money that he took, without a fucking doubt. Las Vegas, I haven't been there, mate, come back, let us come with you. Fuck the band, the band will be right.

Tim I think he was angry, he was obviously in a fucking weird place and we just caned it for two days. Bought some mescaline of all things, if I remember right.

Noel I was angry; we were better than that. By the time we'd got to Japan we were fucking great. All those years of rehearsals had paid off, we all knew each other, we knew the songs inside out, we knew how to do it. It was like we'd got to America and it had all suddenly gone out the window. Everyone had forgotten how to do it because, you know, drugs. You have one shot at it in your fucking life. It seemed to me that everyone else was not taking it as seriously, or didn't feel it as seriously, as I did. Maybe they thought they'd made it, I thought there was a lot more work to do. I guess I left a little bit of me on that stage that night and the relationship between me towards everybody else was never the same after that. I think I probably felt after that night, it was more me and them as opposed to us.

> I think I probably felt after that night, it was more me and them as opposed to us.

Tim It's about six, seven, the sun was going down and it's getting a bit cold. I made a phone call to Marcus and said, 'Where's the band?'

He said, 'Oh, we're on our way to Austin to do the B sides, is there a happy ending?'

I said, 'Well, I don't know, I'm going to ask him now.'

You know, my whole thing was fucking hell, man, don't walk away now.

I said, 'Look, would you do the B-sides for us? John Lennon would have done the B-sides.'

'Alright, but I'm not fucking speaking to 'em. I'll come back and do the B-sides.'

Owen I didn't know this had happened. Marcus didn't tell me because I was booked to fly out to do these B-sides, so they kept quiet that the band had split up. I walk into the fucking airport in Austin, Texas, off the plane, fucking lovely jubbly, business class, fucking love working for Oasis. There is Tim Abbott and Noel Gallagher, I'm thinking, 'You've come to fucking meet me at the airport, nice one, Noel. A bit much, innit?'

Tim Abbot's like, 'No, we've just arrived from fucking Las Vegas. Didn't you hear?' Noel is like, 'Fucking dickheads.'

Phil I think we'd heard about a couple of days before that he's coming back. It means the band's staying together, rather than going home and signing on the dole again, you know what I mean? So, obviously, by the time he's about to turn up everyone's fucking shitting it because he can put on a stern face, you know, he can unsettle you.

Tim We marched back to the hotel and he walks straight past 'em. But they all smiled, they were like beyond relieved, and it was over to them then, really. I'd done my bit. Brought me man in. And that was it.

Noel I remember the first time we met up after that, there was a band meeting, and me saying, 'All I want to know is what everybody else wants out of it. If it's going to be a load of shit-kickers on the road then let me know, I will fucking go and find something else to do. Or are we going to make it the best that it can be? If we're all here just to fuck about and treat it like a stag do then I'm not interested. I'm in it to be great.' At this point every song I'm writing is amazing and I'm not prepared to fucking piss it up the wall. I don't want to be back on the dole in a year and a half, I don't want to be back in the Boardwalk in two years. We had the chance to make it, like smash it; do you know what I mean? Bigger than all of our heroes, bigger than The Stone Roses could ever even fucking dream about. Bigger than all those bands: The Smiths, New Order, all of them. Bigger than The Jam, everybody.

Coyley He'd just got to the end of the fucking road. That was the end of that era and the new era started when he walked back into that hotel with a skinhead. I always thought, when he came back, you fucking changed, man.

Now me, right, I believe in life in outer space and dimensions and different parallel universes and all that. Somebody come and took him. That's what I think, it was that radical. We got a new man back and everything was different after that. We all had to be different, because if you're not with him, you're going home, that was the defining end of the youth of that band.

Liam 'It's going to be like a business and I'm in charge.' Fuck off. What is all that about? I'm all for a bit of fucking discipline, but, 'It's going to be like a business and I'm in fucking charge?' You say shit like that to me and I'm ordering more drinks.

Noel One of the things that I learnt from Inspiral Carpets was if I ever get anywhere, there is no way it is going to be a democracy. They would take forever to decide on anything. That used to drive me mad and I was only a fucking roadie. They used to have band meetings to decide whether to get fucking tea or coffee for the office. I am very good at making decisions. Whether they are right or whether they are wrong, I'll make them on the spot if I have to. I've made some brilliant decisions and I've made some bad ones as well, but at least I've made them. Maybe that's why we got to where we did in double-quick time. Democracy is boring. Democracies are for squares, simple as that.

Jason In the old days it were great; he'd have the best part of a bottle of gin, take his watch off, put it on top of his amp and do the gig. It were great. But then it got a little more . . . As it got a little bigger, I guess, everybody changes.

Maggie He probably thought, this is the point where they need to understand that there are some rules that we have to make. We can't just be this chaotic gang from Manchester going around the world. Yes, you can have fun; yes, there's time for this and there's time for that. There's time for the crystal meth and there's time for whatever they were doing, but not before a gig.

Noel My ethos has never changed from day one. We have the band, we work backwards from that. I don't remember ground rules; I'm not the kind of person who would do that. I think the only ground rules ever set down were, 'We are rehearsing five days a week or you are out.' That's it really. Other people might tell you different because I've not got a very fucking great memory about these things.

Liam I guess we all decided to chill out on the drugs and drinking and everyone just fucking get it together a little bit, I guess we did that.

> I guess we all decided to chill out on the drugs and drinking

Noel I just wanted to know where their heads were at. I don't recall giving anybody an ultimatum, I don't do ultimatums. I am either in or I am out and that is it. Everybody said the right words and then fucking three weeks later it all blew up again.

Lost and found

Phil Being Oasis, they're getting back together by immediately going into the studio and doing some recording.

Noel This was Oasis's fucking cure for everything: 'Let's go in the studio.'

Owen The session was a two-day session in this little fucking shack, brilliant, fucking raining and voodoo dolls and fucking really atmospheric. Noel had his guitar turned up so fucking loud, they're doing '(It's Good) To Be Free' and it's like, 'One fucking take, you cunts . . .'
Shitting themselves, everybody.

Bonehead We're in the studio and it just clicked. I know I, for one, was trying my best and, 'Yes sir, no sir, three bags fucking full sir.' You want me to play that song, yeah, cool, I'll do it, no worries. In, one take, done, yeah. I'm not fucking this one up, ever again, do you know what I mean, no way.

Noel If anything, it was all worth it for that. We did '(It's Good) To Be Free' and 'Talk Tonight'. I'm even thinking 'Half The World Away' was recorded on that session as well.

Liam They were good, they sound dark and all so that was good. Whatever happened was brought out in them tunes, so as far as I'm concerned, job done. We got two great tunes out of that little rendezvous so I'm happy with that.

Whatever happened was brought out in them tunes, so as far as I'm concerned, job done.

Owen 'Talk Tonight' was probably the best recording I've ever done with Noel Gallagher, sensational.

Noel I don't have any recollection of actually, physically writing the song. 'Sitting on my own chewing on a bone,' I remember that line came to me on the plane. I don't really recall writing it as such, but it came together very quickly. Funnily enough it was a song that Liam fucking hated and still hates to this day.

Liam 'Talk Tonight' is a killer tune.

Noel 'Talk Tonight' was written about those few days in San Francisco. Out of that kind of traumatic period of, however many days it was, came that great song. So it was meant to be.

It's not about the girl per se, it's about those few days that I spent with that girl. In the song it says, 'Take me to the places you played when you were young,' or something like that. She'd taken me to the playground where she played when she was a kid and she was making sure that I ate because I was doing so many fucking drugs. It's a document of those few days. I can't even remember that girl's name now. When I close my eyes I can't even see her face.

My wife thinks I'm a fucking lump of wood that walks around the house smoking, talking about football. I counter that I am probably the most romantic man she'll ever know because of writing all these songs. As a songwriter, by fucking definition, you are romancing something, even if it is 'Anarchy In The U.K'.

Coyley It shows a little side to him, that you just don't really see, he doesn't show these emotions. In all the time I've known him, he's never shown these things, apart from when you stick him behind the glass with a microphone and then he can let this emotion loose that he's got. The door opens and suddenly you can see Noel, not the Noel that you might perceive him to be, by reading about him, or seeing him on the TV. You see something else, it's like shape-shifting, you kind of see almost a little boy or something, you know, you see something very innocent and very pure. The veil is just lifted away, and you can get a better sense of what somebody's about. They are my favourite moments, it's like a dark room, the door opens and a bit of light comes in and you just see a little bit, and then the door's shut again and he's calling you a twat.

Noel Buying singles by The Jam and The Smiths is what instilled my obsession with there has to be something as good on the B-side. The Smiths B-sides mean everything to me, The Jam B-sides are fucking unbelievable and it is something I have kept with me to this day, I wouldn't just shove any old shite on a B-side. Unless I had no songs. I had songs I'd recorded, songs that I hadn't recorded, songs I hadn't fully written but it was just a case of finishing them off; in that sense I had a plan of what the first three and a half albums were going to be like. What I didn't know was how great the B-sides were going to be because I was writing them on the way. It turns out the plan was flawed because *Be Here Now* should have been all those great fucking B-sides, but there you go. At that time when you put out a CD single there were two CDs, what the fuck was all that about? Four B-sides. The thing about those B-sides, although they are tucked away on records and America is still immune to most of them, they made the band what they were in England. They sustained the band for years, the fact that you could just throw in 'Acquiesce' and 'Rocking Chair' and 'Talk Tonight' and 'Half The World Away' . . . all those songs from that period were great. In those days I would write every day because I was so fucking driven and, to my own credit, I recognised that I was in a moment. Everything that I wrote felt great. So I kind of recognised that I was on it. We'd be in hotel bars when we get back after the gig and I'd take me guitar and go up to my room. Liam was kind of sinisterly thinking, 'What's he doing up there?' They are all in the bar fighting with lads, fighting with Geordies till four in the morning and I'd be writing tunes. 'What have you been up to? What you fucking doing up there?'

Liam See this is bollocks, I'm not having that. If that's what he was doing then he's a fucking great man and he needs a knighthood, give him one. Fucking put him out of his misery, but when all that madness is going down he is going, 'Oh, you know what, you guys crack on, I'm off to work.' Fuck off, give me a fucking break, who are you trying to kid? I don't think so. Maybe he did write these great songs in the eye of the storm and that, in the madness of parties, but I find that very strange. Having a fucking great time, you're number one, it's all going great, 'Guys, you just crack on there, popping champagne and getting off your box. I must get out of here; I've got a song to write.' Would you? Fuck off. Who are you trying to kid? He just started getting more into the songwriting thing. I guess there are pressures when you've got an album out and it's great and it's doing well. I guess wanting to make a better record will make you go, 'Know what, I'm getting into that.' I was getting into drinking and playing the fucking rock-and-roll star and all that stuff. So me being in my bedroom, that is no place for me. I am mastering my art down at the bar, having it with the fucking people and he's mastering his art up in his bedroom with his guitar. I guess if Noel was in the bar with me drinking and up all night, the songs wouldn't have got written. I get that and it's the big cross that he carries, 'I was in my room doing all the fucking graft.' Well, I was in the bar doing all the graft too, fucking getting mithered to fuck by all the fucking loony fans. While you're sitting trying to get an E-minor together I'm downstairs getting booze poured down my neck and drugs blown up my nose, life's a fucking bitch. It is what it is.

> I guess if Noel was in the bar with me drinking and up all night, the songs wouldn't have got written.

Noel One of the big regrets is not having somebody, when I was writing those B-sides, to say, 'Hang on a minute

– to have "The Masterplan" as a B-side, it fucking beggars belief.' Why didn't somebody say that about 'Acquiesce' or all those fucking great songs? I remember being round my house once and having a cassette of 'The Masterplan' and people were just laughing: 'You can't put that out, what are you doing?' I remember getting angry and thinking, 'They asked me to write a song, so I've written one and that's what I've written so it's fucking going on and that's it, that's the end of it.' Little did I know that that kind of thing would very quickly evaporate or I would have kept all those songs. When you are young you've got the power, and you don't realise that you've got it until you don't have it. And then you look back and you think, 'Fucking hell, wow.'

Liam Never been to America, man, never been. Never been anywhere, so it was fucking great. It was mega.

© Jill Furmanovsky

I don't know what happened to the band at that point, something changed. In some respects, that was the night it finished.

© Jill Furmanovsky

© Jill Furmanovsky

Liam is like a dog

Noel I guess you get a sense of people who you know you have got a great deal in common with, and they are usually songwriters. But I don't consider those people celebrities; Bono's not a celebrity, neither is Johnny Marr or Weller, they are fucking the same as me, do you know what I mean?

© Jill Furmanovsky

HOW MANY $A SPECIAL PEOPLE CHANGE

TO WHAT WE SEE AS STRANGE

WHERE WERE YOU WHILE WE WERE GETTING HIGH?

SLOWLY WALKING DOWN THE HALL?

FASTER THAN A CANNONBALL?

WHERE WERE YOU WHILE WE WERE GETTING HIGH?

SOMEDAY YOU WILL FIND ME

CAUGHT BENEATH A LANDSLIDE

WITH (MY/A) CHAMPAGNE SUPERNOVA IN THE SKY X 2

(WHAT'S THE STORY) MORNING GLORY ?

oasis

E8

ND PEOPLE BELIEVE THAT THERE GONNA GET AWAY

Liam He's cool, a Smedley little mod. When I seen him, I thought 'as long as he can fucking drum, he's in.'

Jason Brothers is on–off. I've got a brother, we are on–off. You get under each other's skin.

About those videos

Noel The making videos thing had already become boring to us by the fourth single, it was like, 'Have we got to do this again? This is fucking shit.' Somebody came up with the idea to hire the Borderline and get a load of fans in and we'll just do 'Cigarettes & Alcohol' about fifty times and see what happens.

Liam Yeah, that was good, we done it with an Australian guy. His wife worked for some fashion magazine so he brought in loads of models to act like they were our fucking mates and shit. You could see in the video that that's not our crew, it was all a bit ridiculous.

Noel We are all supposed to be getting off with these birds in the toilet. Quite clearly, I'd say a healthy 75 per cent of those girls wouldn't have looked twice at anybody else in the band bar Liam, so it's all a bit fucking ludicrous.

Very quickly after that we were spunking hundreds of thousands of pounds on video shoots because he wouldn't turn up. The 'Some Might Say' video for instance . . .

Liam That was a time when I was putting my foot down and going, 'It's a shit idea, we don't have to fucking do it. This is our band, we're fucking in charge now.' We are in charge, we are at the wheel, so if we don't want to do it, we are not fucking doing it. I think we are within our rights. The amount of shit videos we did, they are lucky they got made at all.

Noel You sit in meetings and somebody says, 'This is going to be the idea,' and everybody signs off on it. Then, on the day, while we are all waiting in a motorway service station, he just doesn't turn up. I'm not having that shit. That was a big moment for me. This is going to sound fucking ridiculous; that was the beginning of the end for me. I know the end came a long time after that but I remember thinking, 'If you don't like the fucking idea for the video, say so. Don't have us all sitting here in the fucking rain.'

Liam I wish I'd done it more often, to be fair. And I guess Noel reckons that as well because he hates every video that we've ever done, but why didn't he stand up and say something about it?

Noel He came up with the shitty excuse of, 'It's an important song and it needs an important video.'

I was like, 'Have you looked at the fucking words? Are you fucking taking the piss? It mentions sinks full of fishes and dirty dishes, you silly cunt.'

'No, it's an important fucking song and it deserves an important video.'

Yeah, whatever, so you had a hangover, did you? We ended up cobbling together some video from the American video for 'Supersonic'.

Liam The one of the stuff in America? Yeah, fucking mega! So we come away with a good video by me not getting up and doing the shit one. Whether it cost forty grand or not, who gives a fuck? That's going to be the first number one, so imagine that, we've got a nice number-one song and we've got a shit video to go with it, I think I done the right thing. He would say that I didn't give a shit, but I couldn't see that. I probably give a shit more than I should have. His thing was, 'What d'you care about videos for? Let the video guy do it.'

I would be going, 'I'm going to be in the fucking video, I want it to look cool.'

He would be, 'But you're not a fucking director.'

'I know I'm not a director, but I'm not a fucking actor either, so I think we should get more involved with our videos. You're just leaving it up to these fucking clowns who are just going to do these mad videos and get us in these mad situations and it's going to come across really shit. It's not what we are about. So we should start looking at these scripts that they are giving us before we just go yeah, go and do the video.'

Noel Have you seen how many shit videos we did after? They are fucking all appalling.

Definitely number one

Noel I remember going down to Loco Studios when The Verve were having a weekend off. Owen was doing *Northern Soul* for The Verve . . .

Owen Noel turned up, 'I got a new song. Fucking broke down under the Severn Bridge, in the tunnel. Wrote "Acquiesce".'

Noel 'Acquiesce' . . . it is just so pathetic to me when people say, 'It is clearly about you and Liam.' Oh right, yes, because I forget you were fucking there inside my head when I wrote it, I forget about that so you must be right and I must be wrong. Sorry about that, yes, it must be then. Well, it isn't, in the same way 'Cast No Shadow' is not about Richard Ashcroft. It is dedicated to Richard Ashcroft; it is a whole different thing, isn't it?

Owen So, we record that first, just warm up, one take, boys, here we go. Liam's like fuck it, chorus is a bit high. Noel was, 'I'll fucking sing that then,' you know. Done. Half a day. 'Acquiesce', motherfucker. Then we do 'Some Might Say'.

Noel 'Some Might Say': one of my favourite ever Oasis songs. I remember the demo; I did it on my own, played everything, the drums and all that. I played it on The Verve's equipment because they'd all gone home for the weekend. It's not really a great vocal or anything like that, but the sound of it was great.

Owen Me and Noel listened to it at night. It's a bit fast, because we had the slower version from a year before. But then, the next fucking day, Liam's like, 'That sounds fucking great, I'm going to sing it.'

Midday, cup of tea. Liam destroys it. Fucking hell, we got the wrong backing track, it's too fast. So, it's a really fucked-up recording, but it's beautiful.

Noel There is a strange melancholy to 'Some Might Say' considering I knew it was going to be number one before I even sat and wrote it. It's about the passing of something, a people's anthem about 'one day we'll find a brighter day'. What the fuck, I don't know what all that is about. Looking back on it now, instinctively I may have felt the end of some kind of age of innocence, for us personally, as people about to go and become real rock stars. But when it actually happens to you, you just think, 'Is that it? I don't feel any different.' I don't know what I thought you were supposed to feel; like you were supposed to be sprinkled with some kind of gold dust ... I just felt like me. I guess it's because I knew in my heart it was going to go to number one anyway. Nobody is really doing the conga, everyone is kind of like, 'This is what we expected.' When you see the footage, me and Marcus just

> You are still the same person, it is just that your record is the most popular that week. It doesn't make you feel any different.

have a quick handshake and that's it really. I see people now get very excited about being number one, I just think, 'You fucking square, it's not that big a deal.' I'm living in a rented flat in Camden, it's shit and the front door doesn't lock properly. It was an awful fucking place. I looked around the shitty flat, I was thinking, 'I've got to get out of this place for a fucking start.' I was thinking, 'It couldn't have been like this for David Bowie, it couldn't have been like this for Marc Bolan or Slade or The Jam.' And you suddenly realise that actually it was like that. You are still the same person, it is just that your record is the most popular that week. It doesn't make you feel any different. I suppose there is the temptation to immediately go and buy a feather boa and a Rolls-Royce, a cane and a top hat and be a fucking dick, do you know what I mean?

Bonehead Me and Liam went to the pub to celebrate it, we had a couple of beers. I had me daughter with me, she was only about three months old, I remember she was on the table, bouncing on our knees, it was great. I can't explain the feeling. It was like, 'You actually went to number one, fucking hell.'

Noel Creation had never had a number-one single in their entire fucking existence. They were all really very excited and rightly so. They had a party for us and Blur turned up. We were having a great time, everyone is patting each other on the back. There is a downstairs bit and an upstairs bit, and someone came upstairs and said, 'Blur are downstairs, they want to come in.'

We were like, 'Fuck it, whatever.' I didn't see this take place but legend has it Liam went downstairs and got in Damon's face: 'Fucking number one, number fucking one!' As I understand it, Damon had taken that as Liam throwing down the gauntlet.

Liam I can't remember much about that. I think they'd come in to drink our drinks, they're coming to our party, you're going to have a bit of get-you-at-it, end of. It was just a crack, man, it was never malicious. Unless one of them got a bit lippy and then whatever would happen would happen. It was just a joke, just a laugh, man.

Tony

Liam Tony's one of the lads, he was alright, he just wasn't as mad as us, I guess. If Noel didn't get on with him then I guess that's their thing. Me and him got on. We weren't fucking best of mates, but we definitely weren't arch enemies, man. He was alright, he was the drummer, he just fucking came, drummed, had a beer, talked about Man United. We all went, 'Nah, nah, nah, not listening.' That was it.

> United fan. They are always going to be the first to go.

Noel United fan. They are always going to be the first to go. How Bonehead survived the cull all those years, him being a fucking filthy red, is beyond me because really it should have been a band full of blues. Thinking back on it now, I kind of missed the chance to get rid of the fucker.

Owen I got told that he wound Noel up so much on tour.

Coyley As it went through that American tour, it got really nasty with Tony, but it was unstoppable, and it was very sad, and you'd have to feel for the boy. It manifest itself in verbal abuse and that wasn't very nice but was completely hilarious. Everyone was party to it, I'd hold me hands up and say I give him a terrible time as well, but only for his good and for the good of the band, you know.

I did a lot of shouting at him, just trying to get him going, you know.

Bonehead Tony's the person that I shared a room with in the early days, we didn't all have big hotel suites each, we wouldn't have the budget so we would all share. My roommate was Tony, always. We shared rooms in Japan, America and the whole of Europe and England, Scandinavia. I really got on with Tony, I probably got to know him best in the band, I would say. There were a couple of times when Tony would come in the room and he would just pour it out, 'Fucking hell, Bonehead, people are getting at me and people are doing this . . .' Hard for me, you know, to be the guy in the middle. Maybe I'd talk to Noel or talk to Liam, 'Look, go easy on the guy, man, we're in the middle of a tour. If there's a problem, let's deal with the problem when we come off tour.'

Maggie They'd known each other for a while, so it was all a bit of laddish stuff. They were doing it all the time to each other, so I didn't really particularly find a moment where they were bullying him in particular.

Phil The dynamic between them always seemed like he was kind of the odd man out. I was actually his roadie, so I'm not going to join in, I didn't do anything to stop it, however.

Tony Being in that cooped-up environment, I'm not surprised there were relationships not going in the right direction. There were grudges held, it got personal, and it built from there. I was quite a reserved guy. I think people might look at that as some kind of weakness, but it wasn't a weakness, I didn't want to be the leader, I didn't want to be like that. I'll just sit back here and do me drums.

Noel He did start becoming excluded. You know when a pack of feral dogs exclude one puppy, it became like that, I think. There was a gradual ramping up of, 'This lad ain't going to be here much longer.' Not because of his personality, I don't give a fuck what people are like.

Tony Noel didn't want to have a relationship with me, I do know that. I tried, but it was uncomfortable. Whether the band then followed suit, stayed on the right side, safe side, of the fence, I don't know.

Owen When we were doing 'Some Might Say', Noel was like, 'Fucking last time he's ever in the fucking studio with me.' I was going to Tony, 'You've got to get your shit together, Tony, or it'll be, "Bye, Tony."'

Bonehead They were really struggling with Tony and the drums on 'Some Might Say'. He was too slow, or he weren't in time, or he wasn't doing it right, I don't know. There was a real issue with the drums on it.

Coyley By this time he's history, he is absolutely history, I think they are just looking for the moment where they can just get the scissors out and cut that string and he's gone.

Noel I probably made up my mind, knowing that 'Champagne Supernova', 'Don't Look Back In Anger' and 'Wonderwall' were coming up. He is not playing on them, and if he is playing them, he is fucking not playing them live, because I have got bigger ideas for that. The last throw of the dice for us was to get him drumming lessons.

Tony I thought, okay, I'll listen to everybody. I think I was sent to some kind of drum tutor in Wales, a couple of days. Within the first hour he goes, 'I don't really know why you're here,' he said, 'We're doing stuff that I'd planned for tomorrow evening.' I'm going to sit here and say I could have completed that second album; I know I could have carried on. I had an argument with Noel. He said something and I finally went, 'Fuck you, mate,' you know what I mean, fuck off. As he was soundchecking I told him in no uncertain words what I thought of him. I kind of regret that a touch.

Noel We might have had words, it's quite likely, I don't know. Everybody has their own version of events – Liam, Marcus – and somewhere in between everybody's version is mine. You've got to make your own truth out of it, so I wouldn't deny it at all.

Tony Getting the phone call was something I never expected. I think it was lined up that we were going to start rehearsing for the second album the next week, but Marcus phoned and he said, 'Are you sat down? Listen, I've got some bad news for you, the band want you out.' I was shocked, shell-shocked, I was like, oh my God.

Liam Nothing was set in stone, it's no one's God-given right to be in Oasis, if it changes, it changes. They were Noel's songs, so I guess he had more of a say on who is going to sing or fucking drum. He was going, 'Look, the songs are getting better, he's not getting better, I'm not taking him with me.' So what do you do? You don't turn round and go, 'It's either our kid or it's Tony.' I'm sticking with our kid and as bad as that might fucking seem, that's just the way it is, mate. I was gutted for him, but it is what it is, man.

Noel We couldn't have taken him any further. I showed him the drum fill to 'Don't Look Back In Anger' and the look on his face is something I will probably never forget; it looked like I gave him a fucking book in braille and said, 'Read that for us.' It was then I thought, you know what, this is not going to go any further. When most people in the band are a better drummer than your drummer, and you are about to become the biggest band in the world, then clearly someone's got to fucking make that call, do you know what I mean? I'm not one that sits around fucking moaning about a situation. If something is broke, get it fixed. He was going to hold us back, so he had to go. Things like that to me are not a big deal. A drummer? Fucking hell. Worst comes to the worst we will get a drum machine, the song will still be great and it will be in fucking time and it will be cheaper. We were all quite limited, but we fucking tried to make it better. I don't remember him being the kind of guy that was so arrogant that he didn't give a shit. I just feel that that is the limit of his talents, that was it. He was at the fucking ceiling and that was it. He wasn't going to go any further, I knew that as a songwriter, I was going to go further and he wasn't going to come along. I wasn't the best guitarist in the world, but I fucking knew it and I embraced it. Liam wasn't the best and he knew it. Tony wasn't the best and he didn't know it.

Bonehead Tony was a good drummer for the album he played on. I think if Tony didn't drum on *Definitely Maybe* then it probably wouldn't have sounded like it does. Even though he is not the most technical drummer, what he did was absolutely right for that album, and I don't think anyone else could have made it sound like that.

Noel *Definitely Maybe* wouldn't have sounded as good without him drumming on it, he was part of that sound. He was the right man for the job at that time.

Definitely Maybe wouldn't have sounded as good without him drumming on it ...

Tony Bonehead rang two weeks later, when I wasn't in. Lord knows what sort of phone call that was going to be. But I didn't hear from any of them. Really hurt because it was like one minute I'm surrounded by ten, twelve people that have been your family, if you like, for a couple of years. Then to nobody, is like, fuck. I could never get me head round it and I think about it every day, believe it or not. Still, to this day, it's with me, it's, you know, something missing. But I've just got to accept it.

Noel Tony got kicked out of the band and then obviously it fucking explodes, goes through the roof, so some lawyer contacted him, pissed in his ear, and he thought he was due some mythical figure of £100 million or something laughable. Anyone that ever left Oasis or was asked to leave still gets paid to this day from whatever they played on. We didn't take any of his royalties off him. Anyway, it was going to go to court and he was suing us for lost royalties and all that shit. The amount he was asking for was nonsense. It was clearly nonsense because on the fucking steps of the court he settled for £550,000.

Liam He'd mentioned the confusion over signing the initial record deal and blah, blah. We'd never had a management deal with Marcus, at all. Never signed a piece of paper. We just shook hands down the pub and that was it. So then everybody started to get twitchy, 'Let's sign something.' There were four or five months after that sitting in fucking lawyers' rooms, bored shitless, people clearly speaking the English language, but none of the words making any sense. Forthwith and therefore and blah, blah. Just sitting there and thinking, 'How did it get to this? We signed off five years ago, what the fuck?' Sat in some Gothic castle with a load of lawyers in dickey bows. It's true what they say, that old adage, where there's a hit there's a writ and all that. When shit like that starts happening you do start thinking all the fun's taken out of it. You start a band with the best intentions of just trying to get a big telly and a fit bird and a load of money and the next thing is everybody's fucking hovering round you with briefcases and leather man bags full of shit for you to sign. I guess he felt betrayed, but people come and go in bands and that's the way it is. I don't hold any grudges or anything like that, he does what he's got to do and we do what we've got to do. That's when managers are good. No one really needed to manage the band to do the gigs or get us in a studio, we'd do it ourselves, but when it got to things like that it was 'Over to you, mate. We're out of here.' I guess he's within his rights to sue us.

I guess we are in our rights to have a listen to what he's got to say and then take it from there. I certainly didn't feel like going round to his house and filling him in or anything like that. Tony McCarroll was part of my life, we had some good times, magical times. Times that no one will ever have, so it is what it is, that's the way these things go sometimes.

Coyley The band was never the same when he left. As soon as something changes, it's irretrievably gone, some dynamics change forever.

Smedley little mod

Bonehead Tony's gone. It's like, 'Shit, we need another drummer.'

Liam I know Tony weren't the best drummer, but he certainly weren't the worst. Everyone was getting a bit muso going, 'Yeah, but he can do this?' Who gives a fuck? He sits on it, he hits the fucking thing, you are never going to get Keith Moon. A fucking drummer's a drummer, obviously there's great ones and there's shit ones.

> It was weird having a cockney in the band and all that, but he was great, he was a brilliant drummer.

Noel I was down the Manor with Paul Weller and got talking to Steve White, who says, 'I've got a brother, he plays drums.' So I spoke to him on the phone and said meet me at this cafe in Camden at 3 o'clock, I'll sit outside with a copy of the *Racing Post* and a white carnation, just so you know it's me, and we'll have a chat kind of thing. Now it's a weird way to do business, but there were no mobile phones, no internet, no one had a profile on the web, so it was done the old-school way. I remember loads of questionable-looking idiots – aging mods – walking up and I was thinking, 'This better not be him, this better not be him.' Then round the corner comes Alan and he goes, 'Alright, fucking hell.' He sits down and he starts talking about the drums and I'm like, I'm not fucking interested in how you can play, as long as you look the part you'll do. I don't give a fuck who you've been playing with. What we do is not rocket science, you've heard what we do, I can do it and I'm not even a drummer. As he was getting up to leave I said, 'By the way, you're doing *Top of the Pops* on Wednesday.'

Tony I watched it. It was really hard. I've been sacked for apparently not being the best drummer in the world, but our tune's at number one. We've got a fucking number-one album. Why am I sat home, what's wrong? One thing that really hurt me was fucking Bonehead turning to Alan White and they sort of salute. Fucking hell, you don't take long to forget, like. I was pretty affected by that, yeah.

Noel When Alan joined he was a breath of fresh air. It was a great thing to be in a studio with a drummer who, when you were talking to him about a middle eight, backing off on this bit, speeding that bit up, his eyes didn't glass over like he was thinking about a sandwich or something. He was a fucking good lad and he was a proper cockney. It was weird having a cockney in the band and all that, but he was great, he was a brilliant drummer.

Liam Top lad, Alan. Fucking Del Boy cockney dude. I don't give a fuck where you're from. It's not about where you're from, it's where you're fucking at. So it didn't feel strange at all, he was the man for the job at that time. What does he fucking look like? He's cool, a Smedley little mod. When I seen him, I thought, 'As long as he can fucking drum, he's in.'

Bonehead 'Alan White, he's alright.' That would be the thing every day. To the point of boredom, we would keep doing it. 'Alan White, he's alright.' He was alright; liked to drink and a great drummer. An amazing drummer.

It's Thursday night . . .

Noel I cannot overstate the importance of *Top of the Pops* to our generation. In the seventies it seemed so decadent and in the eighties it seemed so glamorous. I remember being gutted when we didn't get on there for 'Supersonic'.

Jason It is a big thing, *Top of the Pops*, because that's what you were brought up on, that's how you discovered your music. If it wasn't for *Top of the Pops* how would you know what band you like or anything like that? It was part of your childhood growing up.

Noel I used to love doing *Top of the Pops*. They insisted that you mime, so you could just get pissed all day. Then all of a sudden everybody started to get up their own arses and say, 'We're playing live.' Well, fuck you, you are an idiot. Still to this day, 'Would you like to play live?'

> They insisted that you mime, so you could just get pissed all day.

'Not a fucking chance, mate. No way. If you want me to play live it's going to cost £50 a ticket.'

Maggie It's so unglamorous doing *Top of the Pops*. Back then they used to get us in really early in the morning. Seven in the morning, get the gear up there, get them up there as well. Then you sit there all day waiting for your call to rehearse. You rehearse it, then you come back and you wait some more. You're just sitting there for eight hours. There's not a lot for them to do other than drink, to be honest.

Noel We had a great time backstage at *Top of the Pops*, a good laugh. I remember once being at *Top of the Pops* and Jimmy Nail was in the charts with 'Crocodile Shoes'. It was a boiling hot day and we were sat outside the BBC bar getting pissed and Jimmy Nail walked past. We all started singing 'Crocodile Shoes', kind of taking the piss. Jimmy Nail turned round, Liam kind of stood up and, I never forget, Jimmy Nail said, 'Aye, he's up and he's stocky.' I don't even know what that fucking means. We ended up going on the piss with him all day, he was top, man. He looked like he would have kicked the fuck out of all of us. Crocodile shoes or no crocodile shoes. I remember when Jon Bon Jovi went solo, his dressing room was opposite us and there was a knock at the door. He said, 'Hey, *Rolling Stone* are writing about you guys.' He gave us the magazine, it was a review of some fucking thing or other, and as he walked out he said, 'When you get to the States you can tell them Jon Bon Jovi showed you your first review.' And as he went into his dressing room, Liam went, 'Who the fuck is Jon Bon Jovi?'

Whitey's second gig

Noel Alan's first real gig was the main stage at Glastonbury. To think of it now, to put him on him like that, fucking hell . . . He's had one warm up, at Bath Pavilions, which was fucking crazy. We are the big noise at this point, so we are headlining the Saturday night, which is the big thing. We came on and the gig didn't work. We started with a new song. That is cardinal rule number one out the fucking window. Why did we start with a new song? And do you know what, it was a new song that didn't have any words, it was an instrumental. When you are at Glastonbury people want the hits and that is one thing I learned from that night; people don't want to hear your new fucking tunes. The worst thing you can say at a festival is, 'Okay, what I'm going to do now is do a new one.'

'Oh alright, I'll go for a piss then.' We don't want to hear a song that we've never heard of before, fuck that. Play what you are famous for. So we should have done it that night, but we didn't.

> I don't remember the gig man, whether it was good or not . . .

Liam I don't remember the gig, man, whether it was good or not, it was what it was. Glastonbury was never that fucking great anyway. I got psoriasis in my hair so I'd been scratching it all day and I remember some geezer coming up to me backstage after it and going, 'Fucking hell, man, it's Liam out of Oasis.' He's going, 'Come here, man, look, look, he's even got fucking cocaine in his hair,' as if I was Ziggy Stardust. It's psoriasis and he's picking it out of my hair, putting it up his nose, wiping it on his gums, and I was sitting there thinking, 'Alright, now I have seen it all now, everyone has lost the fucking plot.' The occasion is great and all that, but that geezer was the only thing I remember about Glastonbury to be fair.

Noel What I will forever remember Glastonbury for is Robbie Williams. As I recall it, he is hanging round all day and doing his act, the Robbie Williams act. For a while it is funny, but getting into the eighth hour it's, 'Okay . . . wow.' Back then we let everybody stand on the side of the stage. Liam turned round and said, 'Come on, Robbie!' I don't really think he meant for him to come on stage. I just think he meant, 'Come on, hey.' I turn round and Robbie Williams is dancing like MC Hammer to one of my songs on stage at Glastonbury. I remember thinking, 'Oh, that doesn't look good, that does not look good, no.'

Liam Robbie Williams was brought into the camp through Noel's missus back then, Meg Matthews, and all that lot.

Noel A friend of ours called Lisa Moorish is friends with Robbie and she came to Glastonbury. We were hanging around with loads of girls at the time and they are all Take That fans, as every fucking female seems to be – it's some kind of by-law that has been passed. She arrives with him and she is one of our mates ergo we are all hanging out together. Then he proceeded to follow us around the world for about a year and everywhere we went there he was. Him and Liam became the best of friends.

Liam It was nothing to do with me. He was there, just acting like a clown. There are all these pictures of him kissing me, that was like photo bombing, him making out as if he was my fucking mate. It was to do with all these fucking hoorahs down here that brought him into the scene, Noel's mates. He was Noel's mate, not mine.

Noel Fuck off, are you being serious? Oh my God, that is truly fucking unbelievable. I am fucking staggered by that. Seriously, those two were like fucking Morecambe and Wise, except not very wise.

Liam If you look at the backstage footage I think you'll see that I'm not there in this crowd. Fucking nothing to do with it. Our kid laughing, 'Yeah, Robbie Williams, yeah!' Where's LG? Disgusted in the corner somewhere, some geezer's fucking pulling my hair to pieces. Selling drugs off the back of my head.

Rockfield

Noel I don't do things like, 'This is going to be a new direction.' Every time I've tried to do that, to make an artistic move, it's failed miserably because I'm not an artist. I'm just a guy that writes songs; I pick the best ones and then when I'm recording them I take them to the logical conclusion, and then I put them out. Once I put them out I'm going and doing something else. I walk away from artistic decisions, or what's going on in the charts, or he's doing that so I should be doing this. Coming to record *Morning Glory* we are coming straight off the last big, British tour so we are fucking flying at this point. I might have played through them one night on the tour bus on acoustic guitar. I remember one night on a European tour and – most people in bands will know this – you arrive at a hotel at whatever time of day and none of the rooms are ready; you've got to sit on the bus for four hours until some conference for fizzy mineral water has taken place and everyone's left the rooms. I remember Bonehead saying, 'Play us the new tunes

> Is it possible to be walking slowly down the hall, faster than a cannonball? Well, if you do enough drugs it is.

then.' I played the band what I had and there was silence and tears.

Bonehead He actually sat down on the bus and played them us and we were like, 'Fuck, do it again.' It was incredible to hear them in that form. To hear 'Champagne Supernova' sung like that was pretty raw. Yeah, it got me, it hit me, touched a nerve, pretty emotional.

Noel Looking up and seeing him sniffling I'm thinking, 'Fuck me, it's not that bad. It's pretty good, it could be our *Stairway to Heaven*.' Bonehead was quite an emotional dude, he would always end up crying. Liam was quite an emotional dude, he would always end up fighting. Me and Guigs, as I recall, were quite level-headed, just kind of shrugging our shoulders and, whatever, you know. I am sure the drummer was eternally confused by it all and didn't know what the fuck was going on.

Noel 'Champagne Supernova': I've been asked about it so many times down the years by journalists. Is it possible to be walking slowly down the hall, faster than a cannonball? Well, if you do enough drugs it is. What is a Champagne Supernova? You just have to look out to the crowd and think, who cares what it is about? There is a great sadness in that song, like 'where were you while we were getting high' and yet it has generated the most joyous fucking thing ever. I put it down to magic, I really do put it down to magic and really wish I could tell you what the ingredients were for that magic potion. I haven't got a clue, I haven't got the faintest idea because if I did I'd still be doing it.

Owen They had a rehearsal, because Alan White's joined the band, and Noel is like, 'Come on, producer, you turn up for the rehearsal, check the arrangements.' Turned up and Noel was like, 'Yeah, fucking lovely that is. Good boy, he looks alright, doesn't he?'

It was like, 'Oh, that's alright, yeah, off we go,' and that was rehearsals for the album: half a day.

Noel It was the one record I've ever made that I've never done any demos for. I really didn't know whether any of it was going to work. My one reservation was writing those songs and thinking are we a good enough band to pull it off.

Owen It was May: brilliant time to be recording, sun shining. Rockfield: the posh studio, as well-equipped as anywhere in the world. Kingsley, who set up Rockfield, is a farmer and he built a fucking studio on his farm because he liked music and stuff. Fucking 'Bohemian Rhapsody' in his fucking farm sheds. And the accommodation was fucking magnificent, food was good, it was a good place to work. Out of town a bit, so you didn't get in trouble in town. Just a great recording place, brilliant.

Coyley Noel and Owen were in charge of the recording sessions. I wasn't making the record, so I didn't go. I went and made a record with another band instead. Just like that, gone. There is no discussion because what's the point? The decision is already made. Noel knows what he's doing, he knows what is best for the band and there is no time for sentiment or sentimentality, there is no time for anything. I was broken-hearted, absolutely broken-hearted, yeah.

Noel We went in with the idea to do it the same as *Definitely Maybe,* which was live. On the first day we did two takes of

'Roll With It' and what you hear on the record is the very, very first take. On the master tape you could hear Alan saying, in that cockney accent of his, 'Right, boys, first take, we'll get it first take.' At the mastering I decided we can't have a cockney talking at the beginning of a single and wiped it off. I should have kept it, really, because it was a poignant moment. The other songs were a bit more intricate. Owen said, 'Well, how Marc Bolan used to do it' – I still don't know to this day whether it's true – 'he would sit and play it with a click track on acoustic guitar and then build it all up from there.'

'Alright, well, let's try that then.' And it's something that I've done from that day forward.

Bonehead Yeah, it was a different way of working than when we did *Definitely Maybe*, but we had a producer who knew what he was doing, a producer who knew us, we knew him. Alan would come in and do his drums, and we'd have this incredible drum track with this incredibly tight bass track Guigs had put in. Then you had Owen being mister enthusiastic, 'Come on!' cheering you on. He'd be like, 'Fucking yes!'

Noel Owen came up with that way of recording for that record and it suited me. It was great because someone can sit in the control room and learn it while you are playing. If you are all in the same room playing a song only you know, you are going to get about fifty takes because somebody fucked up a little bit, fannying about for fucking fourteen hours getting on each other's tits.

Owen *Morning Glory* was incredibly easy – all my sessions with Oasis were incredibly quick and easy – because Noel had the songs and the arrangements and he'd teach the band the songs very quickly, you know. This is the song, boys, here are the chords, we'll have a few run-throughs, then we're going to record it. Two takes.

Noel *Morning Glory* took maybe sixteen days to record.

Liam To be fair, with all the recording side of it, the lads would go down there and just fucking jam and all that, they would be playing guitars all day. I'd just be upstairs watching the box. Or in the pub and that. So I never was really around it, the recording shit.

Owen We were doing a song a day, finished, completely done. That first week of *Morning Glory*, we recorded 'Roll With It' on the first day, 'Hello' on the second day, 'Wonderwall' on the third day, 'Don't Look Back In Anger' on the fourth day. He is like God, isn't he? Then fucking 90 per cent of 'Champagne Supernova' on the Friday. Extraordinary.

Noel We were never the kind of band to sit in there and theorise and try and intellectualise our music. This is the song, I've written it, this is it. I am going to play it how it goes, everybody join in. We weren't artists, we were just a fucking good band who had good tunes and that was it. It didn't take long. Wasn't really fussed about the surroundings. Even to this day the studios don't bother me; it's all about the songs anyway.

Liam Once there was a song finished and there was vocals needed on it and a microphone in front of me, all that other stuff was out. I had this tunnel vision in getting the best vocal and that was it. I was never thinking about, 'Right, let's get the fuck out of here and do this,' even though on some occasions it would be, 'Football's on, let's get it down.' I was pretty good at just fucking having it, let it all out there and just put it together. I never overthink singing that much, it was just one take, two take, three take.

Noel For 99.9 per cent of everybody in the music business this is how it works: get the vocal on as soon as you can. If you've got the bass, the drums and a good vocal you are halfway there. But no, not in Oasis. No, let's record all the fucking music first, all the overdubs and the hand claps and the fucking choirs and the strings and the bells and fucking whistles and then right at the very fucking end, then let's put the vocals on. That became a running theme with Oasis for years. You never really knew what the fuck was happening until the singing was on and the singing was on right at the very, very end.

Liam I preferred singing live because it was one take, you were on your toes more. It was like being in a boxing match or something, whereas in the studios you can cheat a little bit. You can't really cheat when you are at a gig. I preferred that, to be honest.

Noel The vibe was pretty good, we were rattling through it, there was no fucking about. We were having a good time, the songwriting had taken another step forward. If anybody ever thought I was never going to beat 'Live Forever', we

> I never overthink singing that much, it was just one take, two take, three take.

had 'Don't Look Back In Anger', we had 'Morning Glory' and 'Champagne Supernova' and 'Wonderwall', for crying out loud. I remember being into it, everyone else being into it, and then there was the night where it went off.

Bonehead We were generally under Owen's orders, 'Fuck off, go to the pub. Get out.' He didn't want us there, you know what I mean, that was Owen's way of working.

Noel That gave Liam a lot of time to fanny about in Monmouth and indulge his greatest hobby, which was acting like a fucking buffoon.

Liam That's the problem when you've got these nice villages and nice recording studios, the village, man, it has a pull. You've got to be very strong willed. I always had a pull towards the pub, it was, 'What time we finishing here, shall we go back into town? It's got a bit of a vibe.' I was a sucker for the pub and Bonehead was, Alan was, and all the crew obviously. Guigs wasn't that much and Noel wasn't, so it would be always like, 'He's doing his guitars, he'll be in there all fucking day, won't he, Slash? We could go to the fucking pub.' He would come out and be, 'Right, guys . . . where is everyone?' They are all in the fucking pub. So it would be that kind of thing. I like them kind of vibes but it did cause arguments.

Brian Cannon What a night this was, Liam and I went into Monmouth and we bump into John Robb.

John Robb[*] I was in the studio next door to Rockfield, Monnow Valley, producing this band called Cable. We'd just

***

[*] *Musician and award-winning journalist and author*

finished recording, we went to town for a couple of drinks and there's a bloke with two girls in the seat in front of us. Oh Christ, it's Liam. I go, 'What you doing here?'

He goes, 'We're in Rockfield, we're just doing the album, come down, we're having a party.'

So, we went down there.

Bonehead We knew John Robb, and we invite them all back, drunk. Probably a bad move, because Noel was still working at the studio with Owen, you know, and we bring a bunch of guys we've never met in our lives.

Liam There is a lot of sitting around so what do you do? It's not prison, if I'm not needed today I'm hardly going to sit and fucking watch you play guitar. I'm going to the pub. Obviously you go to the pub, you get wankered, and I probably did bring a few people back one night to have a party; he weren't happy with it and then we smashed the place up and stuff.

Noel He came back with a load of fucking scruffy-looking cunts. They came into the studio, Owen kicked them out and sent them up to the farmhouse.

John Robb Liam goes, 'What do you think of this album?' He's dancing round, 'It's great, isn't it?' And a bloke goes, 'It's crap, it sounds like The Beatles.' The bloke was pissed out of his head, and then he starts prodding Liam with his finger, you can see Liam get rattled. I think, 'I'm just going to leave them to it.' Then there is this massive crashing sound, and the fighting kicks off.

Bonehead It was kicking off outside, big time. I think I hit one of this band that had come down, they were gobbing off, so I punched him.

Liam I liked bringing people in and going, 'Have a listen to this.' Back then it was different. You couldn't do that now because everyone would fucking record it and everyone would take pictures. I shouldn't have brought them back, but I thought we were a rock-and-roll band. I thought anything goes in Oasis. Obviously other people had rules . . . Fuck the rules, man.

Noel I am not generally an obnoxious, belligerent dude. I know people are going to think, 'Fucking hell, I've read your interviews . . .' but generally I'm not. Somebody must have got on my tits. My thing is, when I am working, I am fucking working, I don't particularly want people there fucking about. I am in the studio, I am in and out. I don't want to be fannying about spending five years making a fucking album.

It might have been the biggest fight we ever had.

Bonehead It just exploded into a big, fucking bunch of chaos like you've never seen, man.

Noel Why I had a fight with Liam that night I couldn't fucking tell you, I think maybe one of my guitars got damaged.

Liam When we had fights we had fights, but we didn't have loads. We had raging arguments, but we weren't fighting. We probably had about five physical fights. We've had hundreds of big, 'Let me at him, hold me back.'

Noel It might have been the biggest fight we ever had.

Liam Probably me not giving a fuck and him trying to write 'Bohemian Rhapsody', and me going, 'Bollocks, let's have it.' That kind of thing. Ying and yang. Him being professional, me being unprofessional. Him turning the band into a square band and me turning it into a fucking oblong band. That kind of shit.

Noel Guigs always used to bring a cricket bat and a set of cricket stumps with him because he is obsessed with cricket. Him and Bonehead playing cricket is a sight to behold, I might add. I remember smashing Liam's head in with a cricket bat.

Liam It definitely went off that night, it was bad, man. There were loads of little bits in the corner going 'pfzzz' – electrical bits – loads of broken shit. Terrible. The whole studio got smashed to pieces. I think Whitey was locked in a room while I was going to town on the living room. Everything just got fucking blitzed. Noel got Whitey and I think he drove him home, that was it.

Noel Me and Whitey left in the middle of the night. As we were leaving the studio Liam appeared out of nowhere and threw a dustbin at the car. I think it was Alan's car and we'd only known him about two weeks. He was going, 'Fucking hell, mate, what kind of fucking band is this?' He was saying, 'Is that it then? It can't be over, I've only just joined.'

'No, no, don't worry, this is going to happen all the time.'

He was like, 'Fucking hell man, have I joined the fucking Troggs?'

Liam It happened, man, but there was no need for the cricket bat round the head.

Owen Next morning, what was that then? Liam's broken his foot, Bonehead's nose gone. I missed it completely, flat out, I was knackered. Strawberry fucking bubble bath from Bodyshop, very nice too, thank you. That was a good week, into bed, zzzz.

Michael Spencer Jones I can remember waking up in the morning and walking into Liam's room, I just couldn't believe the scene of devastation. I wish I had taken a photograph of that room, you know. TV was out the window, still plugged in, double bed was in half. I mean, it was just like, you know, a hand grenade had gone off in the room or something.

Bonehead The studio staff come in and they were cool, like they'd seen it before. They were just like, 'Right, yeah, okay, looks like there's been a bit of a fight, we'll just clean up.'

Michael Spencer Jones They found this local repair man and he came along, and he was saying, 'Oh, we've not seen damage like this since Ozzy Osbourne and Sabbath were recording here, this is nothing.'

Noel There is a cooling-off period. I went to Jersey, I believe. I don't know why the fuck I went to Jersey. I think Liam went to Portugal.

Liam I remember going home and I think my foot was fucked and my arm was in a plaster.

Noel Every time there was a scene in Oasis, when we all got back together it was like nothing had ever happened.

Nobody would ever mention it. I don't ever recall there being heart-to-hearts. 'Where've you been?'

'Fucking Jersey – where've you been?'

'Been in fucking Portugal, haven't I?'

'How was it?'

'Fucking sunny. How was Jersey?'

'Shite.'

I don't remember a sit-down airing of your grievances, it was always like nothing had ever happened.

Liam Me and him are like telepathic. I felt that we didn't really have to speak to each other half the time because we just knew, you know what I mean? People have that with their brothers and sisters or family and whatever, we didn't really talk that much. I don't think me and our kid ever sat in a fucking room on our own and had these one-on-one questions, nah, fuck, that would be well weird. That would be weird as fuck.

'Hey, Noel, do you believe in God?'

'Hey, Liam, can I just have a quick chat with you there, do you believe in God?'

What is it all about? That would be fucking weird, man. No.

Noel We were not brought up in that kind of family. There are five of us in our family: me, two brothers, my mam and dad. We are all close to our mam individually, but not any of the five individuals, none of us, are close to each other. I don't know why that is. That doesn't seem that odd to me, do you know what I mean? Now as you go on through life, involved in other families, you see the Swiss Family Robinson. They are all in each other's pockets, that kind of freaks me out. That's just the way we were brought up.

Bonehead I don't remember it being bad when we got back, I don't remember it being like, someone sulking in that corner. I think it was more of alright, we're back, we're here, we've got a job, let's do it. I don't think there was any bad atmosphere.

Noel We were working-class lads, all of us had Irish parents, so we were little paddy fighters. We didn't give a fuck. We weren't nice, sensitive, middle-class boys that go off sulking if something ain't going right. The kind of band we were, rightly or wrongly, if anybody was ever asking for a smack in the mouth they got one, and then we moved on and that was it.

> We weren't nice, sensitive, middle-class boys that go off sulking if something ain't going right.

Liam That's the way I see it, man, that's my mantra: live and let ruck.

Noel The thing blew up that night, and after that we are fine, just normal. Same as things leading up to the night at the Whisky, we are fine. We never let any of it fester. If there was bad blood between anybody it was happening at that particular moment and then when it was gone, it was gone, and we got back in the saddle and did whatever we had to do. We weren't artists. None of us. We didn't give a fuck about that, we were grafters. I never had the feeling that it was over until it was. I never had that feeling. Who was going to leave, Liam? What is he going to do? What was I going to do? I didn't have a band, I couldn't sing . . . it was just shit blowing over. I recall buying him a Beatles belt buckle. Maybe I was feeling guilty because I'd fucking broke his arm or something. Maybe I bought it for me and it wouldn't fit.

Liam About £13 they cost, you can get them anywhere. Made up, nice one for that, our kid.

Owen They came back and they had songs to get on with. The sessions slowed down, we did the main tracks in that first week, but then there was a bunch of tunes to do. Like 'Morning Glory' and 'She's Electric'. We were still doing the B-sides, there was a lot of recording to do. We filled up the time.

Noel I live day by day, I don't carry shit with me. Once it's done, it's done. I am not a sulker. When I get back to the studio I forget what went on two weeks ago, I have to finish this record off. We rattled it off pretty quick after that. We weren't the most experimental of dudes anyway. Bonehead had one guitar, I think I had two, we had about four amps and that was it, what are you going to do? Now, when I make records, I am obsessed with FX pedals; I didn't know what they were then. I had a tuner and a digital delay and that's all I had way up until after Knebworth. It's embarrassing.

Liam I knew the songs were a lot richer than *Definitely Maybe*. 'Wonderwall' was the only one that I didn't get at the time, I was, 'I don't know about this, man.' It just didn't seem right. I thought it was weird. Then when I heard it I was, 'Ah, now I get it'. I was totally wrong and that's fucking right. I love that tune. Growing up we didn't have much money or anything, there was no carpet or shit like that, no wallpaper and we would just write shit on the walls and have posters up. I always thought that was our 'Wonderwall'. But it's obviously not; apparently it's about some bird. Or maybe not.

Noel In the case of 'Wonderwall' and 'Don't Look Back In Anger', I wanted to sing one of them. Liam hated 'Wonderwall' when he heard it. He actually said, 'I'm not singing it, it's not fucking rock and roll.' I'll sing it then. When it takes shape and everyone is going, 'This is going to be massive,' he decides that he's going to save it from mediocrity and make it what it was. So I said I would sing 'Don't Look Back In Anger'. I'm definitely singing one of them.

Liam I don't really remember the actual day going dum, dum, dum, like a fucking gameshow kind of thing. 'You've got five seconds to fucking pick your song.' I don't remember it like that. I think, if it was, I would have fucking picked 'Don't Look Back In Anger' because, like I said before, at the time, 'Wonderwall' was a bit peculiar. I certainly didn't have the choice of singing both; I've never sung 'Don't Look Back In Anger', not even in the shower. I would have fucking nailed it without a doubt. I'd have sang them, easy, but he wanted to sing them, whatever he sung he sung and whatever I sung I sung. I definitely didn't sit in my room crying or ordering up more crystal meth going, 'I want to sing "Talk Tonight".' Did he sing it anyway? Yeah. Done a great job.

Owen Liam was extraordinary, I mean he had this freaky thing where Noel would play the song once, on acoustic guitar, in the control room to Liam, give him the words and then he'd go and he'd fucking sing it. Noel would listen to it to check Liam's got the phrasing for the entire song that he's only just heard the once, melodies, phrasing, the whole fucking caboodle. Noel would go, 'Nice one, Liam.' Noel would fuck off, Liam would just bang another four tracks down. This would be like one in the afternoon, cup of tea, lead vocal done. What the fuck? He's only heard the song once. Five songs, five days, man, fucking amazing.

Liam We'd have a beer, slag our kid off as he'd walked out the door and go, 'Fucking check him out, Slash,' and then we'd get down to proper business. We'd have a laugh, just fucking do it as loud as we could and as raw as fuck. As time went on, some producers were talking this mad language, fucking musos, whereas Owen was, 'Right, take me head off,' and I'd do that. Then that would be it really, we wouldn't sit around and scratch our chins about how great the vocal was, we'd just be raw as fuck.

Noel He was, at that point, great at that, the best in the world. But it's not complicated, it's not jazz fusion. I would write a song and immediately know Liam was going to sound great singing it. I wouldn't have the power for it or the attitude to give it the snarl that was needed, and by the same rule . . .

> I would write a song and immediately know Liam was going to sound great singing it.

Liam There was always this thing, 'You can only sing the rock–and–roll songs, your voice ain't up for it.' Leave it out, mate, I'd sing that in my sleep, but he obviously wants to sing it, he wrote it, do what you want. That was definitely the start of Noel picking and choosing the songs he wants to do: 'I'll do this one.' I think, once you open that box . . . It got to the point he was singing half the albums, he is just trying to put me out of a job, the fucker. That's when it started going a bit pear-shaped for me, musically. You've got me in the band; I should be singing all the songs, end of.

Noel One moment that sticks out for me in Rockfield is when we get to do 'Wonderwall'. Outside of the main studio is a wall which is about six foot tall. I don't know who came up with this idea but, 'Why don't we record on the wall?' I was sat on top of a wall with a huge microphone stand facing the acoustic guitar, and headphones going into the studio. I was sat getting the sound right thinking, 'This is fucking amazing, this is like transcendental fucking Beatles shit this.' Then I open my eyes and there's four sheep stood looking at me sideways, chewing grass in the way that they do, 'What the fuck are you doing on that wall?' I vividly remember thinking it was a great idea until I was being given a withering look by a farmyard animal. Actually no, this is shit, can we go back inside now, please, I'm cold?

Owen We were probably a bit young and enthusiastic and dumb and it probably could have been recorded a bit better or posher, but it worked, and we got it down.

Liam I like Owen, he doesn't bullshit, he was just a fucking geezer who knew how to do his thing. To be fair he was winging it just like us. It felt like he was in the band. We'd come back in and he'd go, 'Have a listen, what do you think?'
I'd go, 'Sounds good to me.'

He'd go, 'That's that fucking done.'

If our arms were down we knew that song weren't going on the album or that take was shit. If our arms were in the air, and your drink was in the air, and you'd got a fucking joint in your mouth, you knew we were on it and you go, 'That's done, can we go to the fucking pub now?' It was like that. We'd never sit there and overthink it and go, 'Tell you what, let's just do another fucking five takes or sing it like this.' If it was there, we would be out the door. And that's the way it is, we never judged it, we never thought of going, 'I wonder what the manager will think of it, I wonder what the record company will think of it, I wonder what that kid in fucking Doncaster will think of it?' It was like, fuck them, it was just, 'Does that sound the bollocks to you?'

Noel I want to get in and I want to get it done and I want to get out as quickly as possible. I don't want to sit around for four months fannying about with a bass drum – that is for fucking knobs. Life is too short for that shit. Fucking football is on. I wouldn't argue with Liam's opinion on that.

> I want to get in and I want to get it done and I want to get out as quickly as possible.

Brothers

Liam Noel: geezer, brother, dude. Miserable bastard. Funny cunt, funny, but miserable . . . Love him dearly, man. Without me he wouldn't be the man he is.

> Love him dearly, man. Without me he wouldn't be the man he is.

Noel I don't love Liam and I don't hate him. We are just family and families are different; family cannot be summed up in one nifty sentence. What does your mam mean to you? That is too fucking complicated a question. What does your dad mean to you? You can't just say that in an interview. So it's easy to say you love them. But I know what love is. I love my wife. And if that is what love is I certainly don't love Liam, do you know what I mean? I don't hate him either. There is like a bit in the middle that's just . . . you tolerate their shit and vice versa.

Liam He's a great fucking songwriter. He is my brother first off and that's that.

Noel We used to fight all the time. All the time.

Peggie They are two big egos, the two of them and none of them will back down. Noel is stubborn, always was stubborn. Liam, I know Liam has got a mouth on him.

Jason Brothers is on–off. I've got a brother, we are on–off. You get under each other's skin. You know exactly where to poke that pencil, give it that little nudge and it will just tip it over the edge.

Liam We definitely had little arguments, but I think people are blowing it up a bit too much. These things get blown out of proportion. It's not that bad. The press love it, they love this Mick-and-Keith, Ray-and-Dave kind of thing. It's just the way it is and I didn't mind. If people want to write bullshit, let them write it. I haven't got time for the bullshit.

Maggie When you have that kind of relationship within quite a closed environment like a band, sparks are going to fly somewhere.

Noel I hate the term sibling rivalry because it just sounds ridiculous, but that's effectively what it is. It is a shame because when we first started and we got interest from Creation, Liam would say to me, 'I'll leave everything up to you because you know what you are fucking doing.' Then it turned on a sixpence when he moved to London. He would question every fucking thing. If there were teabags in the rehearsal room, 'Why is it Yorkshire tea?' Well, because it just fucking is, because it's the best tea in the world, ladies and gentlemen. 'No, I'm not drinking it, get the fucking coffee.' I am exaggerating there, but it was a bit like that.

Liam I think it all stems back to when he bought a stereo, years ago when we shared a room. I've come in one night stoned and, you know when you are going, 'Where the fuck . . . I need to get up and have a piss.' I think I've got up and I couldn't find the light switch so I've pissed all over his fucking new stereo. He's woke up and he's gone, 'What the fuck are you doing?'

'Having a piss.'

I think it basically boils down to that. He's held that grudge. Need to let go of them grudges, brother.

Liam, clearly, would have liked to have had my talent as a songwriter and there is not a day goes by where I don't wish I could rock a parka like that man.

Noel Liam was always cooler than me, I think. He had a better walk, clothes looked better on him, he was taller and he had a better haircut. And he was funnier. I guess I was more articulate. Liam, clearly, would have liked to have had my talent as a songwriter and there is not a day goes by where I don't wish I could rock a parka like that man. Nobody can rock a parka like Liam. Even in leopard-skin slippers and a parka – nobody gets away with that shit.

Liam He's a great musician and all that and he's got that on me, but believe you me, when I'm stood next to our kid he doesn't get a fucking look in.

Noel I guess the fights are not specifically about the thing that sparked it off really, it is about a power struggle. It is about me being in charge and everybody – from the fucking woman who makes the tea to the guy that signed us and everybody in between – directing everything towards me and Liam being pissed off about it. That is basically what starts it all and, right up until the end, that's what it was. A power struggle is what it is. Any psychiatrist will tell you that.

Liam He's a middle kid, isn't he? I guess maybe if you are going to start looking at it in a psychological way, the middle kid's thinking it's all stopping, he's the main man and that and then I fucking pop up and shit on his parade. Psychologically I guess it could come from that. It could come from the fact that I pissed on his sound system one night. It could come from that I'm just better looking or whatever.

Noel There was a period where he was the greatest singer in the world, added to that the greatest frontman, added to that he was a fucking good-looking boy as well, with great interviews and wore great clothes and all that, it was perfect. They were the magic years. There were points where he'd sing 'Rock 'n' Roll Star', 'Live Forever' or 'Morning Glory' and it would be blistering. Nobody sang like he did.

Liam I know Noel thinks I'm brilliant, at the end of the day we didn't need to pat each other on the back and go, 'Oh, you're great.' He gives me the song and I deliver it. I didn't need the pat on the back and neither did he.

Noel Liam is like a dog and I am like a cat. Cats are very independent creatures, they don't give a fuck, right bastards. Dogs: 'Just play with me, play with me, please, please, please throw that fucking ball for me, I need some company.' It is as basic as that. I'm a cat, okay, that is just what I am. I've accepted it, I am a bit of a bastard.

Christine Mary Biller[*] They are two brothers. Grew up together. One's one way, one is the other. Noel has a lot of buttons. Liam has a lot of fingers. It's that simple really.

Liam I didn't want to hang out with him as much as he didn't want to hang out with me, I had me own fucking mates. None of us are into this kind of sitting around on Christmas Day having dinner with your family. For us it never happened and that's a shame. It's certainly not like we all run around going, 'Come on, Noel, come over, let's go and watch a film, let's go for a walk in the park, show us a picture of your kid and I'll show you a picture of mine.' None of that shit. We weren't like that.

Noel We've never been that close, never been that way. So it fascinates me that people find it fascinating, but that is not weird to me, that's just the way it is.

Paul Nobody expresses themselves in an Irish family. They don't go, 'I love you, brother,' nobody does that. I think later on in life you have a grudging respect and go, 'He's alright, I suppose.'

Liam I would much rather get on with my brother. Would have much rather got on with him than hate him, but we didn't hate each other for the cameras. We would have

[*] 'Rock chick' and friend of the band.

disagreements because we'd have disagreements, we are not the same person. He is a bit different, I'm different, and we didn't throw our arms round each other for the cameras, we did it because it was real and that's the way it is. I would much rather not argue with our kid, I'd much rather have good times, go out and have a drink and have a laugh than fucking not see each other. That's shit.

I'd much rather have good times, go out and have a drink and have a laugh …

Coyley's last stand

Noel The way it works in Oasis is we don't care about where we play or who we play to, just point us at the stage and we do it. We trust the people that work with us, we trust Marcus and our promoters and our lawyers and Alan McGee and all that; that's just shit you don't need to be getting involved in. I remember walking into Sheffield Arena and actually laughing and saying to the promoter, 'When is this going to take place?'

'We are thinking eight weeks from now.'

'You are fucking mad.' It was a huge arena.

For all the bravado in the press and giving it the big one and all that, we always really underestimated what we were worth, which is why bands should never get involved in any decisions like that.

Liam I remember that gig. I remember telling all the crowd to come down from the seats and it went right off, I fucking loved it. I remember I was a bit pissed off because they have bits at the front that are for all the people who have paid more money, I remember it just being a bit quiet down the front and everyone was having it in the stands. And I was thinking, what the fuck is all this about? Everyone's down the front just stood there and everyone's having it at the back. I just asked everyone to come down from the seats and fuck these off from the front and have it a bit. Everyone was just diving out of their seats, coming down the front and then it went off and that was great. That's what them days were about. When we started playing arenas and that the crowd were

Coyley Slane Castle, that's my last gig. I never worked for that band again after that. When I get home, I went to see a doctor with ringing ears.

Noel I remember them being great gigs. I probably said something outrageous in the press about one of the greatest gigs of all time.

© Jill Furmanovsky

Knebworth

© Brian Rasic/Getty Images

© Brian Rasic/Getty Images

© Jill Furmanovsky

fucking going mad. I've been to some arena gigs and it's just boring, man, it's like being at Badminton or whatever, it's just boring. Our big gigs didn't lose the fucking chaos. Our big gigs got more chaotic. That's what I felt anyway, I loved it, fucking watching about 20,000 people just fucking all swimming about and going mad. I'd have that any day over 800 or 2,000. The more, madder people in one room the better for me. All the stands were going off, everything was going off, it was just going off and I fucking loved every minute of it. The shittest part about being in a band is not being in the crowd – you want to be part of it. We were up there doing it, and it was all great, and then you would come off and you would be like, 'Fucking hell, them lot looked like they were having it,' and then the crowds were getting bigger and stuff like that. What's going on? At the end of the day you are still just five fucking idiots from Manchester so what were they seeing? Is there something else going on behind us? Part of you just wanted to get in amongst them and see what they were thinking. I don't think we ever captured on record how good we were live really in the early days – we were like a punk band, we were ripping it up, man. No one could fucking touch us. There was all this Britpop going down, everyone was farting about, and we were like a steam train, just ripping your fucking head off. We were like a Rottweiler and then it all kind of got a bit 'Beatley' and a bit more melodic and that.

Jason You certainly need some presence there; he is what fronts the band and no matter who writes the songs or who does the lyrics or whatever, he is the front person. You need somebody with some balls and a bit of character up there, not somebody who is going to whistle a tune in a safari jacket or something. You need somebody who is going to belt it out and get a bit of attitude out.

Liam My mantra was just go on, be your fucking self and all will be good in the world. So I'm pretty good at being me. So it was a piece of piss, it was a doddle, man; all of it was a fucking doddle. If you go on there and you're not being yourself, you're going to get found out, aren't you, and rolled over, so it was a piece of piss, man. Anyone that played with us got a lesson in how to do it, we were a mega, mega band. We weren't frilly or anything like that, we were just like a fucking juggernaut.

Noel Within eighteen months, two years we were selling out football stadiums, but again, with the power of youth and all that, you don't think about it. You don't think about it, you just do it. We didn't really have the foresight; we became an arena band almost immediately, then we became a stadium band almost immediately after that. We jumped ten levels almost immediately, it took U2, fucking hell, twice as long to play stadiums. But no one was really arsed about the show, we were still behaving like we were playing in nightclubs.

Liam It felt beautiful, it felt massive, the sound was better. I could sit here all day, I guess, and play it cool and that, but without a doubt it was fucking amazing playing arenas and that. I didn't feel nervous about it and I give you that straight, it didn't feel like it was too big or anything, it was like, 'Fucking bring it on, can't fucking wait.' But then always thinking on to the next thing, going, 'Right, so we are having a bit of this, what's fucking next after that?' and then we proved it. Knebworth, stadiums, there was always something in the back of my mind or in my soul going, 'This will fucking do for now, can we just get on with it and get to the next thing.'

Noel I don't ever remember being nervous about those shows. I remember being more nervous looking at the itinerary – it just had the word 'helicopter' in it every fucking other page. I was thinking, 'Fucking hell, I'm spending a lot of time in helicopters in the next few months.' That ramps up the odds of dying quite fucking sharpish. Rock stars, baby. We were helicoptered everywhere: helicopter to Slane, helicopter to Loch Lomond, helicopter to the fucking chippy. I was sick of it at the end. Fucking hell they are a pain in the arse. Wearing them fucking headphones . . . helicopters are not great.

Liam Getting off a helicopter the only thing I'm thinking is, 'If that fucking blade messes my hair up, man, I'm walking home.' It was like that, fucking stupid fucking helicopter, fucking messing me hair up. That is seriously where my head would be at.

Noel I remember having a cig on a helicopter on the way to Slane Castle, shouting at the pilot, 'Is it alright if I smoke in here?' I lit up a cig and I don't know why, I asked him if he had an ashtray. He said, 'Open the window.' Flying over these farms in Ireland flicking this cig out of the window, thinking this is fucking bananas.

Liam There were a few people around then that just weren't too clever with the flying business. But getting in a helicopter at your gig? I'm in.

Bonehead We'd done a gig in Belgium the night before, so me being me, I had the world's biggest hangover.

Noel He's quite an emotional dude, Bonehead; honestly it was like trying to get a young calf on to the back of a wagon. 'I am not going on, I am not going on, I'll get a car.'

'It's nine hours in a car.'

'I don't care.'

'Well, we are on in three.'

'Well, I'll run then.'

'Just get on the fucking helicopter.' He wasn't a fearless flier.

Bonehead I'm sure the pilot knew because he just started doing Vietnam fucking stunts, I hated it. Fucking helicopter, stupid invention, what's that about?

Noel I remember we got helicoptered in and congregated at the back of the castle. As we were waiting Johnny Depp appears and introduces himself like we didn't know who he was. And he's going on about 'Live Forever' and *Definitely Maybe*, 'Oh man, those songs.' I was like, wow, fucking hell, holy shit, man. Anyhow, the way Slane is, you look out on to the crowd and it is a hill. Flat down the front, then this big steep hill, and then for some reason the crowd then snakes round this tree and the bars are right at the top. So when we went on, seemingly 80,000 people were at the bar. We came on and plugged in and everybody ran down this hill. It wasn't scary for us, but it was a real sight to see, it was amazing. The gig had to be stopped, there was crushing going on and all that, and it was fucking wild, man, but that's what it was like at our shows.

Peggie It was a great time that, because I had all the family there with me. We had a police escort through Dublin and flying all over, because me sister and her husband had come from a different part. I thought it was great, to me, it was so good, I was so proud of them.

Noel Liam was being a cunt all day, I don't know why. He gets nervous at things like that, I think. See that is the difference between me and Liam, I would just embrace the bigness of it all, I love that fucking shit, 80,000 people, 150,000 people, fucking bring it on, I love that. I couldn't understand why he was in a fucking bad mood all day. I do remember there being an altercation afterwards. I am proud to say, or glad to say, I wasn't involved in this particular one. I don't know what had happened, if you are telling me it was him and our Paul then, well, that is nothing new.

Peggie Paul had the sleeve of his jumper all ripped where Liam must have got a hold of him. It wasn't serious, I think it was just something that Paul said to Liam, something was said in jest and that was it. It was forgotten in no time at all.

Liam Cannot remember a fucking thing.

Noel I often wonder what it must be like to have your two brothers be just two brothers and then, on the fucking turn of a sixpence, become these two that are in the press and all that.

Liam Never spoke about it, but he's not that kind of brother to go, 'Look, can I come with you?' He's just like, 'I'm happy for you, go and do your fucking thing.' He was never tagging along like some soppy brother. I guess I'd have killed the pair of them if it was them two that were in a band. There would have been trouble. But he's not like that.

He was living in Manchester, so all the shit we were getting up to, being out and about, he'd have people coming and going, 'Your brothers are fucking knobheads.' I guess it was hard, but, like I say, he never come up to me with a sob story, we never even spoke about it. He was always with girls and shit. Don't listen to his stories, sob stories; he had a good time as well.

Noel He has got a unique taste in music, shall we say, and he could talk the fucking back legs off a donkey. I don't really know what that saying means, talk the back legs off a donkey, but he could do it anyway. He very rarely draws breath.

Paul Feel left out? Only when they became huge and then certain people didn't put you on the guest list after you'd travelled fucking 200 miles.

Coyley Slane Castle, that's my last gig. I never worked for that band again after that. When I get home, I went to see a doctor with ringing ears. The doctor says to me, 'If I was in your shoes, I would stop doing this because you will go deaf.' So, I left and that was the end of my live life. I'd had enough as well, I think.

Noel I do recall Mark coming up to me after Slane Castle and saying, 'I don't think I can do it any more.' It was a loud gig. You could feel the fucking volume of it from the stage. Towards the end of the *Definitely Maybe* cycle and starting the beginning of the *Morning Glory* cycle, people were regularly coming into the dressing room going, 'Fucking hell, that was loud.' Now that is alright if it happens once or twice, but it was happening all the time. It means somebody has lost control of the sound out front and they are just turning it up.

Jason Noel's rig just got louder and louder and louder until it was 120-odd decibels in front of it . . . probably shake your trousers with that.

Coyley My favourite gigs when I was growing up, always left my ears ringing for three days. Three days, so loud, it was bordering on the painful, but you wanted a little bit more, I don't want anybody being able to have a conversation while that band's on.

Noel I think he's said in the past it had got too big for him, which is great, I really admire him for that. I wasn't upset. The thing that upset me the most – not that I was upset crying – was that he was one of my fucking best mates and he wasn't going to be on tour any more. I was gutted that I wouldn't get to hang out with him and listen to his sage advice about various things – which pretty much amounted to a lot of swearing and smoking weed and calling everybody a cunt. If I could have got him a job doing anything else I'd have done it, could have sacked somebody, but he didn't want to do monitors. So he retired disgracefully and that was it.

Liam I think he had had enough of the management. They were calling the shots a little bit. People were going, 'It's not a band thing any more, why don't the band tell the fucking management to fuck right off and look after their crew a little bit better?' I think it was just getting a bit too corporate for him. I don't blame him. One minute you're with the band, and there are five lads, seven lads, ten lads on a bus, you are all having a crack and you're mates. I was never a boss of Coyley and he was never one of my or our employees, we were just all doing it, having the crack and seeing where it went. Then when management come into it, it changes. So one minute you are hanging with your mate and next minute you are in a different hotel or you are on a different bus or you are being told how your day is going to be by some fucking team instead of your mates. I think the fun goes out of it a bit and you kind of think, 'Fuck this shit.' It felt like all the people that were with us at the beginning were kind of getting pushed out a bit. I don't know how and I don't know why, but it felt like it was a bit, 'That fucking Manchester lot that are with them, get rid of them now, get someone else on board.' We should have trapped them, never let them go. Give them a pay rise and just robbed them and kept them there. You'd be like that on the tour bus: 'What do you think you're doing, you cunt? Sit the fuck down, no one gets out of here.' Of course I took it hard. It's a terrible thing that we let them go.

> It felt like all the people that were with us at the beginning were kind of getting pushed out a bit.

Bonehead I remember it was just like, fucking hell, we got some news, Coyley's going. That's it, he's done. Gutted, oh fuck. It really was like losing a member of the band.

Noel If anybody was a sixth member of that band, it was Mark. We were roadies together with Inspiral Carpets; the first or second batch of demos I ever did were at his house, 'Married With Children' was recorded in his bedroom. He was heavily into Neil Young, Burt Bacharach and all that, and I got a lot of my musical influences from Coyley. I wouldn't have wrote 'Slide Away' or 'Live Forever' if it wasn't for Mark. I wouldn't have wrote 'Half The World Away', I wouldn't have wrote 'Talk Tonight', I wouldn't have wrote the track 'Morning Glory'. He was one of us. The band, Coyley, Phil and Jason, that was it.

> If anybody was a sixth member of that band, it was Mark.

Bonehead He wasn't just along for the ride, thinking this could be a good thing, a few quid in the pocket and I'll get to travel around the world with these boys. He wasn't in it for that, that wasn't Coyley's thing. He was there pre *Definitely Maybe*, pre getting signed, he put the time in before any of that happened. Like I said, he believed in what we were doing with a passion, he loved it. He believed it like the sixth member of the band, he really did. I think it meant as much to him as it did to us in that sense. He sacrificed a lot to sit in the Boardwalk every night and develop this sound through Noel's songs. He'd be there with us, he'd record it and he'd help us. He had a great ear for our sound, he really got it, and he was a sound engineer to boot.

Paul To have a sound engineer, that's half the battle. If you've got a sound engineer who knows your sound and can set it on any desk you go to, you're away. But he is a miserable United fan and that has never changed.

Bonehead Even when we had no money, we could bring our own sound engineer with us. Most bands can't afford a sound engineer, so you've got to rely on the guy in house at whatever gig you are at. He's never heard you before, he's just thinking, 'Another twenty minutes of this lot and I'm home for my fish and chips; turn the drums up, turn up the guitar. Bothered if there's a guitar solo there? Fucking arse. Just give me my money and I'm off.' That is your in-house sound engineer. Not all of them, a lot of them do believe in what they do, but we were fortunate we had Mark Coyle – who totally understood us, who knew the songs inside out – doing our sound when we didn't have the money to pay one. That came across. Obviously we were a great band and well-rehearsed, but he was the guy making us sound like us through them speakers for the people who first initially came to see us, which must of helped.

Maggie It was kind of sad to see him go, because he was one of the original guys on the road with us, but he was having problems with his ears, it was quite genuine. This is a problem sound engineers have in general, but I think there was also an element of it becoming a bit too much, it wasn't the vibe that he had originally bought into, you know what I mean?

Coyley I think the best times are when everybody's together and that gang is out on the road, they are the best of times. Doing them little gigs and living in each other's pockets, it's lovely, it's just absolutely fantastic. And then, it does lose something when, you know, the industry grabs hold and all of a sudden, the band are not in your hotel, the band are not on your bus, and in some respects, it's like going to work. Now, I'm not in this business to go to work, I'm in this business to make me feel good. I absolutely love it and live it and the minute I feel like I'm going to work, I'm away. There was a lot of little issues at that time. But you know, the machine goes on and the band goes on, the band had business to do. I am not getting in the way of that.

Noel It made me a little bit sad that he wasn't going to be around because we knew it was going to explode at this point, that it was going to go through the fucking roof. It is a shame that he wasn't around, but there you go. I have more respect for him for bowing out gracefully than waiting to get sacked. I still speak to him regularly. I was a drummer in his band Tail Gunner. We never got to do any gigs, but we did put a record out. It's pretty good actually.

Liam Coyley was cool. Man United fan, deaf as a fucking lamp post man, but I love Coyley.

Coyley Broken-hearted, man, you know, never get over it. Walking away from that. I'm not over it now. But it was the right thing to do.

Say what you say . . .

Noel That whole episode, the 'Country House' thing, it was the best of times and the worst of times.

> Rivalries with other groups and all that, it doesn't really interest me.

Liam There was all this Britpop thing bubbling up at that time and we were getting lumped into it. I was like, we are not Britpop, we are not Camden; I always fancied us as a proper fucking rock-and-roll band, a bit more real. They were a bit more flimsy and a bit fucking stupid, a bit silly and, I don't know, there was something comedy about it all. Pulp and all that, they are good bands, but I never felt like we were part of that, I felt like they were just some fucking weird shit going on over there.

Noel I really respected Pulp, still do, I like Pulp and The Verve, but we didn't have a great deal in common with all the bands that were lumped together for the Britpop thing. The northerners we always got on with, everybody south of Watford, quite frankly, you can fuck off as far as we were concerned.

Liam We weren't from London, so people would be, 'Come to this boozer.' Maybe people might have been trying to stir something up, trying to get something going, but it wasn't from us. I remember going to The Good Mixer and just playing pool. It was just another fucking pub to us. I didn't hate them, maybe I fucking did, I just thought we were better than everyone.

Noel Graham Coxon happened to be stood at the bar and we didn't feel like we were giving him shit, we were just being us, do you know what I mean? Kind of taking the piss, but not taking the piss out of him. I didn't feel we were being cuntish towards him. He might have took it the wrong way, but that's not where that rivalry started, that started further down the line. I've always like Graham and he always liked us. I don't know, I think I'm going to blame it on Liam; it's usually his fault.

Bonehead I quite liked them as a band. As people, didn't get on with them all; liked Damon, drummer's alright, Graham is a top guy, bass player is a prick. I like the music, they are alright people, used to bump into them quite regularly in London.

Liam We were just little fucking shits, but fuck it, why not? It needed shaking up. Everyone was just fucking licking each other's arse and patting each other on the back and it was like, 'You know what, have that fucking tomato on your head,' or whatever it was. It was harmless fun, no one got hurt.

Bonehead Liam's a champion at winding people up, you know, and building it up and getting them going, you know, and he probably genuinely fucking hated them. Or did he? I don't know, I was never driven by that whole rivalry thing.

Liam It was never malicious, it was just like, you would throw a grape at his head or something when he come in the room, or flick Alex's cigarette out of his mouth or whatever. Just fucking pull Graham's glasses off, it was just a joke. Pinch them up the arse, it was just a laugh.

Noel We weren't competing with anybody and everybody knew it. Rivalries with other groups and all that, it doesn't really interest me. But some lines are just too fucking good not to say them. You can't keep that shit unsaid, do you know what I mean? We were not in competition with Shed Seven or anyone, we were in a different league to that. And even if we actually weren't, I can assure you that everybody in the band absolutely believed that we were in a league with the greats, and at the end of the day that's all that matters. If you believe it, it is. The end.

Liam Looking back now, Blur are alright; when you get out of the bubble they were good. But to me they were a jokey band. There was always a bit of a fucking joke going down with it. We were deadly, deadly fucking serious. Maybe a bit too serious. We thought we were on a different planet

> Looking back now, Blur are alright; when you get out of the bubble they were good. But to me they were a jokey band.

compared to them. I classed us as classic Led Zeppelin, Pistols, Beatles, Stones, Kinks, a Who kind of band. I never honestly thought of us as that Britpop thing. I was 'Fuck off; you're not putting us in with that lot.'

Noel Why on earth 'Roll With It' is picked as the first single, to this day, blows my fucking mind. And I would have been involved in that decision. Out of all the least favourite of my Oasis songs that would rank pretty fucking high. But anyway, it is chosen. I remember Dick Green coming down and saying, 'We've got a problem with the release date, Blur are planning to release their single on the same day.' So we decide between ourselves we're going to move it back a week. A week later Blur move theirs again. So, alright, somebody wants this face-off in the charts. I am assuming it is Damon because at that point I am not interested, it doesn't mean anything to me. Once they have shifted their single twice I was like, 'You know what, alright then, okay, fucking bring it on.' I quickly ran away with it and got right stuck in.

Bonehead I think it was a clever marketing ploy on the part of Damon, what a clever move, well done, Damon. Didn't harm anyone, did it? That hadn't been seen since The Beatles and the Stones, you know, it was that type of thing.

Noel What really fucking annoyed me was the way that the press connived the story that it was us that was moving our single. Call me many things, gobshite, whatever, I am not a liar. And the story was perpetrated that it was us that was looking for the fight, but it wasn't. It was a couple of knobs at the *NME* goading Blur into it as I understand it.

McGee It made us bigger, it's a bit like a boxer taking on a lesser boxer. The minute he put us in the ring, he made us the contenders.

Noel Every interview you are goaded into saying something about Damon and I didn't have enough restraint or self-awareness to think, 'This is a bit unnecessary.' And I am sure the same was happening to Blur. We would get magazine editors asking, 'Will Oasis do the cover?' And we'd say no. 'Well, if you don't do it Blur are going to do it.' The media was playing everybody off against each other. It wasn't manufactured, it was very, very real. Some of the things that were said were totally unnecessary. I was personally as high as a fucking kite most of the time and bang up for a verbal ruck. I remember doing an interview before going on stage and because when I start interviews, I rarely know when to stop, I said, 'I don't mind the guitarist, I've never met the drummer, the other two, I fucking wish they'd get AIDS and die.'

Liam That was a little bit fucking harsh, wasn't it? Mine was more like, I hope they break a fingernail or get a fucking paper cut. I hope they get a boil on their nose the day they were doing the new video, it was always that kind of thing. It was never I hope they fucking die.

Noel It was said with sarcasm and fucking taking the piss. The way she wrote it was quite sinister and then the way it blew up was just the press fucking being the press. She knew it was meant sarcastically, but she chose to write it up in a manner which wasn't. Which is fine, I fucking said it, I accepted all the shit that came with it.

Liam I don't think people should be getting upset about it; it was what it fucking was. I didn't like them; they thought we were loud-mouth cunts, end of. I thought we were better than them, they thought they were better than us, it's just tit for tat nonsense. But I enjoyed it, it was a laugh more than anything, I didn't go home at night and lose sleep over Blur. I'm sure they didn't over us.

Noel Looking back on it now, I think it's one of the greatest episodes ever in British pop music, I think it is amazing. The country came to a standstill for music and wouldn't all of us, as music fans, give anything to be back in those days now? Now music is shit; the charts are flooded with meaningless, media-trained halfwits and the songs are awful, written by songwriting teams in converted garages out in the Home Counties somewhere. Music made by idiots, for idiots.

Liam Thank fuck there were two bands like us around at that time, it would have been very fucking dull, all you would have had was Shed Seven and Echobelly, leave it out.

Noel It was great because it was all about fucking music and all taking place in the charts and on *Top of the Pops*. It polarised everybody: you had to be one or the other, you couldn't be both. In the schools and playgrounds it would be the dude with the side parting, 'Well, actually, I like both groups.' Fuck off, you can be one or the other. I was sat by a hotel pool in Sorrento in Italy on holiday when somebody rang me and said, 'I think it is going to be number two.' I remember feeling slightly disappointed, but not banging-my-fist-on-the-table disappointed. I remember thinking, 'That's a shame.' To be number two in the charts is not a big

It was a brilliant and incredible time to be young and have a vested interest in the charts ...

deal. 'Wonderwall' never got to number one anywhere in the fucking world and that is the song we are most famous for. 'Strawberry Fields' had come out the same week as some tune nobody can remember by Engelbert Humperdinck and only got to number two. It is nothing to be ashamed of. It was a brilliant and incredible time to be young and have a vested interest in the charts, if you were a fan. It's all being played out on *Top of the Pops*, on the news, at award ceremonies and all that. Everybody larger than life, high as fuck; it influenced a whole generation like Kasabian, The Libertines, Razorlight, Arctic Monkeys, The Coral. Yes, we sold a lot of singles off the back of it, but what is important though is *Morning Glory*, the album, has more than stood the test of time. We are all pals now. We straightened it all out with Damon and it's all cool. We seem to have become quite friendly.

What's the Story

Noel I wasn't expecting the success of *Morning Glory*. I remember Marcus coming down to Rockfield and listening to what we had done in silence and I think Marcus's quote was, 'This is fucking serious now.' I've got to say I didn't think that, I was just writing another load of songs. Marcus was, 'Wow, this is really mature songwriting.' And of course I couldn't be more immature at that point. I remember everyone being knocked out and me being the least impressed by it all. Which is the way it should be, I think. I suppose they were blown away because they were expecting another set of 'Rock 'n' Roll Star' and 'Cigarettes & Alcohol' and all that kind of thing. If you do listen to the two albums back to back it is quite a leap going from 'Supersonic', and that kind of thing, to 'Wonderwall', 'Don't Look Back In Anger' and 'Champagne Supernova' barely a year later. It's almost like there was a link that had been missed. We mixed *Morning Glory* at Orinoco Studios in South London. We were on a festival tour and I would fly back on the days off to attend the mixes, and then fly back out to the tour with cassette tapes. I remember Paul Weller seemed to be on the bill everywhere we were; we was sitting in the back of somebody's tour bus with a mix of the track 'Morning Glory'. I think Weller couldn't have thought much of the guitar solo because he said, 'I'll play guitar on it.'

'Oh, alright, cool.'

Somehow we happened to be in London on the same day and I was thinking, he isn't playing on 'Morning Glory', fuck that, but 'Champagne Supernova' could do with a fucking great guitar solo. I remember picking Weller up in a taxi and going to the studio and Owen was lying unconscious on a couch surrounded by tissues. He'd done a bit too much bugle the night before. Weller said to me, 'That is the downside of drugs, my friend.' Weller did the mouth organ on 'Swamp Song' and the guitar solo on 'Champagne Supernova' and the little whistling bit that he does.

Owen I mastered it there myself, pure panic, and thinking this fucking doesn't sound as good as *Definitely Maybe*, fuck, it will be alright, it will be alright.

Noel What people don't remember is that album got universally panned by the critics. It is a cliché and truism in the music business that you get ten years to write your first record and ten minutes to write your second, because, if your first record is a success, back the way that the game was then, you want to follow it up immediately. Which is why, I suspect, that on most of the songs on *Morning Glory* there's a verse, then there is a chorus, and that thing is just repeated. There's not a lot of second verses on that record, which would lead me to believe that, 'Fuck, we are going in the studio . . . well, that's what I've got, let's just do that.' I often think back to it now when I am labouring over songs, 'Well, nobody mentioned it at the time; nobody mentions that there's only one verse and one chorus in "Wonderwall" bar the odd word.'

Liam I expected people like the *NME* to not get it and not dig it, because half of the shit that was in their paper was fucking ridiculous, so why would they get something that's great? We were on a different page, we were making classic rock-and-roll music that hadn't been made since the Stones or The Beatles, as far as I'm concerned. They just wanted some fast food. I'm glad they didn't get it. As long as the people got it.

Noel They were all expecting another *Definitely Maybe*. I don't really take much notice of reviews, good or bad. I've never read a great review of anything I've ever done. *NME* give it six out of ten. *Definitely Maybe* across the fucking board was a nine-out-of-ten album. That is not what made that record great or what broke that album, it was getting in the van and doing it, the spirit of the group and the chaos that surrounded it, somehow managing to reach people and connect with them. Reviews in *Sounds* or *Melody Maker* or fucking whatever magazine was on the shelves at the time, doesn't mean shit to anyone. I'd re-record the entire fucking thing. I'd do it now if somebody would let me. Because the songs were written and cobbled together on the hoof. We recorded it in sixteen days, we were all pissed, fucking gacked up, fighting, all that kind of thing and we were having a fucking good time. The record is not really about the songs, it is about the meaning people attach to those times. Long may it live, but the record is irrelevant really. It always comes in the top hundred albums

> The record is not really about the songs, it is about the meaning people attach to those times.

of all time, it's always in there. But the best album of all time is not the best album of all time because it's the best album of all time. It is the best album of all time because of the way it made people feel at that time, I think.

Bonehead You feel a bit invincible, don't you, anything you're going to do is going to turn to gold, and all of a sudden, slap. No, no, no, you can be put down. But then, you get up on stage, after reading some of these scathing reviews, and you look out and there is all these people bouncing to the ceiling and singing every word and you think, 'It ain't all bad, is it?'

Noel I remember the launch party, which was another epic disaster . . . somebody explain to me, whose fucking idea it was to have a launch party in the morning, just because it's got *Morning Glory* in the title. What genius fucking came up with that? I remember getting up and it's 10 o'clock in the morning – what the fuck. My mam was there and a string quartet playing all the tunes, which sounded pretty good as I remember, I don't remember the football, I vaguely remember the gig at the record store, we'd have been fucking wasted by that point surely. That must have been dreadful, one can only imagine what nonsense we came out with that night.

Liam I remember wearing a cool jacket and there was an ice sculpture, which I thought was very posh. There was an orchestra, and that's about it really, I think. As soon as a line went up my nose I could have been anywhere, mate.

Noel If your lead single off an album is 'Roll With It' you are not expecting great things, I wouldn't be and I was in the fucking band.

Owen When we were recording it, our main thing was to not fuck it up, and hopefully for it to do as well as *Definitely Maybe*. So, it came out, and there was all the Blur shit and all that, and the bad reviews and all that, but it just kept fucking selling and fucking selling. It turned into the Oasis nation, everyone's buying it, incredible, brilliant. But it wasn't expected, we were just hoping for it not to fuck up.

Noel I remember getting all the phone calls: 'Morning Glory has gone eleven times platinum.' Forty minutes later, 'It's gone fucking fourteen times platinum,' and thinking, 'Alright, we are watching the match, fucking whatever, great, well done, buy a new car, fuck off.' I am not in it for that kind of thing. I make the records and the records are great, and that's all I care about.

Coyley It's a fabulous record, *Morning Glory*, but I think the stamp of that band was *Definitely Maybe*. The two records sound completely different and I always thought that it was so brilliant that they didn't sound the same. I just think that's the greatest, greatest thing.

Noel The week it came out I remember going on stage, plugging in, playing *Morning Glory* and everybody knew all the words immediately. I remember thinking to myself, 'Wow, this is amazing, this really is.' It took ages for people to get *Definitely Maybe*, constant touring for people to know the words; this was instant.

Guigsy

Noel We were rehearsing in Brixton Academy, me and Guigsy got in a taxi back to where we lived. The whole taxi ride he stared out of the window with his back to me. I never thought anything of it; I am a cat, I don't give a fuck. That was just Guigs, probably thinking of the cricket as we are passing the Oval. Go back for the rehearsals the next day, Guigs just doesn't show up. We all wait around; Guigs is half an hour late, then he is an hour late, then it's two hours. Then Marcus arrives and says, 'Guigs wants to leave the band.' I thought, 'Oh fuck, shit, man.'

Bonehead I don't think I noticed it but it'd come to a point where Guigsy just, like, couldn't come on tour. Fuck, what's happened to Guigs? He's had a bit of a fucking breakdown or whatever. And that's when you kick yourself. You're like, shit, we were that blinkered that you couldn't stop and notice that your mate wasn't feeling right or looking right or acting right. There was something wrong with him, could we have grabbed him and sorted it, you know. I don't believe it happened overnight, that sort of thing develops over time, you know, and it builds and it builds and builds until it fucking pops. I think, whatever happened to Guigs, probably was a combination of constant touring and massive pressures to deliver. All eyes were on us; that's not Guigsy's style.

Liam Guigs maybe just didn't like the fame side of it, whereas I fucking absolutely fucking loved every minute of it. It was like, bring it on, let's have it. That ain't going to get in my way. I think he had just had enough of it, I think it all got a bit on top. Guigs is a gentle soul, he wasn't lairy or brash, he was a chilled motherfucker. If anyone was going to fucking flip out – with all that thing that was going on, all this fame and all these people and all that stuff – it would have been him. I could have told you that before I was born, he would be the first to flip out. Maybe I'm wrong and I'm being harsh, but I think he just had a bit of a breakdown, kind of. Just got the fear about going on stage and stuff. Maybe smoked too much weed, maybe just needed a breather, but you would have to ask him, I don't think we ever really talked about it.

Noel Guigs is a sensitive soul, any kind of chaos going on, he would shut down. He was suffering from nervous exhaustion, as rock stars always are. My nerves are exhausted or my exhaustion is getting me fucking nervous, I don't know. I've never had it myself, it is a funny thing.

Liam He wasn't like me and Noel, or like Bonehead, we were pretty mental and Guigs was always sort of like the quiet one in the corner, that was his choice. He'd have a couple of drinks and he'd be, 'I'm fucking going to skin up.' So that would be his mood. I think maybe it all got a bit too much for him, or maybe he needed a break – maybe we all needed a fucking break – and he thought, 'Fuck this shit.'

Bonehead Should we have had a bit of time off? Noel's plan of attack was keep it going, got to work, work, work. Fucking hell, we grafted for that. That was our work ethic: play a town, go off and do the next, do the next, then come back to that one we did a few weeks before, do it again before they forget about it, and then go back and do it again. That was our method.

Noel It was in the days of no internet, no social media. Our manager's theory on breaking a band was you have to do the fucking work. We loved it, we weren't a band that couldn't play, we weren't a band that were uncomfortable about playing, we were a band who knew exactly what we were and what we were good at. It's a thing that we kept up right till the end: touring, touring, touring. That's what breaks you. It was gruelling, but you know, if you want to recuperate, that's what time off is for.

> A couple of weeks off wouldn't have done anyone any harm ...

Liam I loved touring, but there were certain things where you've got to go, 'Look, this is more important.' We've done that fucking graft, so we need to have a bit of a break. You can go on these tours sometimes and you're not in the right mind and you need a break; your voice fucking goes or your head goes or whatever. A couple of weeks off wouldn't have done anyone any harm, but then I guess it was all about fucking rinsing everything, just getting as much as you can in before it all goes tits up or whatever.

Bonehead Yeah, you get casualties by doing it that way, don't you? Liam's voice is going to suffer, but again, what do you do? Go to bed at 10 o'clock every night? I don't think so, you're not going to stop here, you're going to live it to the full. You only get it once. Have it, and we did.

Liam Being in the bubble was good but you still needed to just lie on a beach, have a holiday with some of the fucking money that you've made. It wasn't necessarily go back to Manchester and sit in a pub with your mates and sniff coke or whatever. It was, 'I just need a fucking minute from all the bullshit, just to recharge the batteries.' You're drinking a lot every night, smoking and all that, and even though it's great, you needed a bit of a break every now and again to then go and hit it hard again. When you don't get them breaks, you end up fucking launching something at someone, having a little ding dong and people are going, 'Oh, they are not taking it serious.' No, I need a fucking break. A little break on the beach with a pina colada. I would have still got into trouble out there, wouldn't I? You could put me on a remote fucking island and I'd still find a chair to throw at someone.

Noel We were crying out for somebody to just say, 'Know what, this is what you should do,' and give you some kind of Churchillian speech about getting your head down and just fucking go away and do some living and blah, blah, blah. But that never happened. It's ludicrous to think that while I was in the biggest band in the world, I still had nowhere to live. I was still living in a rented fucking house in St John's Wood.

Liam When you are in the fucking bubble you rely on your managers to have a plan. They were just going for the money. We could have quite easily gone, 'I'll have a bit of time off,' go and buy a house, sit in the sun. Instead of sitting back and going, 'You know what, I'm going to let some knobhead that I don't know get behind the steering wheel.' I'd rather fucking steer it over the fucking cliff, because if anyone's going to fuck it up, it's going to be me or our kid or whoever.

Bonehead It can get pretty tiring, it can get pretty hectic for everybody. You were never at home, just constantly on the road, gig, gig, gig. You look at the Oasis 'gigography' and it is pretty full-on. And in between that it wasn't days off: you are doing a video shoot here, you are doing a TV show here, you are doing this, that and the other, here, there . . . or you are in the studio recording.

It was hard, it was graft, but when you are on the way up, it's exciting . . .

Liam It was a full-on schedule. I'm very proud that none of us has ended up in rehab or in casualty; we still know what's going on. But all these other cunts are sitting back at home, with their fucking feet up with their families, counting the money, while us monkeys are out on tour losing the fucking plot. Being in the best band – the most important band – of your generation should be a walk in the park. Should be. Things are thrown your way and it's how you deal with stuff like that that makes you great. If any of these bands today or U2 or Coldplay had half of the shit that was thrown our way, fucking hell, they would all be in fucking nobby nuthouses. I'm proud of all the shit that got thrown our way and I'm proud of how we dealt with it. And none of us are in fucking nuthouses, none of us have been to rehab, fucking bang on.

Noel Looking back on it now I never had a day off. If I had a day off on tour I was going to radio stations to do an acoustic session, or I was doing four or five interviews a day. But I don't like days off on tour, they are fucking boring. Once you've been round the world twice they are boring. I've seen Seattle, there is fuck all there. Outside of Tokyo, what are you going to do? Give me work, I much prefer working. It was hard, it was graft, but when you are on the way up, it's exciting because you can feel your thing growing and you don't know what next week is going to bring. Those are the exciting times. You don't know where you are going to be this time next week, you don't know who you are going to meet – fucking John McEnroe one minute and Talking Heads the next.

Liam Hindsight is fucking great, innit? Oasis was about living in the moment and not making fucking plans and that's what we did. For anyone to be fucking sitting there going, 'If someone had told me this . . .' then it is contrived, isn't it. We were flying by the edge of our fucking pants and we didn't know what was going on, we didn't know where we were for the next fucking day and it was great, nothing was planned out, and that was the beauty of it.

Just missing my bird

Noel We weren't the kind of band to go, 'Poor Guigs . . .' It was, 'Fuck that cunt, we've got shit to do, man.' Called one of our pals, Scott McCleod, what an amazing episode this is.

Bonehead We went out for Scott McCleod from a little band that we'd played with in the past called the YaYa's. He looked great, he could play bass. What a great job he got, didn't he, you know. Do you fancy being a bass player in Oasis? Fucking yes.

Noel I remember meeting him at the train station, maybe with Liam, a load of fucking paparazzi . . . He got off the train – a lad from Oldham with his bass guitar and the minute he gets off the train it is fucking chaos.

We must have rehearsed and then gone off to the States. We had done a few gigs and on the way to New York to do *David Letterman*. I'm sat at the front of the bus and Maggie – fucking God bless that woman, we put her through absolute fucking hell – came up to the front. It was late at night, I was up there fucking smoking, pontificating about how many chimps I'm going to buy when I get back to England and how many rocket ships I'm going to own. She came in half laughing, 'You'll never guess what's just happened . . . Scott's just told me he wants to quit.'

Maggie It's really weird, we'd finished a gig, he said to me, 'Can I have a chat with you?' He said, 'I can't do this any more, I want to go home.'

I said, 'Well, why do you want to go home? You're in Oasis, come on, what's going on?'

'I miss home.'

'You miss home?'

Noel Can't handle it because me and Liam are drinking all the time, arguing all the time, which seven times out of ten escalates into fights about what is the greatest Christmas single of all time. Well, it's fucking 'War Is Over', isn't it?'

'What about Slade?'

'Fuck Slade, Slade are shit.'

'Slade are fucking great . . .'

I think that argument actually did happen at one point. I remember going to the back and he said these words, 'I'm just missing my bird.'

Liam There are people that are cut out for it and there are people that ain't. He might have just gone, 'You know what, this is not for me, this is not what I want.' Either that or his bird must have been fit as fuck, beautiful. Hanging out with the likes of us just didn't float his boat.

Noel You are driving to do *David Letterman* and the bass player that's standing in for the bass player who's got nervous exhaustion is saying, 'I can't handle it any more.' I am laughing. Me, Bonehead and Liam are going, 'We must be the biggest bunch of cunts in the world because our mate is fucking sat at home watching the cricket, this fucking clown here, who's on the dole in England, he doesn't want to be in a band with us. What are we, the biggest three cunts in the world? I think we got slaughtered and high-fived each other.

Bonehead And he went. Tour fever, cabin fever, he couldn't handle it. Why not, I don't know. It wasn't hard. Four gigs.

Noel Marcus was saying, 'Okay, look, this is what we are going to do. We'll just cancel everything,' to a chorus of, 'Whoa, whoa, what the fuck, no fucking way.' That's not how we run shit. If he can't do it then we'll get someone else. Bonehead got up, what's happened? Scott's fucked off home. What? Scott's fucked off home. How are we going to do the show? You are playing bass.

Bonehead We had a run of gigs and the *David Letterman* show, which is a massive, massive thing to do, you know, you don't miss out on that. So it was like, 'Bonehead, can you do the bass?' Course I can do the fucking bass. So we went to New York and we did the *Letterman* show with me on bass. It was great, I was comfortable with it and it actually worked.

Liam David Letterman, I've never, ever found him funny. But it's the place where The Beatles done the Ed Sullivan show and all that, so we all go over and stand in a corner where Lennon had and that was great. The best thing about them fucking shows was the mixes; the geezers who used to mix it on American TV made everything sound fucking great. When you do one of them TV shows in England it just sounds like we're in a block party or something. You'll be fucking having it on stage, you go back and listen to it and it will be like two different bands. So I loved doing all them TV shows out in America because you sounded pretty close to how you were live, which was a good thing.

Noel What annoyed me most about it was he borrowed a leather jacket off me, right, which is a Levi's leather jacket, it was a fucking beauty. He's still got it. I think that is what wound me up the most. Wasn't bothered about *David Letterman*, we blagged that, any day of the week; I want that jacket back.

Earls Court

Noel We come back to England, got these gigs coming up, they're sold out, they're going to be monumental. It was all gearing up to be this great thing and we didn't have a bass player. I remember being wherever I was living and the phone going. I picked it up and it was Scott and he said, 'I think I made a mistake.'

I said, 'Fucking too right you have, son.'

'I've thought about it now and I'm up for it.'

'Too late now, see you later.'

> If my fucking mam has got to play bass, I'll teach her to play the bass, that gig is happening.

Bonehead I seriously thought that everyone was going to turn around and go, 'Bonehead, get the bass on.' Surely not. We can't do Earls Court, two nights as a fucking four-piece.

Noel I think we gave Guigs the first refusal and said, 'Are you going to do this gig or what?' We are doing the gig no matter what. If my fucking mam has got to play bass, I'll teach her to play the bass, that gig is happening. There was a funny request, which the twat in me was thinking I should have accepted: Bruce Foxton offered his services. I was thinking that would be the fucking ultimate to fucking wind Weller up. 'Sorry, man, can't be done.' Peter Hook offered his services. 'Fucking what? Are you taking the piss? No, thanks.'

Bonehead We could have got anyone, we really could. We could have got anyone to just stand in. Choose your bass player, they'll come and do it, surely, we're Oasis.

Noel Guigs was put on medication and he just got back in the saddle and was the same as he had ever been.

Bonehead I remember just getting a message like, 'Guigs is going to do it.' What? Guigs is going to come back and do the gig? It was just like, 'Hallelujah!'

Liam We never fussed about it. It was, 'Have a nice fucking rest, did you, you lazy fucker.' It was kind of that. 'Where have you been?' or 'I didn't even know you'd fucking gone. What, you had a breakdown, when did that happen?' It was shit like that, banter. We never rolled out the carpet or anything. We might have skinned up a few joints for him, but then again we might not have because it might have tipped him back over the edge. It was, 'Hey, you're back, let's get back on with it.'

Noel I've got to say, me, Liam and Bonehead, to this day, remain pretty straightforward guys. We just weren't that kind of band. I just don't countenance that shit; if you are in a band and you are feeling a little bit down, man, thank God you are not playing in the Boardwalk. It is the survival of the fittest. For my own part in it, most of it is on me. I am writing the fucking songs, everybody defers to me for all the decisions, creatively, fucking everything. I haven't got time to worry about whether the fucking bass player is having a bad day. Just get on with your own shit.

Noel Even if, best-case scenario, Guigs is going to come back, is he going to be up for the biggest gigs of his life?

Bonehead I was really looking forward to it: the brass section were on stage, grand piano, orchestra, Bootleg Beatles supporting us. Real good vibe around the gig. I was just really looking forward to it, buzzing for it, yeah. I used to love, just before the doors open, getting out from backstage and getting into the foyer and watching everybody coming in and filling up. Then I'd get straight back backstage and then, when the lights were down and support bands were on, I used to often get out and get right up to the top, get in a seat or just stand at the back, and watch what was going on, just soak it up.

Tim They hadn't stopped for two years solid, and they got there, it was amazing. One of my greatest memories ever will be walking out Earls Court, first night, with the boys, ready to take on the world. There is a classic one-liner from Liam: I said, 'How you feeling?' I was literally fifty paces from however many thousands of people are out there and he's . . .

Liam 'Here we go, another day, another dollar.'

Bonehead It was good to show a lot of people who might slate you and say, 'Yeah, they are going to burn themselves out, they're going to be over in a year, you won't see them again.' So, it's good for that because it's just like, 'All you lot out there who said that, watch this.'

Maggie It was a big gig. I think it was one of the biggest standing gigs in Earls Court, or something like that. It was like 20,000 people on the floor. It was amazing, but the neighbours didn't like us. We were very loud.

Noel At one point the pogoing started a bit of wave and the ground shook. The residents complained because they thought it was an earthquake. Really it was just 'Cigarettes & Alcohol' kicking in. Those gigs were unbelievable. Unbeknown to us, Kasabian are there, two young lads, Tom and Serge, only fourteen and fifteen. Their mum and dad has picked them up outside after the gig. Obviously we have since become friends and they said that's what kind of sparked it for them, what kicked it off.

Maggie We had loads of complaints from neighbours, but you know who the neighbours are. They're all Chelsea, you know? It was all very 'my candelabra moved across my table while I was eating dinner.'

Bonehead There ain't many bands that can go out and do Earls Court the way we did it and get that reaction from a crowd. It was pretty dull on stage, you know. Thank God we had a good light show going down, because we weren't doing much, there was no choreography involved, no nothing. Liam was prowling about, he was cool, but they just go berserk. There was a big element of danger. I'm sure people were like, 'What's going to happen next?' Even I did on stage. You never knew what was going to happen, it could be all hunky-dory backstage before you go on, and then it just goes off. That danger combined with the music and just, I think, the presence, the attitude of us, you know. The crowd just reacted.

Noel I remember them being great gigs. I probably said something outrageous in the press about one of the greatest gigs of all time. I am not sure at the time you really appreciate it, they are just more big gigs. I've got to say I don't remember Bono being there, I don't remember Madonna being there, I don't remember Elton John being there. I only recently read that all those people were there. I kind of remember some of the gig because I've seen bits of it on the telly. I don't remember it because we were fucking hammered, I suppose, for a couple of days afterwards. I think we played 'Hey Jude' over the PA at the end, we all came out of the dressing room and the entire crowd had stayed behind and were all singing it. So there was something in the air celebrating something or other.

I would just be stood completely fucking still, like a boxer

Liam There were days when you were in the zone where you could just stand perfectly fucking still while there is all this chaos going on around you. All these kids are just leaping about and the sound's pumping, roaring, and I would just be fucking stood completely fucking still, like a boxer, thinking this is the best feeling in the world. Pure control, not feeling the need to join the madness or bust a move, just absolute fucking still, but yet all this craziness is going on around. When you had them moments, where it was pure still while all this shit was going on, that was like nirvana, the highest peak, man, it was the bollocks.

On the list

Noel Famous people had started turning up. There was a show in New York when John McEnroe traipses into the dressing room followed by Duran Duran. As they walked in, I would always walk out. Not because I don't like John McEnroe – I fucking love John McEnroe – or Duran Duran, but I just don't have anything to say to them. So I would kind of pass them on to Liam and then do one, sharpish.

Liam I remember John McEnroe coming, he was fucking cool. Dave Gahan was around at the time, he was pretty scary, but a top guy.

Jason Where you are getting actors and models and pop stars and rock stars and people like that wanting to come along to see the show, it changes the dynamics of it. You are hanging round a different set of people and different ideas.

Noel We are in L.A. and we are out with Kate Moss and Johnny Depp. I think it was Johnny who said, 'You should play at the club tomorrow night, a secret show.' Now if Liam hadn't been in the car that gig would never have happened, but he was, 'Yeah, yeah, let's do it.' I can't be fucking arsed, it's the size of a shoebox, who gives a fuck, a load of rich kids, 'Yeah, yeah, man, fucking hell, Oasis.' Honestly, he was like a Jack Russell with a chicken leg on Christmas Day. So we had to go and do it. I don't like doing secret gigs, I'm not getting paid, fuck that. I'm not doing it for a laugh, I'm doing it to be mega fucking wealthy. Has it gone down in the annals of being a legendary gig? No, it's forgotten. There were about sixty people there. A waste of a fucking night out. On my night off an' all. I just want to go out and get hammered and go back to the hotel and swan around in an expensive robe and drink fucking red wine and smoke a cigar.

Liam I think we did a gig somewhere in L.A. and then I think we done a second gig that night at the Viper Room. I don't think we could get all our gear across so we just used what was there, which was pretty shit. But we done a little mad, raucous gig; it was good.

Noel I liked Evan Dando, still do to this day, he's a good lad, heart of gold, it's like having a huge hound dog on tour with you, a lovely guy. I love Evan, I fucking do love him and I love his tunes and he is a fucking good guy, man, but he was a bit crazy for a bit.

Liam He was well off his box and I loved every minute of him. He was a dude. I don't know what we were doing with him, what he was doing there or why. He was mad and he was a lovely guy. We were just getting off our tits and doing drugs and getting wasted, man. I remember he would always break up TVs and fucking phones and put them in his bag. And then we would be going through airports and they would be, 'You can't go through, this is like a bomb!' We would be saying, 'What you doing?' He was a bit weird, man. I can't remember much about it but we had some good times. I've not seen him fucking since. He sort of just come in, caused a bit of chaos, beautiful chaos, and fucking left.

Noel I guess you get a sense of people who you know you have got a great deal in common with, and they are usually songwriters. But I don't consider those people celebrities; Bono's not a celebrity, neither is Johnny Marr or Weller, they are fucking the same as me, do you know what I mean?

Peggie I just love meeting them. 'Oh, you're awful small, you're not like what you look on the television.' I said to Noel, 'How is that Bono?'

He says, 'Oh, he's fine, Mam.'

I said, 'He's a small little fella, isn't he?'

Noel I do remember one gig in Manchester, being in the dressing room afterwards and going to get a drink, going for the bottle of whatever it was, and George Michael getting there before me. I was kind of looking, 'Fucking hell, there's George Michael in our dressing room. How fucking mad's that?' Mental.

Liam I remember George Michael used to come to some of our gigs. I remember going into a bar and he was sat there with fucking Bananarama. He started popping up at a few gigs, he was into us. I liked George Michael, he was cool. Bananarama cool, still cool. People just want to come and have a nosey, don't they? They didn't get the red carpet rolled out for them. We'd

> I guess you get a sense of people who you know you have got a great deal in common with, and they are usually songwriters.

never really get into arse-licking them. I've been to gigs to see big bands and the red carpet is rolled out and it's all a lot of fucking, 'Oh great,' slapping each other on the back. We didn't give a fuck who was coming to see us, how many films you've been in or how many records you've sold. It was, 'Oh look, there's such and such over there,' and that would be it. I was never fazed by it because I was never impressed by it. Only Paul McCartney. We were in L.A. and he was mega and I was proper freaked out by it, but he was great. I met Ringo. Anyone else I was never star-struck by. Certainly wasn't star-struck by Bono and I mean that, and that's not a diss on him. I was more struck by John McEnroe, to be fair, he was cool. But I'm not really fazed by these people that come to see us.

Noel If John Lennon walked in here now I'd shake his hand and all that. It was his music that matters to me, you have got to understand they're just like you, but more talented versions of you. Paul McCartney is a fucking Scouser with a bass. There's fucking millions of them, but he is more talented than all of us, you know what I mean? Paul McCartney doesn't have the answers, Paul Weller doesn't have the answers, Peter Hook certainly doesn't have the answers, Johnny Marr ain't got them, George Harrison never had them, Iggy Pop, Lou Reed. They are just like you, but a different version of you.

Making headlines

Noel They were crazy times. There was a period of about six months where it was everything that I said or Liam did got on the news.

Liam You give a lot of your privacy away when you are a band like that. I think what you get back from it is well worth it: you get to travel the world, you make shitloads of money, you make great fucking music, you touch people, you change people's lives, you make their lives more important and they make your lives that little bit more important.

Noel There is a saying within the music business, 'I only release records to promote my latest interviews,' which is true, because really I'd much rather be doing an interview, to be honest. Writing songs is difficult; talking shit is easy. In fact that is going to be the title of my audiobook: *Talking Shit is Easy*. In that period, it seemed that everything that I said ended up on the front page of the newspapers. People started to think it was an act. I remember somebody saying in an interview somewhere: 'the master of manipulating the press', and I was thinking, 'I am just answering stupid questions with stupid answers.' Interviews are fucking nonsensical most of the time. Until it gets to be really fucking important, like, 'What do you think about Rwanda?'

> ## Writing songs is difficult; talking shit is easy.

'Does she sing with the Happy Mondays?'

'What?'

Whereas at the beginning it's like, 'Where do you get your flares from?' So I was well prepared for the silly questions, which, still to this day, do get a silly answer. When I am doing an interview with a journalist, to me that is as important as the records. I am there to be a gobshite and cause as much fucking trouble as possible. That was my thing, and to polarise opinion, so when people put a microphone in front of me, I would have said, 'The Beatles, who the fuck are they? Fucking better than them and the Sex Pistols; we're the Sex Beatles, fuck them all.' That is what I would have said.

I would dread picking up the *NME* because I would think, 'I know this is going to look bad in print.' But it's usually all said with a smile on my face, just taking the piss really. I was always 'blasting' people: 'Gallagher Blasts Royal Family'. Or 'ranting': 'Rocker's Amazing Rant About Gerbils and Bourbon Biscuits'. I get bored in interviews very quick.

Maggie When they got to the stratospheric era of '95, '96 they were in the press all the time. And they were still quite young, really, to be thrust in that kind of spotlight without having any sort of knowledge of how to deal with it.

Noel We never started an interview by saying, 'By the way, you do know that we use cocaine?' Somebody asks you, 'Do you take drugs?' and you say yes. I never boasted about it at all, but I won't tell a lie in interview, I try not to anyway. I'm not saying, and I wasn't saying at the time, 'This is a fantastic lifestyle choice and everybody should fucking get involved in this shit.' Clearly I wasn't saying that.

Liam Drugs were just done because there was fuck all to do. That's what people do, innit? Before you go up your own arse, you take whatever's there, don't you? It wasn't a big deal. Started off with, I guess, weed, partial to a fucking can of gas every now and again just to blow your head. I was doing mushrooms at the age of fifteen so a little bit of acid every now and again was like nothing. My mind had already been fucking tilted to one side, so a little bit more won't hurt . . . a bit of coke, a bit of speed and bit of everything, man.

Noel You grow up on a council estate in Manchester, you are surrounded by it. I used to bunk off school to glue-sniff. Then speed and weed, or draw as we used to call it, and magic mushrooms and acid and fucking cocaine, ecstasy. They were all just there. But it wasn't like it was our whole fucking reason for being. Nobody was on heroin, nobody fucking died. As far as I can remember, the only thing that died was my creativity.

Liam People would be going, 'You can't be fucking saying that.' Well, I ain't going to lie about it and then get caught out doing drugs. Yeah, I do drugs; write about it and fucking move on. That's the way it is. I know loads of people that are in the public eye that are secret little sniffers and that. The minute it comes out on them, they are fucked. Do you do drugs? Yes, we do and I will do them off your fucking head in a minute if you fucking carry on fucking asking silly questions. Yes, we do; move on.

Jason Wow. Rock-and-roll band taking drugs and drinking, are you joking? Good God, people will be reading in libraries next.

Noel The *News of the World* once ran a story that I had a £4,000-a-week cocaine habit, so we worked out that if it is so much a gram, it meant that it was something like sixteen grams a day you were doing. Now, twenty-four hours in a day . . . you work it out. I managed to keep a very successful band going, all over the fucking world! It's not nice for your mam to read because the next time you see her she is going to think you are going to look like a fucking big, fat, plastic bag full of piss or something.

Peggie I used to go to the shop and see them on the front of the paper and think, 'Oh God, is there anybody looking at me buying the paper?' Then you would go out and somebody would say, 'I've seen your boys in the paper,' and you think, 'Oh God.' There's always someone out there to say, 'That Liam is a right so and so, who does Noel think he is?'

I'd read it and then I'd think, 'Is it true?' Then I'd say to Liam, 'Is that true, Liam, what's in the paper?'

'No, no, no, Mam.'

You think, 'Well, is he telling me lies?' You think to yourself, 'Something must have happened for it to be on the paper.'

Paul I suppose it wasn't nice for her. It would have been nice to know what was going on, but all you get out of Liam is, 'No, Mam, don't believe what you read in the press,' and all you get out of Noel is, 'Wasn't me.'

Liam I certainly wasn't hamming it up because we were in a fucking band. I was doing more drugs before I was in the fucking band. You don't join a band to do drugs, if you do that you're a fucking sad cunt. I've never hyped anything. That was my life, man, that's how we behaved. If I'd seen it from any other band then I'd go, 'Yeah, they're hyping it,' but we had a laugh. Play a great gig and then you get fucking drunk and then shit would happen, that's life. I was getting up to shit like that before I was in a band, that's what my life was.

Noel Whatever I do is not an act, if I am being asked a question I give an honest answer, apart from when I'm lying through my teeth, which is a good 75 per cent of the time, I have to say. Or making shit up. I might bend the truth, or spin a good yarn for a laugh, but I'm not a liar. If there is one thing I have always been, it's true to myself. That's the way we were and if people didn't like it, fuck 'em, I'm not asking anybody to like it, I'm not asking anybody to like me. I'm just asking them to buy my records and, more importantly, buy the merchandise because that is where the real money is. Liam has that thing where he is the nicest guy in the room, then he's had a drink and he will pick a fight with a microphone, for no reason. There isn't a person in the Oasis organisation that's not been on the end of some of those moments, but that's just the way it was.

Liam I didn't need pushing. If anyone had said, 'Can you go out and drink tonight and go and start a ruckus?' they'd have got the sack because it would have been like, 'You're not right for me.' We didn't need pushing in that direction, that was there whether we wanted it or not. There's always some fucking crackpot around the corner, just waiting to get inside my head, or maybe I'm the crackpot around their corner, waiting to get inside their head. I remember going to the pub some days at

11 o'clock, by half twelve people would be dancing on the tables and snorting cocaine. Come in for a quiet pint and read the paper, now all hell's broke loose. One thirty in the afternoon, everyone's just fucking having it. Good times.

Noel I'm not a tragic character and I can handle drink and drugs, I don't have a problem with any of that, I can go toe to toe with anyone. I'm not a tragic fucking Pete Doherty character; I got most things in my life under control. I can't give you a story about my drug hell. I can't because I didn't have one. It was fucking great up until the point where I just said, 'That's it, no more.' But I can't sit here and tell you I had a shit time because I didn't, it was a great time.

> I can't give you a story about my drug hell. I can't because I didn't have one.

Liam I was too off me tits to care. Obviously it pissed you off when there is people trying to trip you up . . . I kind of loved all of it, that is what I signed up for. They are outside me door because I am fucking interesting, not because I'm boring, so let's have it.

Noel I've always been able to get up in the morning, look myself in the mirror, and the same thing at night. I'm fucking cool about it, I really don't give a fuck. It means nothing to me what people write about me or say about me or feel or believe.

Liam I'm the frontman, I'm the face of the band, so I guess they are going to go for it. Fuck it, let them have it. It would do your head in at times when they were writing shit about you and fucking waiting outside your house, but it happened and it come and it went. I guess when you put yourself out there for it you are going to get shit.

Noel I don't know what I was going to see him for, but I remember having to fight through a scrum of photographers. I thought my house was bad – there was quite a few outside mine – but there was tons of them outside his house. I thought, 'Fuck that, I couldn't live like that.' Poor fucker.

Liam The only thing I didn't like was people with cameras putting it in your face. If you are going to take a picture, take it from over there; don't be putting it in my face. That ain't being a moaning fucking famous person or whatever, it was just 'You are in my fucking personal space here, knobhead. Get out of it.' If there were people with cameras in my face and I'm a bit drunk, my thing is, 'You are in my space, you are going to get a fucking clout.' They invented a long lens for a reason, to stand over there and take a fucking picture, not to put a long lens up my nose. I enjoyed that as well, even though it cost me quite a few quid and that, but I enjoyed a photographer having a dig every now and again.

Noel I'm going into these interviews thinking, 'This is it, I'm a fucking rock star, this is it.' And I'm sat opposite a journalist and within thirty seconds I'm thinking, 'You're a fucking knobhead,' asking me the same questions as a guy asked me two months ago. I get bored quickly and think, 'Alright, I'm going to jazz this up a little bit now and fucking threaten to kill Prince Andrew or something, see if that gets interesting for fifteen minutes.' The journalists were either trying to be on side with you by, 'Yeah, man, fucking hell, it's so rock and roll, dude, got any coke?' Or they were trying to get you to slag Liam off, or Damon, all the time – I did enjoy slagging Liam and Damon off, I have got to say. It wasn't till much later on in the game that I became at peace with it and thought, 'Okay, a silly question deserves a silly answer so fucking here goes.' One of the most notorious quotes was 'taking drugs is like having a cup of tea'. And it was, and it is to young people. That fucking story went all over the world and it was crazy for a bit. It was at the *NME* Awards, and I remember saying I'll only do interviews in the toilets. All the cubicles are full of people doing drugs so I said, 'Drugs are just like having a cup of tea, everyone's on fucking drugs; all these people here are taking drugs, I bet there are people in the Houses of Parliament on drugs.' I didn't think anything of it. I went home and I drove up to Birmingham with Paul Weller, we were recording a Ronnie Lane EP for some thing or other. I didn't have a mobile phone, so the next afternoon somebody is flicking through Ceefax to look for football scores and I see my name pop up on it. I said, 'Whoa! Go back . . . what the fucking hell is that?' And there was this story. So I drive back to London and I got the driver to drive past my house. Honest to God it was insane. There were TV presenters with the lights on, fixing themselves to go live to the fucking 6 o'clock news. About six weeks before, Brian Harvey had been kicked out of East 17 for saying something about ecstasy. I'm watching the news in Tim Abbott's office and Michael Howard, the then Home Secretary, is on the TV giving an interview about what I'd said. Fucking hell, this is insane. Michael Howard came out with, 'This is a disgrace. I hope Oasis see sense and send him the same way as Brian Harvey.' Fucking hell; we laughed out loud and went out on the piss.

Liam It was a headline and bring it on; I'd rather that than, 'Oasis went to bed at 9 o'clock with a cup of cocoa and were up at six in the morning doing yoga.' It had all been done before and it will all get done again. Listen, if anyone in this band turns round to you and tells you that they were not happy with these kind of headlines, they are fucking liars. We were going, 'Yeah, cool. Nice.' It's better than having some fucking Tory MP, or whatever, on there doing coke. I'd rather us be on the front than any other cunt. I loved it.

Noel The thing that was funny was the hypocrisy of the British press who would write these things, this outrage. Well, I've taken drugs with you. I have been in toilets in clubs in London with you, you fucking liar. And although not everybody in the House of Commons is on drugs, clearly, as the years have gone by we've come to know some people have been and are. It is the hypocrisy of politicians who are up to far worse than some rock star trying to live his fucking dreams. Hypocrisy has never been in short supply in England, particularly in the media and in politics.

> # Hypocrisy has never been in short supply in England, particularly in the media and in politics.

Liam They loved it as much as us, because there was nothing else about. It was boring and it ain't big and it ain't fucking clever, but it was right for the times. They might have been exaggerating, but there was definitely some truth in it I guess.

Noel It did make life quite difficult, though, getting around was difficult, couldn't go out of the fucking house because you got followed everywhere.

Liam There are some days where you go, 'Fucking hell, I can't go down the fucking shop, me private life is fucking all over the papers,' but that's just the way it is. I got used to it very quick and moaning about it ain't going to fucking change it. There is two ways to go: I stop being in a band and go be a hermit and then that's my dream over, or I fucking shut the fuck up, get down to the pub, have a pint, chill the fuck out and just fucking get on with it. No one's stopping me from doing what I am meant to be doing, and that was being in the fucking greatest rock-and-roll band of my era. A couple of little shitty stories here, a couple of little fucking digs by the press, fucking water off a duck's back, give a shit, bring it on.

> # My band is better than every single tabloid newspaper put together.

Noel The *News of the World* and all the Sunday papers and all the fucking tabloids were out to get a story because surrounding the band was chaos. Stories were regular fucking occurrences and here was a band who were bigger than anybody else who didn't give a fuck. The drugs and fucking women and all that shit and the chaos and all that. I was always of the opinion, this shit doesn't matter, we're better than this. My songs are bigger than your newspaper. My band is better than every single tabloid newspaper put together. It doesn't matter to me. We were better than that.

Liam Whatever they were saying, it was pretty much true. I was a bit lairy, I was out taking drugs . . . it's all there to see, it's pretty much true, but I wouldn't say I'm a cunt. They were going, he's this and he's that and it's like, no, I'm a good person. But all the rest of it is true, without a doubt. But I didn't care what they wrote, I'd never sit there and go, 'I'm fucking suing them, they've said this about me.'

Noel Wherever we went the press followed. So I got the big house in Primrose Hill, turned it into a nightclub, then never went out for two years. When you have got responsibilities only to yourself, fucking live life to the full, man. Those parties at Supernova Heights went on forever, forever and ever. There were quiet times, but they were only to clean the place up. Everybody was round at my house all the time. I can't name names, but we all had a great time. It brings a smile to my face when I think about it, and outside the house was never less than fifteen, twenty kids, the press, all the time.

Liam I went round a few times to lend some sugar and shit, but never got the invite. I might have wrote on his wall every now and again on the way back from the shops. Liam is God. Liam is cool – kiss kiss.

Noel They weren't 'parties'. I don't remember there being any loud music. It was where everybody that I knew hung out. I remember once there was a random scruffy guy sat at the kitchen table. 'Excuse me, mate, do I know you?'

And he said, 'No.'

'Well, what are you doing here?'

'I delivered pizzas here about six hours ago.'

'Well, what are you doing?'

'Everyone said it was alright to stay.'

'Take your fucking crash helmet with you and your moped and get out.'

Phil Obviously, they took guitar music as far as it's been in Britain since The Beatles. I know Led Zep were doing that, but Led Zep were never that visible, you know. They were the most visible band since The Beatles and the Stones, because everybody knew who they were. They weren't just the biggest band, they were the biggest people in Britain at that time, Noel and Liam, without a doubt. Everybody had an opinion on them. Everyone in the street is treating you different, your world is different.

When people ask you for your autograph for the first time it is a fucking bizarre thing.

Noel When people ask you for your autograph for the first time it is a fucking bizarre thing.

Liam If people stop and ask you for an autograph, it takes you two seconds to do it. You can make or break someone's day, and I'm not about breaking people's day. I never, ever go out of my way to make people feel bad. I hope I didn't anyway. I rarely have a shitty day, nine out of ten I was buzzing. I was always up and still am. I've had a lot of shit go down and that and so have other people, but I always try and keep a positive outlook, it will all be right tomorrow.

Noel I kind of envied the rest of the band for being able to take a step back. I think for me and Liam it was slightly different, we were in it, immersed in it, and probably still are. So it must have been nice to take a step back and just go, 'Holy fuck, how did it get like this?'

Bonehead We were kings, yeah, we really were. We were just living that dream and that's exactly what we wanted, that's why you join a band.

Liam I did exactly what it said on the tin: rock-and-roll star, that's me, boom. I just absolutely fucking love it, and loved it, and still do love it. I wake up with a smile on my face. I'm always out to have fun, definitely.

Noel He's into the chaos for sure; he causes a lot of it.

Jason Chaos just came their way constantly, it was quite an interesting band like that. If it wasn't one thing it was another and it just kept on coming and coming and the band were getting bigger and bigger and more and more chaos ensued. When you are involved in it, it doesn't faze you. You just think, 'Oh well, another incident, another issue, another something that's happened. Surely nothing else can go wrong. Oh, it can.'

Liam As much as it was getting big, I still was trying to keep an element of fucking rawness to it. They wanted to drive the rawness out of it, hence the rule book getting invented, and shit like that.

Maggie Anything that starts becoming stratospheric has to become a business, unfortunately. That's the harsh reality of life. Things that do stop being fun, which is quite difficult when you have one of the main band members thinking of it as a rock-and-roll thing, it's quite hard to say that the rock-and-roll image doesn't really exist. It is a business, at the end of the day. There's a part of you that has to accept that.

Awards ceremonies

Liam Always had a good time at awards ceremonies, was never there for the whole 'Aren't we great' business, we were there for a piss-up and a night out sitting round a table with your mates. Getting drunk, hurling abuse at a load of people that are not as good as you. Amazing.

Noel The first year at the Brits was great. We were there, Blur were there, Pulp, all the new wave of bands and there was a sense that at some point, some woman is going to come in with a clipboard and say, 'Hang on a minute, you lot are not supposed to be here.' The Brits were something; it wasn't even that popular then, it was just something you'd seen on the telly that fucking Take That were on and dippy boy bands. I think Suede were on it once and it was like, 'Oh my God, Suede are on the Brits. Wow.' Then, for want of a better word, indie music started to become mainstream. My management said, 'You have to be there by such a time so the car's coming to pick you up.' I remember it was just a minicab. I get to Alexandra Palace before the fucking doors open. I get out of this taxi, streets are lined with all these people, I don't even think the photographers have

> We were there for a piss-up and a night out sitting round a table with your mates.

turned up yet, and I go up to the door and they wouldn't let us in. I had to sit in the kitchen with the fucking staff making the dinner for an hour and a half to wait for the show to fucking start and then come out and go up the fucking red carpet thing. Sat next to me was Annie Lennox. She was saying 'I really like your work,' and I was like, 'I haven't got a job, what you talking about, work?' We were doing fucking gack under the table and all sorts, it was insane . . . Annie Lennox was fucking disgusted.

We got presented an award by Ray Davies and I am sad to say that I didn't fully appreciate that at the time. I mean, I love their music so much. If it wasn't for Ray Davies there wouldn't be Britpop, he's one of my fucking idols. He's written some of the best songs that this country's ever produced. Then the next year by Pete Townshend. Pete Townshend, one of my other idols; if there wasn't Townshend and The Who there wouldn't have been punk rock. I remember Damon getting Best Band and saying, 'We should be sharing this with Oasis.'

Liam I remember running over to their table – I was doing a Kanye before he was doing it – I remember going to Graham, 'Give us that, that's ours, that,' and he's going, 'Fuck off, man.' I was going, 'You know it's ours, though,' just winding him up, just taking the piss basically. Yeah, I had a good night, we drank lots and lots of stuff, it was great.

Owen The Brits in 1996, that was a night. Off our tits. Fucking Guigs had some really strong fucking skunk. It was so big that they had to give them everything, didn't they, but they didn't give us best producer, you know, Brian fucking Eno won it. Me and Noel were like, 'What the fuck?' He gave me their Oasis Best Album award, 'You have that,

Owen.' Next day I had Creation on the phone going, 'Can we have the award back?' I was like, 'No, he fucking gave it to me.' Fuck off. We were on the table next to Tony fucking Blair. Tony, come here. Cherie, give us a fucking cuddle, love. Oh, what a night, Jesus Christ.

Liam I didn't even know who Tony Blair was. What's his record, like? Is he a jazz musician or something? Who the fuck's Tony Blair? Never heard of him. I'm not into politics in records, full stop. Give a shit about John Lennon's political side, Bono's and all that? I am not into it, man. We make music to have a good time, all that fucking shit is a personal thing. I think it shouldn't be involved with music. I've always thought, 'Once you start opening that box you are going to end up like a self-righteous fucking idiot,' and my words have come true. Once you go down that route of politics, man, and all that bollocks, you ain't coming back, mate . . . If there's anyone who can bullshit you more than yourself, that's a politician. You sit round a table with them, they will fucking get inside your head, mate, and before you know it you will be one of them. You know what, you can fucking enjoy your canapés and your champagne, I'm off to Wetherspoons to speak to the real people. We must have really got on people's tits. The likes of Michael Hutchence must have been just like, 'Oh, for fuck's sake, these cunts are going to be here.' But that's the way it is, man. We earned our right to be there. As much as they were thinking that, we were thinking, 'Are these cunts still fucking here? Have we not got rid of these lot yet? Who let these lot in?' We would always flip it back to them.

Noel In the case of Michael Hutchence, the week before he'd said something about Oasis and I used to live for shit like that. I've never really picked a fight with anyone but I used to live for the day people say, 'Fuck, have you heard what what's-his-name said about you?' I'd just be like, 'Oh, he has no idea what's going to happen to him now.' Before we went on stage I met him backstage and he kind of apologised, 'I was only having a laugh,' and I was saying, 'Mate, we'll fucking see who's having a laugh in about fifteen minutes.' Some lines are just too good not to say.

Liam God bless his soul. He did nearly get brained because he was being a fucking cheeky cunt. I think it was something about Paula Yates, God bless her soul, I think someone had said she was getting a bit frisky and that. I was pissed and he said something like, 'I'll fucking come down on you like a fucking can of Fosters,' something like that. 'Well, fucking let's have it,' and I picked the fire extinguisher up, but didn't hit him with it. That was the end of that, but he was having a bit of me and I was having a bit back.

Noel I remember at the Brits once we were just sat round the table talking to our pals. Somebody came and said we had got to leave. The award ceremony had finished, everyone had gone home and we were just sat round these tables like the fucking guys from the Monty Python sketch, just talking shit. It was like 3 o'clock in the morning or something, we'd been there all night.

Liam We were a bit arrogant, I guess we were a bit cocky and that, probably had too much to drink. Every time we did an awards ceremony we definitely didn't just sit there, I don't think I ever ate any bit of food at these awards ceremonies, I think it was just proper fucking sessions. We just drank too much and we would hurl abuse at people, it was just fucking banter, man. Come on, everyone needs to fucking lighten up. Maybe we went a bit overboard every now and again, but where I'm from we just give each other shit on a daily basis and it's just a laugh. People from up north can take it a bit more, I guess some people couldn't take it. It was never malicious, we were just having a fucking laugh.

> We treated being the biggest band in the world with the contempt it deserved and deserves.

Noel I don't have any of my awards, I give them away when I get them. If you are sat besides me at a table at an awards ceremony and you ask for it, I'd give it to you. I think I kept one Ivor Novello and that's because my missus put it in her handbag. That was it. I've given the rest away, they don't mean anything. I don't have any of my gold discs. It doesn't make you any better, any greater a person or better a songwriter, or the record any more popular. It's what you're doing on stage that matters.

Liam You come to my house, there is not one award up, there is not one fucking disc up of our great achievements. They're all under the fucking stairs, just sitting there. I've never put them up because that's not what I'm about. I've been round some people's houses and it's like there are all the fucking awards up. What is this, the fucking eighties or the seventies? Mine are just under the staircase. So award ceremonies are good just for the simple fact – to get wasted and hurl some abuse at some poor shit indie band.

Noel We treated being the biggest band in the world with the contempt it deserved and deserves. There was a lot of, 'I can't be arsed doing that.' Do we want to do the Super Bowl? That's a ball ache, no, takes two weeks. So we never played the game in any way, we couldn't be bothered. Too busy having a good time. We won five MTV awards one year and we forgot to go to the ceremony. We just went to the pub, and we were kind of, 'Aren't we supposed to be doing something?'

'And the winner is Oasis . . .' and there are five empty seats. We were in the fucking Warrington pub in Maida Vale getting pissed. We never got a single fucking play on MTV after that, they hated us. MTV fucking hated us, the *NME* fucking hated us, Epic, our record label, loathed us, but the people loved us and that's what carried us through to this day.

Take that look from off your face

Noel *Morning Glory* took on a life of its own after 'Wonderwall' and 'Don't Look Back In Anger' came out consecutively as singles, then it just blew up all over the world. I wrote 'Don't Look Back In Anger' and I didn't think anything of that song when I wrote it. I thought, 'Yeah, that will be good, I can hear it live, it's got a great chorus and I think that will be great for the next record.' As I recall it, we were doing this gig in this strip club in Paris. I can't remember the gig, but I remember that there'd been a fight – there seems to have always been fights, fucking mental. I decided I wasn't going to go out that night. I took my guitar and went back to my hotel room. If I'd have known that night what I know now about 'Don't Look Back In Anger', I would never have finished it. The lyrics would never have been right. If you were to think that night, this song is going to outlive me, you'd think I'd better come up with a better first line than 'Slip inside the eye of your mind', whatever that is supposed to mean. I sat down and I wrote it and it took me one night, not even all night. It took me a couple of hours maybe to write that song, give or take a few words – Liam came up with the Sally bit – and I didn't think anything of it. Then you put it out and it takes on a life of its own.

Liam I don't remember it being in Paris, I can remember this distinctly, it was in America. I was sat at the back of this hall and I heard him playing this fucking tune and I was going, 'What's he singing there?' And in my head, this is my version, I've gone, 'He shouldn't sing that there, he should sing "So Sally can wait . . ."' Maybe I was stoned or maybe it was just a dream. But it wasn't about 'I wrote that bit' or 'I want credit for that' give a shit. Then next minute that comes out. It was a top tune.

Noel When I am frustrated with the songwriting process, or I feel like I'm not cutting-edge enough, I always go back to that night and think, 'No, just write it, let the people decide.' That song is played at weddings, funerals, football matches, concerts . . . It's an extraordinary song and it's extraordinary because the people made it extraordinary. I say to people, 'I only wrote it, my part in it was that minimal.' The way that I write songs is just to write it, fuck it, just let it go. Then record it and when you are recording it, make it the best that it can be. Then let other people decide if it's great or shit, if it's their favourite song or it's their worst song. Years later I was at an Ian Brown gig and a girl came up to me and she said, 'Can I ask you a question? Is Sally in "Don't Look Back In Anger" Sally Cinnamon?' And I thought, 'Fucking bastard; why didn't I think of that?'

The Point

Noel I remember those gigs at The Point being, like, wildly emotional with the crowd and all that. I remember it being breathtaking, the energy and the vibe in the room, it was unbelievable. You could feel it, and it was almost like we were not worthy of that.

Peggie I remember in The Point them all shouting, 'Peggie! Peggie! I was up in the balcony with all these fans down in the thing screaming, 'Peggie! Peggie!' Let me move away. I was so embarrassed.

Bonehead My family, when we got six weeks off school in summer, we'd spend that whole six weeks without fail in Ireland, as did Noel and Liam.

Liam Beautiful, it always just seemed really sunny, and we used to get there and go up to my uncle's farm, fuck about in the hay. He lived a bit outside of town so we would walk into town and shit and just fart about. Robbing cigs and stuff and just messing about really. Me old fella would never come with us so it was always, like, pleasant times, me mam would have a good time with her family and that, so that was good.

Peggie They used to love going over to Ireland, they'd run wild over there, out in the

> The energy and the vibe in the room, it was unbelievable.

fields and doing all sorts of things. That was their summer holiday, never went nowhere else.

Noel There is rage in Oasis music and let me explain that to you. If I say to people there's rage in the music, people might think about screaming and shouting, but you can rage joy. When the Irish are sad they are the saddest people in the world, when they are happy they are the happiest people in the world. When they drink they are the most drunk people in the world, there is one rule for the Irish and different ones for everybody else. Oasis could never have existed, been as big, been as important, been as flawed, been as loved and loathed, if we weren't all predominantly Irish.

Paolo Hewitt[*] It's that immigrant thing. It's that sense of identity. Ireland saw them as their own and everybody was in such a good mood. So we got back to the hotel, there were loads of us in the bar.

Paul That hotel was on Grafton Street and it's pretty open; anyone could walk in off the street because Ireland didn't really have security around rock bands in them days. My dad, we'd seen him skulking around and I thought, 'What the fuck is this going on?'

Liam All I remember is someone turned round and said, 'Your old fella's over there with a journalist trying to get summat goin'.' I was about to kill him. I just thought it was a shitty thing. I'm there with me mam's family and all that. He

---

[*] *Journalist and author of* Getting High: The Adventures Of Oasis *and* Forever The People.

was from Dublin so they just turned up, trying to get some fucking vibe, just to get a story. It's the cheapest shot, cheapest bullshit. I thought, 'You are going to get it, you cunt.' If he thought he was brave enough to come up and have a bit of a fucking square-off, then he's fucking foolish. In front of the press, with your son? It's just pathetic, what a sad cunt. See you later, mate.

Maggie It's really quite a tasteless thing to do, isn't it? Obviously they were setting this up and they were banking on a confrontation that they wanted to film and get in the papers.

Noel The thing with me old fella turning up is, no one had actually seen him. I never actually saw him. I was coming out of the bogs and somebody says, 'Don't go out there because the *News of the World* are out there and we think your dad's with them.'

I was like, 'Okay, cool, whatever.' I don't want to cause a scene. I'm kind of long since over whatever was going on with my old fella, that doesn't bother me in the slightest. I don't know what our Paul was doing. Me mam had clearly gone to bed. I did think Liam was a little bit upset.

Liam There was a scene and I was trying to take the dignified approach. Fuck him, he doesn't mean anything to me any more. We were better than that. I was fucking steadfastly not going to get involved.

Paolo Hewitt Noel was saying to Liam, 'Do not react.' He's at one end of the bar and Noel and Liam are at the other. Liam's going 'I'm going to fucking kill him'. And that's when they locked horns, 'Don't fucking react, you're not going to react.' To give Noel his due credit, he contained Liam, because Liam would have gone for him, and Noel protected his brother. Got him out of there because the press were obviously looking for the big fight.

Liam Without a doubt, I was ready to fucking kill him. Without a doubt. But then the only people who would have got that would have been the *News of the World*. I would have killed him if I'd got near him. I got calmed down by our kid, I think, but, no, I didn't dwell on it, just moved on to the next fucking heap of shit.

Noel You don't really know what the papers have said to your dad. They might have spun him some yarn about, 'I know Noel and Liam; I know they'd really like to meet you.' You don't know. Tabloid journalists – the ones who are out there to set people up, secret filming, phone tapping and all that kind of shit – are, as we've since found out, fucking scumbags. I can only say the only way to deal with it is rise above it.

Liam Round about that time there was a story every couple of fucking months. Poor old fucking dad's trying to get in touch with his famous fucking sons, but they are cunts because they don't want nothing to do with him. All that bollocks.

Paul That is not cool, turning up with the *News of the World*. I was in that hotel and he still never mentioned me. It doesn't bother me, but if you are going to have a reconciliation, we are three, not two. Or is there only two that makes money?

Peggie Oh, that was awful that. Really, I couldn't believe that happened, because it really spoiled their night. He knew how Liam would get up on his high horse, because Liam was just waiting for something like that. I think Noel was more nervous because Noel doesn't like anything like that. He had no intentions of making up with them. That was his last thought, but of course he got paid from the *News of the World*. And then, of course, it was all over the papers the next day. He's always said it was me and the three kids that ruined his life. But I would just like him to know that it wasn't us that ruined his life. He ruined his own life.

Noel You know, it was kind of long since over, whatever was going on with my old fella. All I care about is the music. In the end none of this will matter, when it's all said and done, what will remain is the songs.

> All I care about is the music. In the end none of this will matter, when it's all said what will remain is the songs.

Home fixture

Noel We knew that the two records had captured something, probably we didn't even know what it was. I would probably hazard a guess we were as amazed as anybody else really, but not overwhelmed. We were never that blown away by it. When Maine Road sold out – fucking hell, it sold out in twenty minutes, a football stadium – I don't ever recall going, 'What? Wow! Fucking get my mam on the phone!' I just wanted to say, 'When is it? April? Right, well, give us a fucking shout in January.'

> It was our first stadium gig and it was kind of a celebration of an era ...

Liam Maine Road was a great gig, man. Just playing there – getting on the pitch, going backstage in the ground and all that – was great. I used to go and see City there all the time. I first got into City through a teacher who was at St Bernard's. I think, it was Mr Walsh. He was a City fan and he'd get tickets to give to kids and that. He'd get ten tickets and he'd bring along whoever had not been a cunt that week. I don't know how I got one. Anyway we'd go and sit there behind the goals and just have it and that. It was great, man.

Bonehead Maine Road and the streets surrounding it really are a stone's throw from where I was born. I was a United fan as a child, but all my friends were City fans and if City played at home, everybody walked down to the ground to stand in the Kippax and cheer on City, you know. I was really familiar with the ground, inside, outside and surrounding it, so it meant that much to me to do it, and to do two nights.

Noel It was our first stadium gig and it was kind of a celebration of an era and a generation. We still felt like a cult band, we still felt that we weren't really in the mainstream at that point. So selling out two nights at a stadium was cool as fuck.

Liam I remember turning up at the gig, I can't remember what I was wearing, but I think there was an old training kit in the corner in one of the dressing rooms so I thought, 'I'll fucking have a bit of that.' Whacked it on over me gear. 'Yeah, man, we're in. Be playing for them next.'

Noel The fact that I'm a Man City supporter, and have been all my life, to be offered to play a gig like that was laughable, to do two nights was even more funny. To become a stadium band . . . stadium bands were like U2 and Guns N' Roses. Stadium bands have

> We walked into a football stadium playing the same game that we'd played in the Boardwalk two years before.

stadium music and use stadium tactics. We didn't have any of that. We walked into a football stadium playing the same game that we'd played in the Boardwalk two years before. I didn't know what stadium tactics were until Johnny Marr pointed them out to me once. He said, 'How have you managed to do that without resorting to stadium tactics?'

I was like, 'What are these tactics?'

And he said, 'All the people over there, sing . . .'

I was like, 'Oh that, yeah, can't be arsed with that.'

Bonehead We walked out on the stage and it was like, 'Fuck, oh my God.' I could see everything I knew about that place, I could see those houses through the gaps, I could see the floodlights. You know when people say, 'It's a homecoming gig.' I was just getting emotional because that really was a homecoming gig, for all of us.

Noel When I walked out on stage at Maine Road I wasn't detached from it, I fucking loved it. It never paralysed me: the size of this shit or the amount of press or the record sales or the attention that we were getting; that was all great, I loved all that. It never consumed me in any way whatsoever. I felt like a) I fucking deserved it and b) I could get more. I'll have more of that, I don't give a fuck.

Peggie That was the best day, people would be coming to our door and I'd think, 'I can't believe this is happening.' It was great.

Noel You had to queue up and get your guest-list tickets, and people were giving blag names and all that shit. Someone was saying the United players were outside and getting shit off loads of City fans and we were like, 'Good, fuck them off.'

Liam I remember United players wanting tickets, it was like, 'Fuck 'em, always beating us fucking ten nil.'

I loved them gigs, they were great. There was always lots of fighting and shit down the front. I know in this day and age people go, 'Yeah, but I got piss thrown over me one night at an Oasis gig.' You're lucky you didn't get your fucking nose broke. I guess if lads want to scrap each other, let them fucking scrap each other. If they start hitting birds and shit like that, then that's out of order, but if people want to get a bit argy down the front, I fucking loved it.

The chaos surrounding those gigs was fucking insane.

Noel The chaos surrounding those gigs was fucking insane. Maine Road is right in the middle of Moss Side, a great place for a football ground, not a great place to do a gig. It's a tasty area and it was a bit of a scene outside. Helicopters all over. Even friends of ours from Manchester were coming in saying, 'Man, it's fucking rough out there.' We didn't see any of it going on, but you read it in the newspapers and all that. I remember playing on stage and looking down towards the north stand and there are people on the roof who couldn't get in.

Maggie Outside was like Beirut. You stepped outside and there was people hanging off fire engines, trying to get into the venue. We had a fire alarm go off in one of the stands so obviously the fire engines were coming in and they looked at it as an opportunity, to jump on and try to get in. At the far end people had gotten onto the roof over the terrace. I don't know how they got up there, but they found some ladder from some neighbour. There was like fifteen of them dancing away. The police come, they take the ladder away. It was like, 'Oi, you're supposed to get them down. They might hurt themselves!' It was absolute chaos.

Noel The songs were made for the stadium environment. They sounded good in my flat, then they sounded good in the Boardwalk, then they sounded good at the Apollo, sounded better at GMEX. Then they sounded better at Maine Road, and better at Knebworth.

Liam The small gigs were great and all that because they were a bit punky, but our sound was too big for it, I think. We were better off in arenas and stadiums.

Noel I can understand if a dude is stood on stage, singing an intimate song about how his dad shit on his cornflakes when he was a child and he's never recovered from it, I can understand if the meaning is getting lost when there are 50,000 people. 'Cigarettes & Alcohol', let me tell you, you can't fucking play that to enough people. Seventy thousand people didn't seem enough, 125,000 . . . You was thinking there should be more people here to listen to this. The second night at Maine Road, sitting in a box on my own watching the stadium empty with the floodlights on I'm thinking, 'Where does it go from here?' Slowly watching the stadium emptying, trying to appreciate it, but then, almost immediately, bang, you are into a party. Then you can be anything from seventeen hours on the piss to four days, you know what I mean, so by the time you have pulled your head out of your arse there is something else happening. All of those gigs at that point, were a level up. They just became this massive celebration of the level that we were at. I look back on them all with great pride and fondness and I can only say from my own part, I had a fucking great time.

Knebworth

Noel Somebody suggested that the next thing we should do should be these things at Knebworth and we all just went, 'Yeah, whatever.'

Owen I remember Marcus Russell saying to me, 'Do we book these big gigs while they can? Everyone's going, it's fucking brilliant but it's like a fucking truck going down a hill – it's burning and the wheels are fucking falling off – so I don't know when it's going to end, Owen.'

Noel The band never talked strategy. Ever. I don't remember sitting in a room with anyone mapping out the future. I'd heard of the name 'Knebworth'. It didn't really have much significance to me until somebody said it was Batman's house in the film. I thought, 'Oh, that gaff, nice.' If I'm being taken to Knebworth and asked what I thought, the deal's already been done. They are not taking me there for me to go, 'No, I'm not interested.' Somebody's already made their mind up. But somebody's only got to whisper in my ear, 'These are the biggest gigs of all time . . .' Yes, that's me, you've just sold it to me. Thank you very much. 'You'll be bigger than Led Zeppelin and Pink Floyd . . .' Let's do it. They had been booked. This is what we are going to do. We all know what we are doing, the songs are great, I'm great, you're great, the rider's great. Let's fucking have it. As long as it doesn't rain it should be good.

Maggie Everyone was taking a big leap of faith that they were going to sell these shows out. The first one, I think, went on sale and it sold out in, like, minutes, or something ridiculous like that.

Noel They would be talking figures and this, that and the other; I was worried about where the aftershow was going to be. I remember walking round what became the site having the same feeling that I did when they took me to Sheffield Arena and Maine Road, just laughing going, 'This is ludicrous,' and then, 'Are you sure we are going to sell this out?'

Bonehead We'd reached a level where I was really confident. Two nights, alright, we can do it.

Liam I can't believe that we only did two nights. Whose fucking great idea was that? We should still be playing there right now.

Noel The only time I was aware of what it would mean was when the two nights sold out immediately. I think the idea was put to us that we should put another two nights on sale and I think for the first time ever, we kind of backed away. I don't know, maybe we had got the sense that it had become too big. Then you find out

> I can't believe that we only did two nights. Whose fucking great idea was that? We should still be playing there right now.

afterwards that we could have done seven nights and really we should have done. It was like a year where we went from the Manchester Academy to Knebworth, there were three big jumps: Sheffield Arena to Maine Road to Knebworth. But the shift from the rehearsal room in the Boardwalk to the stage in the Boardwalk with eleven people was massive. Then the shift from the eleven people in the Boardwalk to it being 700 people was huge. They are all massive jumps and none more important than the other, I might add. But the jump from the university circuit to the arenas was huge. I'd only ever seen proper big bands in arenas. Then going from that to stadiums – fucking football stadiums – what? What's endearing to me when I see the footage of the stadiums, is there is no production in it at all, it's just a load of lads on stage playing guitar.

Liam Same performance, but better gear, you know what I mean? And more people. But believe you me, every gig, was treated the same as far as I'm concerned.

Noel Now people play stadiums and it's fucking bells and whistles, lasers up the arsehole and all sorts of shit going on, backing singers and fucking all the rest of it. You see other bands playing those big gigs and it is like fucking Cape Canaveral, it is like NASA. If you do that gig now, fuck me, there would be like a million dollars spent on the screen. We had swirly cardboard cut-out things, they weren't even in colour, they were black and white. There was an atrocious lack of foresight about how it looked. It wasn't a statement at all, we just couldn't be arsed. It's difficult enough to come up with a chorus, far less a meeting about how it's going to look. I am not sure whether it would have worked if there'd been the obligatory second stage down the end of a catwalk. We were still behaving like a bunch of shit-kickers, but I suppose that is part of the charm. Our mantra, I guess, was it's all about the songs. I don't remember, at the time, feeling dwarfed by it and to everyone's credit I don't remember anybody shitting it that much. They might have been shitting it in private, but I guess we were so confident in the songs that we were doing, we were just rolling into it. My whole theory is, don't worry about those people out there, they'll have a great time whatever. The stage remains the same size, don't look at them, just stand there with your head down, don't worry about it. You know the songs inside out, just play them. Maybe buy a new shirt, that's it.

Liam I was never sat backstage fucking biting my nails, nervous, wondering how it was going to go. It was, 'Is everybody in, right, can we fucking get on with it?' and that was it, and still is today. The small gigs I find a bit odd when people are right in your face, I find them more nerve-wracking. The big gigs were a piece of piss. Never had stage fright. Never, ever went, 'Can't do this,' not once. Was never overawed by it. Obviously you have a bit of nervous energy, but we were never going, 'Fucking hell, I don't think I can do this gig. Fuck me, shit. What am I going to do. Fucking hell, I'm going to lose the plot. Fucking head's gone shit.' It was just like, fucking bring it on.

Noel We're going to fly into Knebworth in a helicopter and I said to Coyley and Phil, 'You're getting on the helicopter,' because they were our two oldest mates. 'You should be there to see it with us. This thing that we're all part of.'

Phil We just got in the helicopter with them and flew to Knebworth. It is the only way to get to a gig really.

Noel When we were up at the highest in the helicopter it didn't look that impressive, it looked so small. As we were getting near to the ground it's like, 'Fuck me, it's massive.' There is no fairground, there is not a lot of other shit going on, there is no second stage, it's effectively a load of fucking Oasis fans in a field getting pissed.

Bonehead That was a good helicopter, I was a dab hand by then. Knebworth, how we getting in? Helicopter. It's like phff, cool, I can do them now. When you're flying across the countryside and you can see it in the distance, you're like, shit, is that us? It was a great, great feeling though: helicopter coming down, you can see loads of people, everyone knew it was the band arriving. It was just brilliant, best thing ever.

Liam Being on stage and looking out at them people, it's a fucking head fuck. I guess being in that crowd and watching that band, that would have been fucking amazing, I wish I'd have gone to that gig.

Noel When the people are with you and they've taken those songs into their hearts, it's easy. There is no point in getting nervous, you might as well just be one of them and enjoy the gig.

Phil In the end they're just doing a gig. They just bowled on stage and did a gig, wherever it was, whether it's a hundred people or, you know, 150,000, they didn't seem to bother any more than in the early days.

Noel 'This is history.' By this point we know that nearly three million people have applied for a ticket. It was historic.

It is very unlike me to get swept away in the moment, I'm usually a bit reserved about things like that. I think I might have had a drink before I went on, so I could well have got swept up in the moment of it all.

Phil Probably felt like history in my brain, you know, it was my history. I always believed, I never doubted that that band would do something.

Liam It was biblical, man, it felt fucking biblical. All the rest of it is a load of bollocks really, sitting about all day, doing interviews, talking . . . It felt fucking great. It just felt fucking real. The rest of it, you take it or leave it, but that hour and a half, whatever it was, was just like, 'This is the shit, man, this is really fucking proper.'

Noel Now how does John Squire end up on stage at Knebworth? I don't know, he certainly wouldn't have suggested it. I think it would have been either me or Liam and he agreed to do it. It was a bit odd because he never hung out with us. He kind of turned up, hung out on his own tour bus then did the tune, never seen him again. I thought that was a bit weird – I thought he might be, I don't know, one of the lads for the weekend, but there you go.

Liam John Squire, best guitarist in the world today, and was back then. We were all, 'Fucking hell, man; he's up

> When the people are with you and they've taken those songs into their hearts, it's easy.

for playing with us.' We were made up. We were fucking stoked, man. That was good, he was cool. John's very quiet and you can tell there is a lunatic inside dying to get out, but he's very reserved and chilled. We'd always have to play it cool around him because he is not into fussing about or jumping up and down . . . he is a bit of a chilled guy. We'd always try and hold it down around him, but top man.

Noel It is something you can't define. You can't bottle it and fuck knows how you make that happen again, you just don't try. You are just happy that it happened to you once in your life and I guess if you were in the crowd, you were happy that you were there, in your twenties while the band was there in their twenties, and that's it.

Liam I can't even describe it. I would say that gig was more about the fans than us. The fans: I hate that fucking word. More about the people than the band.

Bonehead It went above and beyond and further than anything I ever imagined, so that was the pinnacle for me.

Noel Even though it's huge, it's a low-key thing. We are still the same band that was playing in the Boardwalk, we are wearing virtually the same clothes. All that's happened is it's caught fire and all these people have got on board. There were no sing-alongs, no dropping down of the chorus from 'Wonderwall' and the singer going, 'Everybody over there . . .' None of that shit. In, out, put the kettle on, there's a rider to get through here. That was the ethos.

Liam After the first night I got a bit carried away. I woke up the next day and there were people knocking at my door going, 'Come on, you've got to go and do a soundcheck.'

I was like, 'What the . . . who, what, where, what fucking soundcheck?' Forgot that we had to do it all again. I remember not having a change of clothes, but I had this big woolly jumper, so I said, 'I'll have to wear that,' because I didn't want to wear the same jacket twice.

Noel Every night after the first night is a breeze because you know that it's steadily going to get better. Whatever sense of anticipation or excitement, and whatever level of nerves you might feel. The second night, honestly, it was like fucking playing in my front room, I was that relaxed about it. How it used to work with Oasis was the second night would always be the first night to go on sale, so you'd go out and you'd do the first night and that would be amazing and then you'd think, 'Fucking hell, all the diehard fans are coming tomorrow, all the nutcases are coming tomorrow.'

Two days after Knebworth I was no bigger a rock star than I was two days before it.

Liam People have come up and gone, 'I was at Knebworth.'

'Alright, cool, me too.'

We never really sat and thought about it. Looking at it, it's insane, it's massive.

Noel Well, yeah, you'd have to be a dick to be in the midst of that and not think that this is significant. Even if you wouldn't be pompous enough to think this is a significant moment in popular culture, you would certainly think it's a significant moment in my life. I knew it was significant. But it didn't change my life in any way. Two days after Knebworth I was no bigger a rock star than I was two days before it. I wasn't perceived any differently, the band weren't perceived any differently. I remember it being immediately slagged off in the fucking papers. Some tabloid journalist was going on about the price of the food or some shit like that, which is a very British thing to do. 'Wasn't it great?'

'Fucking hell, what about the queue for the toilets, though?' Whatever.

Liam It was amazing, it was beautiful, it felt like it was fucking justice, it was us and the world. It was up there with any kind of fucking religion, to get them people in that crowd without fucking religion is something. It's a big, powerful thing. Deep, man, deep but beautiful. I just wanted more of it. I've heard Bonehead bang on a million times, 'We should have split up, blah, blah, blah.' What for? Do what? Go and be a fucking car mechanic? Just have a bit of time off, go and do it all again next year. All them people that were there, or that couldn't get tickets, let's go and fucking play for them next year or whatever.

Noel We should have at least gone away and given the impression that we'd split up. We should have gone away and done a bit of living. A fucking shitload of money was about to fall into our laps: all the royalties were starting to come in from the first two records, the tours, Knebworth and Maine Road, and that kind of thing. We should have gone off and done that thing that rock stars are supposed to do.

Bonehead That was my life. That band was my life. It went above and beyond anything I ever imagined. That was the pinnacle for me. It was like, where the fuck do you go from here? My attitude then was more, give me more, give me more, give me more, I want more of this, keep going. Now, looking back, I honestly think we should have just went, thank you, every one of yous, for getting us here. A final bow, on that stage. We were Oasis and goodnight, you know, and walked off.

Noel Looking back on it now, it did feel like the end of something as opposed to the beginning of something. I had a sense, even at Knebworth, that it was never going to happen again. You couldn't have envisaged it getting any bigger than that. The only thing to be bigger than that would be to do more nights. So it couldn't get any bigger than that, it could just get more repetitive: four nights next year, seven nights the year after . . . It was right on the cusp of the analogue age going

> Looking back on it now, it did feel like the end of something as opposed to the beginning of something.

into the digital age. Walking out on that stage that afternoon there were no mobile phones. It was the pre-digital age, it was the pre-talent-show-reality-TV age; things meant more. It was a great time to be alive, never mind a great time to be in Oasis. We were about to enter a celebrity-driven culture. I've always thought that it was the last great gathering of the people of the old age before the birth of the Internet and phones with cameras and video phones and iPads and all that shit. I do say it quite often, and I said it then, people think I'm a fucking lunatic, I thought we were going to be the last great rock band. What I meant by that was we did it in the traditional way. It's no coincidence that things like that don't happen any more I don't think. I think that the Internet and the digital world has taken a lot of the magic out of rock and roll. The biggest music phenomenon was a band that came from a council estate. I just think in the times in which we live, it would be unrepeatable. We should be worried about that, because where's it going to be twenty years from now?

> I loved every minute of it. It meant the be-all and end-all, man.

Liam I just wanted it all there and then, do you know what I mean? I just wanted it to happen in one big fuck-off explosion of madness. I loved every minute of it. It meant the be-all and end-all, man. Life or death. I'd do it all again in a heartbeat. It's easy to say that in hindsight we should have gone, 'Right, let's knock it on the head.' And do what? Go back to your fucking house and count your fucking money? It doesn't work like that. Bollocks to that. When you score a hat trick in the first twenty minutes against United, you don't turn round to your fucking bench and go, 'Here you are, let me out of here now, I've done my fucking bit.'

Noel I wish I was that cool, back then, to have taken a step back and gone, 'Let's just all go our separate ways for a bit.' Imagine doing those gigs and then just splitting up. We should have disappeared into a puff of smoke. It would have been fucking unbelievable. If it would happen to me again, knowing now what I should have known then, we would have just gone off stage and said something cryptic and then disappeared for five years. Then slowly just made a great album or wrote better songs as opposed to just carrying on, carrying on and carrying on. But, you know, it was my idea to keep going, I keep on fishing for it because I am an addict. I'm addicted to the thing. That's what shit-kickers do, they ride it until the wheels come off then they are desperately running around for the Sellotape, trying to put it back together again.

Liam Just because you can't get any bigger or any higher, doesn't mean to say you can't keep doing it, do you know what I mean? You shouldn't just stop because you kissed the sky. Give it a fucking love bite.

No regrets

Liam People have asked me before, are you surprised at how big Oasis got? No, I thought we would be a lot bigger, that's where my head was at.

Noel I'd often think, 'What was it all about?' It happened in such a short space of time, two and a half years from signing off to walking out on that stage. When we got to Knebworth, we'd only just become rock stars; two and a half years previous to that we were a bunch of shit-kickers. You might think it took a lot of savvy business people saying, 'We are going to do this and we are going to do that,' but there was no smart business moves or anything like that. What happened is just magic. When you say it now, it is so ridiculously simple: you had a band who had the tunes, who were grafters, who came from nothing and wanted it all. Were willing to put themselves out there and inspired a generation of people to believe in them. We were the last. We were the greatest. Nothing anybody does could be as big as Oasis.

> It is about the way that we made people feel, and people will never forget that.

Liam Just pure self-belief, man. Self-belief, not arrogance, self-belief. Arrogance is someone who turns round and goes, 'Oh yeah, we're going to be the best band in the world,' knowing deep down that the tune you're writing ain't even going to get out the studio. It was pure, pure fucking self-belief and that was it. It would never get repeated. Not because we were greater or better than anyone else, but just because we didn't actually give a flying fuck. We've definitely got a table upstairs with the big boys, whether they like it or not.

Noel I guess if you were to rationalise everything that we ever did, you couldn't say that anybody that was ever in Oasis, me included, was the best in the world at anything. As a lyricist, I wouldn't even come in the top twenty; guitarist, wouldn't even come in the top twenty. Liam as a singer, not the best. Bonehead as a rhythm guitarist, wasn't even the best guitarist in Oasis, never mind the fucking world. Guigs, no chance. But when it all came together, in a venue or in a field, it did something that was great. We made people feel something that was indefinable. I thought we were the greatest and I still do and that's because of all the elements. Because of Liam and me and the songs and the words and the fans and whoever else was in the band at the time. We made a thing and it was great. I don't consider myself to be that great. I wrote the songs, but to me that is a very small part, that's just kind of like giving birth to a child. This thing goes on and becomes fucking huge because of the people. I do believe that certain songs have written themselves, like 'Slide Away' and 'Don't Look Back In Anger' and 'Live Forever' and 'Wonderwall' and 'Champagne Supernova'. I do believe that if I hadn't had written those songs that night, somebody else would have written them somewhere else. Neil Young calls it sitting beside the rabbit hole, and when the rabbit pops up you are quick enough to grab it by the ears. Keith Richards says they fall out of the sky. I liken it to going fishing, if you are not fishing you are not catching anything, and if I hadn't have been writing and hadn't picked up my guitar on that particular day, then that song would have sailed on down the fucking stream and somebody else would have written it.

Liam We were properly, properly into it and we weren't fucking lazy; we grafted like fuck and we weren't cunts. We took the piss out of people and we had banter with people and obviously we got shit back if anyone was funny enough to take us on, it was just a crack. Yeah, we took drugs, we fucking slapped a photographer, all fucking true, but that is it.

Noel It is not about the songs and it is not about the fucking clothes and the attitude and the headlines and the scandal. It is about the way that we made people feel, and people will never forget that. Don't ask me to intellectualise it because I don't fucking know. I was only on the stage and in the studio, but people will never, ever, ever forget the way that you made them feel.

Liam We had a laugh, man. Anyone who says we didn't have a laugh obviously weren't there. It was twenty-four hours of the day fucking fun.

Noel If it wasn't a proper fucking laugh – regardless of all the getting kicked off aeroplanes and thrown out of hotels at 4 o'clock in the fucking morning – we wouldn't have stayed together for eighteen years or whatever it was. That in itself tells you something.

Liam It was everything and more than I asked for and I wouldn't have changed a fucking thing. I enjoyed the chaos, I enjoyed the hard graft, all the riches, I enjoyed all the fucking nonsense.

Noel There was chaos fucking surrounding the band and right in the middle it was fucking worse. Whatever the chaos going on, screaming kids and this, that and the other, in the dressing room it was worse. There was shit getting smashed up and people fucking pissed falling over and it was great. We didn't have that calm in the eye of the storm, in the eye of the storm was a worse fucking storm, it was pissing down.

Liam The wheels were never on the fucking bus. We were on the bus, but the fucking wheels were rarely on it.

Noel In the end, when it is all said and done, what will remain is the songs and you can have an opinion on them for as long as you like. None of that stuff about hotel rooms is greater than the impact that 'Live Forever' had on a generation. None of that stuff about drugs and not turning up for gigs and what was said in the press will ever be as great as 70,000 people singing 'Don't Look Back In Anger'.

Liam We just knew that we were here to take this band as far as we could without turning into knobheads and licking arse and being what all these other fucking clowns had been before us. We had to keep it super, super fucking real, for us first of all, and for the real people that are out there. The real people that needed something, instead of some fucking soft-soap bullshit band. We were a Mike Tyson band; just come in, fucking blazing, knocking everyone out.

We were never going to do ten rounds and it was never going to get to points, we were just going to come in and fucking have it. No regrets, no fucking regrets. Even the fuck-ups were great. When we fucked up, we fucked up fucking great and we did it with a laugh. Even the shit bits were great. It was just mega.

Noel Oasis's great strength was the relationship between me and Liam. It is also what drove the band into the ground in the end.

Peggie Sometimes I do look back on it and I wish it had gone in a different way, but it hasn't. It's caused a lot of problems with them two. But it's their lives and you have to just let them get on with it.

Liam I get where she's coming from, because obviously me and our kid ain't got a relationship any more, but who is to say if we had been a pair of fishmongers we'd not have still slapped each other with a bit of trout every now and again. I know people in all walks of life that don't speak to their brothers for a long, long time and they are not in rock-and-roll bands. At the end of the day I weigh it up and I go, 'Did the good times outweigh the bad times? Fucking 100 per cent!' I'm happy with that. As far as I'm concerned I'm still fucking up. I come in with nothing so if I leave with nothing – even if I leave with 10p in my back pocket – I'm still up, man. It's all good, man. I didn't join Oasis to fucking make lots of money, we did it to make music and whatever comes with that. We were never driven by money, I certainly weren't anyway. It was more about just having a good time and getting in a bubble and playing your music and having a fucking laugh. The money side of things, I don't know how much money we made, I don't know how much money we lost, didn't care. I've had big houses and I've had small houses; I've had big bar bills; I've had this and I've had that and it doesn't really matter. I've had good times, I'd rather that than a big bank account, sitting there going like, 'Yeah, I was in a pretend rock-and-roll band and I got up to fuck all really. I've got 90 million quid in the bank.'

I'd do it all again in a fucking heartbeat, the exact same way.

Noel People make the mistake of thinking that the people on the stage are defining something; what if no one turns up? The people who are making it what it is are the people in the crowd. So we can all sit here and suck each other's ball bags about fucking 2.6 million people applying for tickets, but, you know, what's great about that is the 2.6 million people. Not anything that we did. It means shit without the people. The people were with us and I felt that, and I felt quite invincible in feeling that. Really, the people are as important as the songs and the chaos and the nonsense and the interviews and the fucking drugs and the fucking this, that and the other. What should never be forgotten is what the fans did, or how special they made it. The songs are not great because of anything that I did, I only wrote them. They are made special night after night after night, decade after decade, because of the people. When I sing 'Champagne Supernova' on acoustic guitar in a soundcheck and there are eleven people there, it's good, it's fucking good, but it's not extraordinary. When you are singing it five hours later to 12,000 people in

Glasgow, *that's* extraordinary. Not because of anything I'm doing, I'm playing it the same, it's the love and the vibe and the passion and whatever it is, the rage and the joy that's coming from the crowd, if anything that is what Oasis was. There's a chemistry between the band and the audience. There's something magnetic drawing the two to each other.

Liam We meant every fucking last fucking breath of it. Everything. Every fuck that got fucked, every fucking swear word that come out of my mouth, every fucking table that got chucked, every fucking drink or whatever that went up our nose or in our mouth, I meant every fucking minute of it and I wouldn't change anything. I'd do it all again in a fucking heartbeat, the exact same way. It was a miracle that we even got there. It was everything and more than I asked for.

Yeah, we felt untouchable, man.

Supersonic, even.

Simon Halfon's Acknowledgements

I'd like to thank Noel and Liam for their support on this project from its inception – initially as a film and now in book form – and all those who contributed along the way: Tim Abbott, Christine Mary Biller, Bonehead, Clint Boon, Brian Cannon, Mark Coyle, Paul Gallagher, Peggie Gallagher, Paolo Hewitt, Johnny Hopkins, Johnny Marr, Tony McCarroll, Alan McGee, Owen Morris, Maggie Mouzikatis, Jason Rhodes, John Robb, Phil Smith, Daniela Soave, Michael Spencer Jones and Debbie Turner. Their time and support is very much appreciated.

Additional thanks first and foremost goes to Mat Whitecross who really exceeded all our expectations in delivering quite simply one of the great rock-and-roll documentaries! A huge thank you to all the team that made the film: Fiona Neilson, James Gay Rees, Paul Monaghan, Marc Knapton, Rael Jones, Arturo Antolin, Hannah Green, Asif Kapadia, Julian Bird and Joe Berry.

Many thanks also to Debbie Gwyther.

To Marcus Russell, Alec McKinley, Daisy Blackford, Sarah Mansfield and Kat Killingly at Ignition; to Martyn James, to Jill Furmanovsky; to Dan Newman at Perfect Bound Ltd; to Tim Bates, Jon Fowler and Daisy Chandley at PFD; and all the team at Headline, especially Sarah Emsley and Emma Tait.

Special thanks to Robby Elson for his fine editing skills.

And finally to Joe Halfon for all his help, and not forgetting the rest of the very special team: Lev, Ira and Anat!

Picture Credits

Section One 1: Paul Slattery/Retna Pictures/Avalan.red. 2–3 (background): Kevin Cummins/Getty Images. 2a: Dan Callister/Liaison/Getty Images. 2b: Courtesy of Paul Gallagher. 3a (photo strip): Noel Gallagher. 3b: Kevin Cummins/Getty Images. 3c: Tom Sheehan. 4a: Peter J. Walsh/Pymca/Shutterstock. 4b: Peter J. Walsh/Avalon.red. 5a: Roger Sargent/Shutterstock. 5b: Paul Slattery/Retna Pictures/Avalon.red. 6a: Glasgow montage: Marc Knapton The Brewery VFX. 6b (Alan McGee cut-out): Courtesy of Alan McGee. 7 (all): Kevin Cummins/Getty Images. 8a: Jill Furmanovsky. 8b: Christine Mary Biller.

Section Two 1: Courtesy of Big Brother Recordings Ltd. 2: Kevin Cummins/Getty Images. 3 (all): Kevin Cummins/Getty Images. 4–5: Christine Mary Biller. 6: Courtesy of Big Brother Recordings Ltd. 7a: Paul Slattery/Retna Pictures/Avalon.red. 7b: Kevin Cummins/Getty Images. 8: Courtesy of Big Brother Recordings Ltd.

Section Three 1: Jill Furmanovsky. 2a: Paul Slattery/Retna Pictures/Avalon.red. 2b Background: Robert Landau/Alamy. 2c Ephemera: Courtesy of Big Brother Recordings Ltd. 3: Jill Furmanovsky. 4–5: Jill Furmanovsky. 6a: Brian Rasic/Getty Images. 6b: Jill Furmanovsky. 7a (song lyric sheet): Courtesy of Big Brother Recordings Ltd. 7b (album cover): CBW/Alamy/courtesy of Big Brother Recordings Ltd. 8a: Courtesy of Big Brother Recordings Ltd. 8b: Paul Slattery/Retna/Avalon.red.

Section Four 1 (all): Jill Furmanovsky. 2–3: Jill Furmanovsky. 4: Ilpo Musto/Shutterstock. 5a: Stephen Sweet/Shutterstock. 5b: Dave Hogan/Getty Images. 5c (ephemera): Courtesy of Big Brother Recordings Ltd. 6–7 (background): Stefan Rousseau/Alamy. 6a: Courtesy of Big Brother Recordings Ltd. 6b: Mick Hutson/Redferns/Getty Images. 7a: Jill Furmanovsky. 7b and 7c: Brian Rasic/Getty Images. 8a: Jill Furmanovsky. 8b: Andre Csillag/Shutterstock.

Additional Credit
Section Two 1: Extract from interview by Chris Salmon.